When the Korean World
in Hawaii Was Young,
1903–1940

When the Korean World in Hawaii Was Young, 1903–1940

SEONJU LEE and
ROBERTA CHANG

This book was supported by a National Research Foundation of Korea (NRF) Grant funded by the Korean government (NRF-2007-361-AL0015).

Published in association with
Ewha Institute for the Humanities
Ewha Womans University
11-1 Daehyun-Dong Seodaemun-Gu
Seoul 120-750 Korea
http://www.eih.ewha.ac.kr/

This publication is printed on acid-free paper and meets the guidelines for permanence and durability of the Council of Library Resources.

Print-ready copy prepared by the authors.

Distributed by
University of Hawai'i Press
2840 Kolowalu Street
Honolulu, Hawai'i 96822
www.uhpress.hawaii.edu

CONTENTS

PREFACE

Ewha Institute for the Humanities at Ewha Womans University in Seoul, Korea, with the support of the Korean Research Foundation, began in 2007 to collect and preserve materials related to Korea's living past: its people, government, and culture. In 2008 Roberta Chang, a Korean American born in Hawaii, was invited to speak at Ewha Womans University about Koreans in Hawaii and presented a documentary, *The Legacy of the Korean National Association*. At that time Ms. Chang also donated copies of video interviews she conducted with direct descendants of the first Koreans in Hawaii, who emigrated between 1903 and 1924. Most of the interviews were done in Hawaii over a span of nearly twenty years. After studying the interviews, I obtained Ms. Chang's consent to transcribe the nineteen I deemed most valuable. It took me three years to select, study, and transcribe them and to document my findings. The result was the first edition of this book published by Ewha Institute for the Humanities.

The Korean Americans interviewed were the daughters and sons of the first Koreans to arrive in Hawaii in large numbers and whose immigration was sanctioned by the Korean government in 1903. In fact these Koreans were the first to arrive and settle officially in a U.S. territory. Observing that many of the second generation were passing away (most of them had been born in the 1910s and 1920s), Ms. Chang felt a desperate need to record their stories. Other research has been done on the first Korean migrants to Hawaii and their picture brides based on photographs and written records; however, this book is composed mainly of transcripts, in which nuances of feeling in a person's voice are often apparent. Ms. Chang has also added photographs from her sizeable collection on subjects discussed by the interviewees.

Oral histories are often records of everyday experience—they have none of the glamour and abstraction of accounts of historically significant events. People describe a specific point in their lives affected by the tenor of the times that becomes a part of history. The personal histories in this book show

how people, far from home, gathered together and came to depend on each other; how fear and vulnerability aroused their religious faith; how they firmly united as patriots to help their homeland; and how, under opposing leaders, they turned against each other. These interviews with early Korean migrants to Hawaii tell of private experiences, yet they are also vivid records of Korea's history.

Korean migration to the U.S. started at the end of the Choson Dynasty, when a small group, mostly men compelled by current events and poverty, answered the call of recruiters seeking laborers for Hawaii's sugar plantations. Those who landed in Hawaii without spouses started families with picture brides, who began arriving in 1910. After Korea became a Japanese colony in 1905, the struggle to liberate it came to rest more with those living abroad than those within. Hawaii Koreans supported the March First Independence Movement in 1919. The Korean military in Manchuria was aided by funds gathered in the form of tithes from Hawaii's Korean Methodist churches and donations from the Korean National Association and other newly formed organizations. The leaders of the Korean community in Hawaii appealed directly to Washington for political support. After liberation from Japan, Dr. Syngman Rhee was able to become the first president of the Republic of Korea because he was recognized by the U.S. government. His political and economic foundations were established in Hawaii. All of the interviewees were involved in some way with Rhee, either as supporters or detractors, revealing again that their own accounts are linked to a critical time in contemporary Korean political history.

The stories in *When the Korean World in Hawaii Was Young* are archetypical of modern diasporas; they tell of both the tragedies and successes involved in the struggle to acculturate and assimilate. We learn that Korean immigration was encouraged to keep the increasing numbers of Chinese and Japanese in check; that first-generation immigrants were denied permanent residency status for forty years; that those visiting Korea during the Japanese occupation could only re-enter Hawaii with a Japanese visa. Although the lives of early immigrants were difficult, it is clear from the interviews that, in contrast to those who remained in Korea, Hawaii Koreans were able to take advantage of their relative freedom and feelings of self-realization: They believed they could do anything or become anything if they possessed the will and worked hard. Maria Whang, for example, left her patriarchal husband in Korea and took her two children to Hawaii, where she taught at plantation schools and organized the Korean Women's Association. Dorothy Kim Rudie's father, Kyung Pok Kim, a sailor on the *Mongolia*, landed in Hawaii in 1901—well before the majority of Koreans arrived as laborers—and went on to help dozens of his newly arrived countrymen; it was said that his funeral was well attended by those who had received his assistance. Nora Pahk, who followed her parents to Hawaii, became the first Korean teacher at an American school. After she was dismissed when it was discovered that she was not an American citizen, Nora went on to nursing school and became the first Korean nurse supervisor. Manuel Kwon, born of a Korean father and a Spanish mother, became the principal of Wahiawa High School and the chairman of a Korean association.

There is a saying that when an elder passes away, it is as if a library has disappeared. While watching Ms. Chang's interview of Mary Hong Park—a lively woman with an unaffected, innocent laugh who will turn 104 years old this year, I reflected that Mary is not just a library, but a part of history itself. It is a blessing that Mary and others documented by Ms. Chang will be with us for a very long time.

I want to thank Roberta Chang for devoting her life to recording the lives of Hawaii's Korean Americans. I also thank the Korea Research Foundation for providing the financial support that made the first edition possible and express my appreciation to Miyoung Jang, Director of Ewha Institute for the Humanities, Ewha Womans University; Professor Youngmi Kim; and Professor Byoungjoon Jung of the Ewha History Department, who supplied much encouragement and introduced Ms. Chang to our faculty. I thank Soyoung Lee and Junghae Sung for their assistance in transcribing the interviews; without them I could not have accomplished this task. Finally, I deeply appreciate the efforts of Colins Kawai of the University of Hawai'i Press, who was instrumental in getting this new edition published.

Seonju Lee

It was a great honor to work with Professor Seonju Lee of Ewha Institute for the Humanities. It was Professor Lee who first alerted me to the importance of my interviews of Korean Americans in Hawaii. Eighteen of the participants were sixty years of age or older when they were interviewed. Most of them were born in Hawaii during the 1910s and early 1920s.

It should be noted that the second generation of Hawaii Koreans spans four decades, from the 1900s to the 1940s. Each decade was colored by the political struggles in Korea at the time. Older second-generation Hawaii Koreans were, like their parents, engrossed in the Korean Independence Movement, while their younger counterparts could only vaguely recall their parents' dedication to Korea's liberation.

Dr. Syngman Rhee was invariably mentioned by every interviewee. Ten of them had direct contact with Rhee or their parents were close friends of his. Because political organizations became enmeshed with religious and educational ones in the Korean community, Rhee played a large part in the lives of many older second-generation Hawaii Koreans.

To gain a clear understanding of the history of Koreans in Hawaii, one must recognize the importance of key churches and associations established from the 1900s to 1940s:

Korean Methodist Church (1903)
Korean Episcopal Church (1905)
Korean National Association (1909)
Korean Military Brigade - Kookmindan (1914, a subsidiary
   of the Korean National Association)
Four organizations founded by Dr. Syngman Rhee
   Dongji Hoi (1918)
   Korean Christian Church (1918)
   Korean Christian Institute (1918)
   Korean Residents Association - Kyomindan (1921)
Korean American Club (1925)
Korean University Club (1926)
Taeguk Club (1933)
Delta Fraternity (1934)
(Photographs of the above can be found in the Appendix.)

The first eight were created by the first generation; the last three were established by the younger members of the second generation born between 1915 and 1925. Of course an in-depth discussion of these organizations will not be found in the interviews presented here; that must be accomplished in another publication.

It is my hope that *When the Korean World in Hawaii Was Young* will help future researchers gain a better understanding of the role of Hawaii Koreans in the Korean Independence Movement. Therefore, I thank Professor Seongju Lee and Ewha Institute for the Humanities for recognizing the value of the interviews as well as undertaking the arduous task of transcribing the interviews and publishing the first edition of this book.

I also wish to thank University of Hawai'i Press' Colins Kawai, Stephanie Chun, and Mardee Melton for their work on the new edition and to acknowledge Cynthia Ong for her assistance in selecting the documents for this publication.

Roberta Chang

Interview with Mary Hong Park

My name is Mary Hong Park. I was born in Seoul, Korea, on May 3, 1909 on a Sunday morning. My brother, Tae Hee Hong, was also born in Seoul, in the Myong Dong area; he was two years older than I. My father, Rev. Han Sik Hong, was assigned by the Methodist Mission at Myong Dong in Seoul to go to the Korean Methodist Mission in Hawaii alone. The rest of the family followed him a year later.

Myong Dong 1911; Rev. Hong Han Sik, with infant son Tae Hee, before he left for Hawaii. Korean Methodist Church in Seoul.

Rev. Han Sik Hong and his family in front of the Maui Korean Methodist Episcopal Church, circa 1912.

I was three years old and my brother was five years old when we arrived in Honolulu. We were in quarantine a few days because both my brother and I had come down with measles on the ship. Dr. William Wadman, who was the superintendent of the Methodist Mission in Honolulu, got us out of the quarantine station, and we were taken to the Methodist Church compound in the Punchbowl area in Honolulu. I don't know how long we stayed there. Maybe a week or two later, our whole family was sent to the Honakaa, Papaloa, area on the the Big Island [the island of Hawaii], where my father started his first preaching mission for about a couple of years before we came back to the Punchbowl compound area in Honolulu.

Family photo; left to right: Mary, Rev. Tae Hee Hong, William Hong, Hannah Chung, Hei Ja Chung, John Hong, circa 1922.

2

As I recall, we first lived on Liliha Street because by that time, I was about five years old, and I remember having attended a kindergarten on Liliha Street. We may have not lived there too long, but I remember my first Christmas gift from my father. He had us hang up stockings up on the porch, and I found a doll the next morning and my brother found a pistol. I always cherished the idea of gift-giving because that was our first Christmas gift. Then we moved back to the main compound near Punchbowl, where we stayed until maybe 1915 or 1916. That is where my brother Bill was born. He was named after Dr. William Henry Fry, who was the new superintendent of the Methodist Mission.

Then we were sent to Maui and we lived there for about four years, and at that time I attended Maui Spreckelsville Public School from second grade to the mid-fifth grade. My brother was already in the seventh or eighth grade. But because Spreckelsville School had classes only up to fifth grade, he had to go to Wailuku by train daily to attend school, but I was able to stay in Spreckelsville to continue my grade-school education.

Then my father's mission assignment was changed again, so we had to go to Kauai, another island north of all the islands. Later on, I graduated from Lihue Intermediate School and went on to Kauai High School. I was in the second semester of my sophomore year there when my parents were transferred again back to Honolulu. By that time, the Methodist Church had been moved from Punchbowl Street to Fort Street because the old property was bought by the Hawaii Territorial Government to establish public offices in Honolulu.

So we lived on Fort Street on the Methodist Mission grounds for about four years. By that time, I had graduated from McKinley High School and had entered the University of Hawaii. Just before my graduation, my father gave up the pulpit because of a transition between the first immigrants and the young Korean Americans in the Methodist Church's congregation. The Methodist Mission realized that the growing new congregation was increasingly young members who needed an English-speaking minister. So they had Rev. Fritz Pyun be the minister. We still continued to live on Fort Street and Rev. Fritz Pyun lived in the back of our quarters, which was the dormitory for boys who were attending the University of Hawaii. These boys were from the other islands or from the rural areas of Oahu. I think it was after I graduated from the University of Hawaii, when we moved out of the Fort Street Mission house, and we went into a rented house. The Mission demolished the old parsonage quarters because it was too old.

3

Rev. Fritz Pyun did not stay at the Hawaii Methodist Church Mission long. The young people could not accept him because he was too fanatically religious. He was too strict. He returned to Korea. A new minister, Rev. Doo Wha Lim, was sent to us. He and his family also lived in the new dormitory, which was converted into a two-story building. The upstairs was for their lodging and the lower floor for parishioners who visited the pastor or who lingered in the compound after services or social gatherings.

In the meantime, we lived in a rented house until my father bought a property in Kaimuki. We moved to Pahoa Avenue in Kaimuki. We owned that house until it was passed on to my oldest brother. I stayed there until I got married in 1934 to Ernest K. H. Park.

I can remember the days on the island of Maui when we were very young. We were happy there. It was a plantation home, a three-bedroom house. Of course, we were given a better home than the average Oriental immigrants because my father was a reverend and the Methodist Church supported our family. We had a kitchen with a wooden stove with a iron-cast range. They delivered logs once a week, and my father had to use the axe to chop up the wood to use in the iron range. We did not have a sewer system. We had a pipe in the kitchen. We had an outhouse. The toilet was outside the house and flushed with flowing underground water. The water used to fall from the sink down to a cement trough on the ground and, when the trough got really moldy, once a week a plantation worker would clean up the trough for all the residents in the camp, which was a Portuguese camp. The Portuguese camp was on a higher level than that of the ordinary Oriental plantation workers. The ordinary plantation worker had a kitchen outside of the living area, and it was on a dirt floor. The chickens would come in and out of the kitchen area, and we would just throw old rice on the ground. The chickens would just help themselves. We did not have refrigerators or iceboxes in those days, so we kept our food all in the "safe," which was made out of wood and a screen.

In those days to preserve the food, we made *jang-jorim*, which is meat cooked in soy sauce, which could be kept for about a week or so. The butter would stay a little more firm in the safe because the air would pass through the cabinet. In the Portuguese camp, between every few houses, they had a cement-cast outdoor oven because the Portuguese ate a lot of bread. They use to bake their bread once every week or two weeks in the same outdoor oven. My mother got to learn to make bread from them and they let her use their oven. But since we didn't need that much bread, she would wait for the

4

Portuguese to bake their bread first, and she would put one or two loaves in their oven for our family. Now I will tell you how they prepared the oven. It was a round dome-like thing, the height of your standing height. It came up to a little higher than your hip. They would burn all their wood inside the door and close the door, which was made out of iron. And they would burn the wood for maybe a couple of hours until it became charcoal. They would wait with a long handle. They would mop the floor of the oven and then put the bread in, and after maybe a couple of hours, the bread would be all done. We all would look forward to those days because my mother kept some dough aside and we would have a feast with raised donuts.

You mentioned something before about your mother preparing rice for you to take to school?

Once a week, the meat truck would come. So she would make *jang-jorim;* she would buy the cheap cuts like the shin of the cow and make a dip after she cleaned the shin. Then she would skin the meat, toes and all. Then she would make a great pot of soup which, maybe, would last about a week or so. It was very nutritious.

Now, when we went to school, there was no cafeteria at that time, so we had to take our own lunch. A lot of times, the lunch can had two compartments, one for the rice and one for the *banchan,* that is, the side dishes which you eat with the rice. So a lot of times we had *daegu* or *jang-jorim* with something salty that would help not to spoil the *banchan.* Since we had no place to hang our lunch bag, we used to hang it on tree branches in the schoolyard. And sometimes, when it was ant season, we would find ants in our rice. So what we did was just pour water in the rice and when the ants floated up, we would just drain the water and enjoy our lunch. We thought nothing of bacteria or thought that it was kind of odd to be eating those things, but the Korean food kept us healthy. We did not have dessert; we never thought of buying fruits because the only time we really did enjoy fruit was on Christmas Day, when we were given apples and oranges at church.

There were quite a number of Korean members in Camp One, which was in Spreckelsfield, but later many of them moved to Honolulu to find better livelihood. So there were very few Korean families left gradually, but enough for us to have church services every Sunday. On special days, like Christmas, New Year's, and Thanksgiving,

Korean people from Paia Camp Three and the Kihei area made a point to come to church services. Other than that, I remember that we learned to sing all of the church hymns in Korean. So, to this day, I can remember some of the songs in Korean words. We did not speak in English at that time. In the same yard of the church there was another building which was used for the Korean language school. We attended that language school just before we were old enough to attend the English school. When we were old enough to go to the English school, we went to the Korea language school after the English school finished for the day . . . say about three o'clock and then we'd stay at the Korean school until around five o'clock in the afternoon. Then we'd all return home, and it was time for dinner, for our bath, and back to sleep for the next day.

Spreckelsfield was a sugar plantation. Last year, when I visited Maui, I wanted to go to see the place where we lived. There was nothing, there's no Spreckelsville now. There used to be a post office, railroad station, church, plantation medical dispensary, a park, and a mansion for managers of the plantation, who were important on the plantation. These and other important persons had their homes there. The Spreckelsville beach was nearby so we were able to go and spend some days and learn to swim there. Now, there's no Spreckelsville. Now, it's covered with wild sugarcane fields which are still owned by the Baldwin family. The Baldwin family were descendants of the first Methodist missionaries in Hawaii. They were originally from the east coast of the U.S. The Baldwins supported the Methodist churches for many years, but for some reason, the Baldwins who ran the Maui plantations supported Dr. Syngman Rhee's Korean Christian Church on Maui years later.

Could you tell us what years these would be? Your memory about Spreckelsville seems so vivid. That town had a fantastic history because of Mr. Claus Spreckels. About how old were you and what years were you there?
This was in 1916. I remember it was during World War I. We were in school. We had to buy war savings stamps. We thought it was a such a great thing when we fill 25¢ war stamp books. It would amount to $5. I was in the second grade so I must have been about seven years old.

Tell us once more your full name and also your Korean name, and the year you were born.

I was born in 1909 and my name was Suk Hee at birth. My English name, Mary, was added later. In my generation, the family name ended in Hee. I was told the custom was that for the first two generations, the beginning is the same and after that the ending is the same. So my father's ending was Sik and his name was Han Sik and his brother's name was Jang Sik. Then, when it came to our generation, we were all Hee. So my first cousins were all named Hee, that is, the name ending was Hee. Now my nephews, their beginnings are the same. My nephew and their first cousins are all starting with Ki, and I found out that their children would start with Suh. My paternal grandfather was Sung Tae and the ending was the same for my father's first syllable. This was explained to me by relatives, and they said that the tribe was the Hong tribe. They meet at least every ten years, and at that time, they all select a chairman.

Let's go on with your personal life.

While on Maui, during World War II, we learned a lot about demand and supply. My brother and I went around picking coffee beans because the horses and cattle needed feeding. Now we did sell some of the beans. I think they were 20 cents a bag. We held back several bags, about fifteen, twenty bags, hoping that the price would go up. Then the war ended. We got stuck with the beans. That was our first lesson in demand and supply.

Tell us about life on Fort Street in Honolulu.

We were in high school and my brother was attending the University of Hawaii. We were pretty active because all our friends about our age used to come to our church. The church was the social center, and we had social parties at the dorm because the dorm had a big area where they always had parties for the church. Now that was when social dancing was quite popular, and we wanted to have social dancing during our parties. We had music from phonographs and we enjoyed ourselves. The Methodist Mission objected to that so they used to send someone to watch whatever we did, and we rebelled.

Finally, I guess the elders gave in, so we did enjoy every weekend. Teenagers and college-age kids came and enjoyed themselves on our mission grounds. Another gathering that we enjoyed was our choir, which met once a week, and Donald Youngak Kang, who had a good ear for music, was our music director. He never played any instrument for us, but he was very good with tones. His wife, Fannie Nam, was our church organist. We enjoyed him for many years. And we used to compete with Rhee's Christian Church choir. We always were better singers.

I got married in 1934 to Ernest K. H. Park, who was at that time working at Pearl Harbor. He had gone to the University of Hawaii but did not finish because his brother Edward, who was also his twin brother, was also attending college, and financially their parents couldn't afford two of them going to college. So, since my husband had an opportunity to work at Pearl Harbor, he quit his school and went to work. At that time, very few people owned their homes so we lived in a rented house on Powell Street. The rent was only $21 a month. From there we moved to Nuuanu and then to Puunui. Later on, when my father built a home at Kam Heights, we moved to that home and shared the house with my brother, Bill, who was also married. [This indicates that the Depression in America also hit the families of Hawaii very hard.]

Could you tell us a little bit about your husband's family? I understand that they were very prominent among Koreans in Hawaii.
Well, Ernest, my husband, had a twin brother, Edward Park. There were three other siblings who were born in Korea and came to Hawaii with their parents when their were very young. Kwan Mo, Kwan Doo, and Esther Park arrived from Korea, so they were aliens. Kwan Mo was sent to a theological college in Kentucky, and when he finished, he returned to Korea, where he got married and had one daughter named Soon Yang. I was informed that Kwan Moo was involved in the 1919 Independence Movement rebellion. He was immediately arrested because the Japanese were arresting all the Korean young men who had Western education. Kwan Mo was one of them. I was told that during his imprisonment he contracted tuberculosis, and in later years, I don't know how long later, he died of tuberculosis, so he died in Korea. Kwan Doo graduated from the University of Hawaii with a degree in architecture, and he was the first structural engineer in Hawaii.

Esther graduated from the university and was teaching in Hawaii until she had to give up her teaching job; she was told that because she was an alien, she would not be able to hold a government job. So she was given a job as a, more or less, matron at private boarding schools in Hawaii. Then she was offered a scholarship by the YWCA to get further training and join the staff of the YWCA on Richards Street. Eventually, she became the director of the YWCA in Korea after World War II.

Eddie, the twin brother of my husband, finished university as a civil engineer. So he worked for the City and County. By that time, Ernest also worked for the City and County of Honolulu. The twin brothers, Ernest and Edward, decided to form a company, which they called Park and Park. And they worked together for several years until they split in 1959. Then Ernest had his own office, and Eddie had a corporation of his own.

Ernest and I adopted three children: Erna, Susan, and Michael Park. They were all three years apart. Erna and Susan were adopted in Honolulu. Michael came from Korea. Ernest did well at work, but he was a compulsive gambler, which I didn't know. So when I found out that we were losing our home in Kahala in 1964, I got a divorce. Now I had to take care of the three children alone because Ernest couldn't afford to take care of them. I was fortunate that I found work at the Palama Settlement and later I was working at Leahi Hospital as a social worker.

I started off my employment life during the depression years, when there weren't many jobs, working as a clerk at the Palama Settlement. The director of the settlement thought I had more ability than just a clerk, and so he gave me permission to attend classes at the University of Hawaii in the afternoon. After I graduated with a degree, Palama Settlement gave me a job as a social worker. I worked there for several years.

At Palama Settlement, I helped Dr. Rhee's wife, Francesca Rhee, get medical help for the children who were at the Korean Christian Institute, the orphanage that Dr. Rhee established. So the Rhees and I knew each other well. Dr. Rhee himself knew me well also because of my father. There was a time my father, although a Methodist Church minister, was a very close friend of Rhee, when Rhee was the principal of the Methodist Mission Boys' School from 1913 to 1915. They were

9

greatly involved in the Korean Independence Movement, but with different views. Rhee and my father broke off their close relationship in 1916, but they were distant friends.

Then I was offered a job at Leahi Hospital. To prove to myself that I could handle it, I accepted the job although I was needed at home to take care of my children. A couple of years later, I resigned and stayed at home to take care of the children until I was was asked to come back again in 1954, which I did and stayed, until I retired in 1975. So now I'm finally comfortable because I have earned Social Security and a government pension.

Did you join any Korean organizations?
During the war years, a lot of our friends were members of the Korean Delta Fraternity and Sorority. They wanted Ernest and me to join. Our initiation fee was $150. Most of the members were Korean Christian Church members from Rhee's church. But we joined, and that's how we became very good friends with persons like Harry Choi and his wife, Komeni Pai, all Rhee's church members. Wilbert Choi, I knew him when he was still in high school. He always took me as an older sister. He used to invite us to go up mountain-apple picking. When he graduated from high school, he was offered a job by Ewa Plantation. As we grew older, he used to invite Mrs. Yang [Polly Tai Yang, Dr. You Chan Yang's wife] and myself to his home for chicken dinner. He wasn't married at that time. He was a good cook, so he was a very good friend of mine until he passed away.

This is how we—the Methodist Church members and the Korean Christian Church members—still could be good friends.

Tell us more about the differences between you, a Korean Methodist Church member, and Korean Christian Church members. What happened there? How did you become friends with the Delta Fraternity, which was a Korean Christian Church organization?
Well, I didn't know very many Korean Christian Church people. There were a few that used to come to the Fort Street Methodist Church grounds just to join our social functions or just to meet some of the girls or boys.

But tell us about the relationship between the Methodist Church and the Korean Christian Church and its effect on the second generation.

I don't know, I was too engrossed in our own activities.

But you do know about the beginnings of the Korean Christian Church.

Not too well because we were living on Maui at that time ... when the church separated, actually separated ...

What church separated?

The Methodist Church and the Korean Christian Church that Dr. Rhee started.

The Methodist Church existed first, right? Then, within the Methodist Church, there was a split. Dr. Rhee had left the Methodist Church ... and began his own church, splitting the congregation of Koreans.

That's right.

So making friends with Korean Christian Church members was kind of unusual.

For me, it was. Because all the time, until I graduated from high school—I mean, just before graduating high school—we were living on a different island so we had no contact with the Korean Christian Church people.

But you were one of those who broke the ice, so to speak, between the two congregations, right?

I guess it was because the other side came around to our Fort Street Methodist area. We had more modern activities in the Honolulu Methodist Church for the youngsters.

So you became friends by accident?

Yes, by accident. There'd be girls coming to our church, not to attend church, but to come around our parsonage, where we had socials, and we became friends. When I was attending the University of Hawaii,

I think the majority were Methodist students. There were one or two that were Christian Church people, like Yo Imi Kim, O'Neil Hwang. They were strong Christian Church members. Other than that, I think the rest were all Methodist.

So there was friction between the two churches?
Yes. Because they got that feeling from their parents. They themselves, I don't think felt it too much. Like the Delta Frat was started, of course, by Donald Kang, who was a Methodist, but those Christian Church people belonged to it, too, as well as members of the YMCA. The YMCA was where the Methodist and Korean Christian Church young people met, and I guess that's how Donald Kang could start the basketball team with both kinds of youngsters at that one place, meeting informally.

What about Wilbert Choi? His family were strong Rhee's supporters. What do you know about his circumstances?
As I told you [earlier], he was the first FFA [Future Farmers of America] representative to go to the Mainland. And because some were not in a financial situation where they could go to college, he was one of those who had to work after he graduated from high school. Luckily for him being a FFA representative without a college degree was prestigious.

So Ewa Plantation hired him because he was the FFA representative. At first, they thought he was Chinese. Because Ewa Plantation managers had a very difficult time with Koreans, they had vowed that they would never hire a Korean. They did not know Wilbert was Korean when they hired him. Later, they found out that he was Korean, but because Wilbert did well for them, they kept him until he was offered a job by Doris Duke, the multimillionaire heiress. He became her head landscaper at her beautiful home along the Diamond Head sea shore, called the Black Lagoon. And then, from there, he became very wealthy.

At that time Wilbert became the unofficial leader of the Korean community, didn't he? He was famous in the Korean community, wasn't he?
Yes. Somehow, because Wilbert worked for USCD [U.S. Civil Defense], he had contacts with Korean prisoners who were in the

Japanese army as laborers. The Korean prisoners were caught in Okinawa and brought to Hawaii for imprisonment along with the Japanese soldiers. But they were not placed in the same prison camp. Wilbert Choi had a soft heart. He made contacts with the Korean prisoners. Wilbert took them on as one of the big projects for Delta Frat to take over. They gave the Korean prisoners Christmas gifts, special food, and other things. So we at Delta Frat made packages of cigarettes, candy, etc. We cooked dinner for them on special occa-

Wilbert Choi, circa 1930s.

sions. Wilbert had the facilities to do these things because he was living in one of Doris Duke's quarters at the beautiful Black Lagoon near Waikiki. He could use the yard space there, and Delta Frat had all the cooking things to be able to handle a big project like that there. We enjoyed doing that.

So Wilbert was sort of like a role model? His family, from Wahiawa, were strong Rhee supporters, weren't they?
Yes, and his family always worshiped Dr. Syngman Rhee. Their relationship was so close that Wilbert got to know a lot of Korean generals who used to come by Hawaii, who were likely sent by Dr. Rhee after he became president.

Because of Wilbert's stature in the community?
Yes. And Wilbert became the idol of many young people. Many years later, Wilbert rescued Dr. Syngman Rhee from the riots when Rhee was deposed in 1960.

What other activities were going on among the Korean societies? You were in the thick of these societies after the war so you must know a lot.

After the war, I was engrossed in University of Hawaii activities, not only Korean activities. While I was at the university, Ms. Ha Soo Whang was on the staff of the International YWCA. At that time, they had all different ethnic groups, separately. She got the high school and university girls to form a club called the Hyung Jay Club. And I think Sarah Lee Yang was the first member. Later on, Rose Shon and myself became members. I was the first delegate from the Hyung Jay Club to go to the Asilomar Conference in California. That was in 1932. Sarah Lee and Rose Shon qualified to be delegates, but Sarah Lee was already on the Mainland, and Rose was on her way to the Mainland. So I happened to be the next qualified person.

Tell us about this seminar in Asilomar. I believe that it was an important event and broadened your experience.
The Asilomar Conference. It was a YWCA conference for young professional working women. It was all in the California area. It was about a one-week conference. I forget now what the goal was or what the theme was at that time. It's been so long ago. That was in 1932. Asilomar is near Monterey and Carmel.

And who was there?
From Honolulu, we had one from the Chinese club, Gladys Chung Tan, and one Portuguese, Roseline Corea. Including me, there were three of us.

It seems that travel broadened the life experience of a young person in those days. Was that an annual thing?
I guess so. That was my first trip to the Mainland—the continental United States of America. Hawaii was American, but it was a territory of America.

There was no plane to go to the Mainland at that time, and I was an alien. So, because I was an alien, I had to get a Japanese passport. Remember that when I arrived in Honolulu for the first time from Korea, Korea was occupied by the Japanese. All Koreans at that time were considered Japanese citizens. So, because I had a Japanese passport, when I went to the Asilomar Conference, I was the last one to get off the ship in California because I was considered a foreigner.

Years later, I had another problem with my citizenship and that was in 1952, when we went to California. We were going to a Rose Bowl game. After that we were going to Mexico, but I couldn't get a visa to go to Mexico. There were four of us: Eddie; his wife, Bettie; Ernest; and myself. I told them you folks go ahead and while you folks go to Mexico, I shall go to Washington, D.C., and visit Polly—Mrs. Yang, the wife of Ambassador You Chan Yang. Polly was my closest friend. So I was fortunate in going at that time, when it was the inaugural year for the President of America. Since the Yangs were invited to the inaugural, I was able to go to the Georgetown Inaugural Ball with them. Also I went to the inaugural ceremony because I was asked to accompany Mrs. Yang. I had a wonderful time and experience.

Would you explain your friendship with Polly Yang and her husband?
She was the ambassador's wife so she was recognized for her high position in Korean society everywhere. Dr. You Chan Yang was at one time a physician in Honolulu. He was quite famous because he is the one who introduced insulin for diabetes, and he treated some of the well-known Hawaiians. He was a popular doctor for the wealthy royal Hawaiians. He was always someone my family knew because he was a Methodist—when he was a child and up to college days.

The Methodist people felt Dr. Yang betrayed the Methodist Church because he and Dr. Dae Bong Kim were the two that were given scholarships to a Methodist university in Boston to get their medical doctor's degree. Dr. Kim remained loyal to his faith in the Methodist Church, but Dr. Yang changed to follow Dr. Rhee.

What happened?
Y.C. Yang was always loyal to Syngman Rhee since 1914, when they both were members at the Methodist Church, years ago. They kept their relationship even when Dr. Rhee broke away from the Methodist Church. Years later, Dr. Rhee appointed Y.C. Yang to become the ambassador from Korea to the United States in 1950. Dr. Y.C. Yang had never become an American citizen. The McCarran–Walter Immigration Bill to allow aliens to become U.S. naturalized citizens wasn't passed until 1952. Since Y.C. Yang remained a Korean citizen, he could be appointed as the Korean ambassador to America by Dr. Rhee.

Let's get back to the point where you said that Yang was a traitor to the Methodist Church because he was educated with support from the Methodist congregation, and after he was educated, he broke away and followed Rhee to his church.

By the time Yang broke away, it was after he graduated from college that the Christian Church had a stronghold on the community.

Then he decided to follow Dr. Rhee. Tell us a little bit more about the ambassador. This is very interesting—you're saying things I've never heard before.

Well, Dr. Yang knew of me, and I became very good friends with him when he married Pauline Tai. Pauline Tai and I were chums at the university, although she was one class below me. It was her first marriage to Y.C. Yang, and this was his second marriage. He had married a Caucasian woman that he knew at Boston University. They had one daughter named Peggie. Peggie just recently died . . . about a year ago.

What happened to his first wife?

You Chan was a widower, quite early. His wife was active in Hawaii local society. She was quite active in the Korean community also. At one time, I think she was the president of the Board of the YWCA on Richards Street. When their daughter, Peggie, was still very young, she wanted to give her some Oriental culture experience, so she took Peggie to Korea. I don't know how long they lived in Korea, whether it was one or two years. That's where and when Mrs. Yang contracted trichinosis . . . pork disease. When she came back to Hawaii, she was hospitalized. She was very seriously ill and she died of that disease. Then You Chan married Pauline Tai, my close friend.

Was Pauline a Korean Christian Church member?

No, her family were Methodists, not exactly strong church members, but strong Kookminhoe members . . . very strong members. Pauline's father was a very good-looking, physically well-built man, unusually tall, more than the average Korean man. And he always had a good position on the plantation staff. Before he retired, he was head luna [boss] at the Aiea Plantation.

You Chan and Pauline had two children, Sheila and Channie. The children resided in Washington, D.C., when they were growing up. They were seldom seen in Hawaii. Peggie, Dr. Yang's first daughter by his first wife, sort of disappeared and so did Channie.

Let's get back to your personal life. Some of the meetings and conferences you attended, especially Asilomar in California, were impressive. Were there other similar conferences that you attended?
That was the only major conference ... that was the only organization outside of a Korean organization we were able to go to in those days.

You belonged to Delta Frat. Tell us a little bit more about it. [This was a Korean association, mainly made up of young Korean Christian Church members. Although the name seems to indicate that its members were college students or graduates, most of them were neither affiliated with colleges nor were they college students.]
When I joined the Delta Frat, it was mostly a social club. In 1959, because Wilbert Choi was very interested in Korea and in President Rhee, he suggested that Delta Frat members make a trip to Korea. He would make all the arrangements. Since Delta Frat had quite a bit of money in the treasury, they divided it evenly, among all the members. There were several members, most of the members, in fact, made the trip in 1959. We took Pan Am, and Pan Am had that airplane with a big belly. It took us, I think, over thirty hours to get to Korea because we stopped in Midway and in Japan, and then Korea. The welcoming group arranged under Rhee's direction gave us a wonderful reception.

Last week you were telling us about your relationship with Dr. Rhee. When you got to Korea, you stayed at the Blue House.
Well, out of respect for my father (who was against Rhee and could not go to Korea because of Rhee), I went to Korea, perhaps unknown to Rhee. I stayed in the background when the group met with Rhee. This was my second trip to Korea. I had already been to Chung Wha Dae when the vice-president had been Lee Ki Bum. His wife, Mrs. Lee, took us and gave us a tour of Chung Wha Dae at that time.

So I wasn't too interested in meeting President Rhee, but I went for the gatherings with my friends in the Delta Frat group. I kept a low profile because I really didn't really want to have pictures taken with Rhee, out of respect for my father. My father and President Rhee, socially they got together, but politically they never did agree.

Ironically, a strange phenomenon happened years later, when they were dying, that put Rhee and Rev. Hong together: Both of them died on the same day. My father died in the morning at Kuakini Hospital and President Rhee died about four hours later at Maunaloa Hospital.

What did they agree on and, politically, what did they disagree about?

Because of the opportunity the Methodist Mission gave to the Korean community to become Christians and settle in Hawaii, my father was always very loyal to the Methodist Church. My father felt that Dr. Rhee should have been loyal, too. My father didn't feel that there was anything wrong for the Korean Methodist Church in Hawaii to be attached to the Methodist Mission on the Mainland. President Rhee's excuse to pull away was that he said that the Mission wanted to keep all the money. Rhee said that the Koreans should handle the money here, among the Koreans, although the Koreans didn't collect so much that they could have been independent.

Tell us a little bit more about your memories of Dr. Syngman Rhee.

Well, I was a youngster, oh maybe about five or six years old. I don't believe I remember seeing him when I was that young, but I do recall when I was a bit older that he used to ask me to pull his white hair. He used to wear his hair short. When he started the Liliha School, he had Mrs. Choi, who was Salome Han's mother, to take care of him . . . like a matron and also cook for the girls' school, which Rhee started.

Because Mrs. Choi and my mother were very good friends, one weekend Mrs. Choi said that she'd let me stay over at the girls' school for the weekend. I stayed and I got the "nits"—lice—in my hair. After that my mother said no more of going to the girls' dormitory.

Then our family was sent to Maui, where my father became the pastor of that Methodist Mission there. [At this time there was friction between Rhee and the Kuk Min Hur. Rev. Hong was the president of Kuk Min Hur.] I guess the separation [between Rhee and Rev. Hong] wasn't clear cut because I remember Dr. Rhee and maybe two or three of his haole—Caucasian—teachers had accompanied him and came to visit Spreckesville, where our family lived at that time. He visited our family. Maybe he came to look around and see whether he could start a Korean Christian Church there, which later on became a very strong area, Paia, for Koreans. I remember having to pull his white hair again there and we also had a gathering at the camp on the beach. That's all I can remember as a child of having seen him.

Dr. Syngman Rhee sleeping at a beach on Maui in 1918 after visiting Rev. Han Sik Hong; Rhee had asked him to be the first minister of his Korean church.

When Dr. Rhee and his wife, Francesca, came back to Hawaii [in 1935] after having lived on the Mainland for several years, they lived in Kalihi at the girls' dorm, and Mrs. Rhee took care of him. [The Rhees met and were married in Austria; they then stayed in California for a short while before moving back to Hawaii.] I guess she was just like a matron of Rhee's girls' school because once a year Mrs. Rhee brought the children to us for their general physical exam [at Palama Settlement, where Mary was a social worker]. Or if something was

The Palama Settlement in Kalihi was an important playground and social service care arena for children who came from plantation families. Mary Hong Park, the first certified Korean social worker in Hawaii, worked there from 1936 to 1940. Palama Settlement Archives.

really wrong with them medically, they also used to come to Palama Settlement. As a social worker there, in that way, I helped Rhee's school very much.

Were these children orphans at their school?

Most were, I guess, orphans, but I didn't know any of the children's backgrounds well. I knew them when they used to come to Palama Settlement, knew that they were Koreans and were from Rhee's school. Mrs. Rhee brought some of them. Also I did see Dr. Rhee visiting Dr. Yang at his office, which was nearby.

During one of Dr. Rhee's visits to our house, he invited my father to go to a movie with him. Whether my father went or not, I don't remember. But I know there was an invitation. So my father always said they were friends and that he had nothing against President Rhee, except that politically he didn't agree with him.

20

Profile of
Mary Hong Park

Mary Hong, right, returning from Asilomar, California, 1932.

Mary Hong Park is the most extraordinary interviewee among the nineteen presented in this book. Born in 1909 in Korea, she arrived in Hawaii at age three. Co-author Roberta Chang has been interviewing her intensely for the past fifteen years, and she and Mary have been friends for more than forty-five years. Since she first formally interviewed Mary in 1993, she has continued to see her almost weekly or called her for detailed information about certain events in the past.

Mary Hong Park is the daughter of Rev. Han Sik Hong, a minster of the Korean Methodist Church who had significant relationships with the major figures in the Korean Independence Movement. Rev. Hong had a close relationship with Dr. Syngman Rhee at the crucial time when the Korean community began to become dysfunctional as a united community.

Mary Hong Park's own life story in Hawaii is very important because she has in-depth knowledge of the various Korean organizations in Hawaii. She was privy to the nuances of the interpersonal relationships among the first and second generations, either immigrants or local born, because she had numerous friends from both sides of the Korean political divide. Her detailed accounts expand nine decades.

Moreover, Mary Hong Park married into another iconic family of the past: She was married to Ernest Park, the son of Chong Su Park, the second commander of the Korean Military Brigade in Hawaii under Commander Young Man Pak. In addition to her own parental heritage, her husband's family history adds to this recollection of the past. The story of Chong Su Park, Mary's father-in-law, deserves a full review at another time.

2
Interview with Mary Lee Moon Han

My name is Mary Lee Moon Han, and I was born in November 1918 in Waialua, Hawaii. My father, Man Kee Lee, came as a sugar plantation worker in 1903 from Korea. He left my mom, Si On Lee, and my older sister and brother in Korea. He came alone because my mother refused to come with him. She refused to leave with him because at that time in Korea, my father was a spoiled child. He drank and gambled, and so she didn't want to come to Hawaii and suffer. She stayed with her mom, and I understand from the story that she told me that during the harsh winter, their son passed

Man Kee Lee (back, standing left) and Seon Joo Choi (back, standing right) families; front, left to right: Mary Lee (Moon Han), Si On (Man Kee Lee's wife), Ruth Lee (Mack), Harry Choi, Wan Soon Lee Choi, Smith Choi.

away when he was an infant. So we never had a brother. Many years later, I remember my mother telling me that my father used to send friends, whoever was going back to Korea . . . he would tell them . . . please go and tell his wife that he had changed and please come to Hawaii with their daughter, but she never believed that he would change and so she did not go to Hawaii. Finally, in 1918, he personally went to get them, and that's why I call myself the "love child" because I was conceived in Korea, when he came to get my mother and sister.

My mother always told me the story that she was very sick coming to Hawaii on the ship because she was pregnant with me. She was sick with me plus being seasick. My older sister was already seventeen and half years old, almost eighteen years old. She came along to Hawaii. The sad thing was that when they landed, my sister couldn't de-board because she had "pink eye" and it was infectious. She had to be sent back to Japan, where all Korean immigrants had to go first for a physical examination. Can you imagine my mom letting her go back to Japan alone? But she had to, that was the law. So, after a few months, my sister came back all healed.

We then settled in Waialua, and this is where I was born. My father worked at the Waialua Plantation mill. I remember that my mother frequently told me she was so afraid of everything because she couldn't speak English. She would dress me in a bright Korean dress so she could spot me when looking out the kitchen window to see wherever I was. So I was really so precious to her, as she always used to say. She was so afraid of everything in Hawaii that she told my father to stay home during the day and to work on the night shift. During the night she used to have a young boy come to spend the night at the house. By telling me all these stories, I realized how precious I was to her.

Finally, my father found Mr. Seon Joo Choi to marry my older sister. The young man was very likable because he didn't drink, he didn't smoke, and he didn't gamble. So my father introduced them. At first sight of my sister, Choi fell in love with her. He used to work at Schofield Military Barracks. He walked all the way to Waialua every weekend to visit her . . . imagine, from Schofield to Waialua Plantation to visit her. Then they got married.

My father resigned from his plantation job, and we all moved to Honolulu and he became a barber for a while. Then later my father joined my brother-in-law in his laundry business; we all moved back to the Schofield Military Barracks area. At that time they called it Leilehua Village. He used to pack the laundry on his shoulders and deliver it. We really never suffered financially.

23

Father Man Kee Lee with Ruth, daughter. Background is Onyong Camp area in Wahiawa, near Wahiawa Elementary School.

Mary Lee (Moon) and Ruth Lee (Mack) at young ages in front of the Onyong Camp, which was originally a Chinese camp in Wahiawa.

We didn't know what the Depression meant in 1929 and thereafter, because the Schofield Military soldiers got paid regularly, they were good customers. The soldiers paid their bills regularly. The laundry and tailor business in that area became very popular among Koreans. Many new families moved there also. Most of them had some kind of laundry business there, too.

Wahiawa, which is very close to Schofield, was called the Korean Town of Hawaii. Most Koreans worked at the tailor or laundry shops in the same area. Then later I remember we finally moved to the town of Wahiawa, where Top-Hat Club is now; my brother-in-law bought a house near there, and we all lived together, and that is where we grew up. We went to Wahiawa Elementary School and graduated from Wahiawa High School.

After graduation, I went to Honolulu everyday with my brother-in-law, where he had another type of business. By that time, he owned a radio store. I went to Honolulu with him to study at a secretary commercial school. After school I waited for my brother-in-law and then came home with him to a good dinner: Mom did all the cooking. It was a long ride from Honolulu to Wahiawa. All I did was eat and study, and then I graduated in 1939 from the Commercial School. In the meantime, I met my husband, Duk Moon. Right after business school graduation, we got married in 1939. Our oldest son, Ronald, was born a year later, 1940.

Duke Duk Man Moon, circa 1934.

Chong Hurn Moon, widower, and children Thomas, Daniel, Duke Duk Man, and Beatrice, circa 1935.

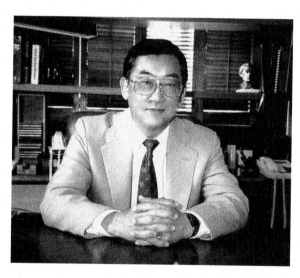

Hawaii State Chief Justice Ronald Moon, grandson of Bok Dok Ahn Moon, a picture bride, circa 2000.

Then World War II began. The military wanted all of us to help in the war effort, so we all had to work for the U.S. Army. I worked for about eight months as a secretary to the chief engineer. Then after eight months my second child, Eric, was born. After working in the army for a while, my husband worked at Ford Island as a time keeper. Then he worked for his father for a while in Wahiawa at a shop he started. Then Duk decided to open his own store. After his father retired, we bought the building his father had rented, and

25

Registration form for alien status issued by the United Korean Committee and certificate of alien registration issued for Man Kee Lee in 1942.

we opened a trading store. In the beginning, we thought of having a toy store, but we found out it was seasonal, so we decided to open a trading store. We added children's, men's and women's goods, trading at a small country store. We lived upstairs until 1958, when my oldest son, Ronald, graduated from Mid-Pacific High School and College. We finally could afford to buy a home on Glenn Avenue, a very nice area in Wahiawa. We've been here ever since.

Chong Hurn Moon's son Duke Duk Man Moon took over his father's shop in 1940 and opened Duke's Clothing, circa 1940. Insert: Chong Hurn Moon tailor shop in Wahiawa, circa 1930s.

As we were growing up, we always had to go to church; it was always the Korean Christian Church. We also went to the Korean language school after the English school. People even now ask me, "Where did you learn how to speak Korean?" or "When did you come from Korea?" I said, "No, I was born here." Those days, as soon as we were at home, we always spoke Korean. I'm very, very grateful that we had that opportunity to learn Korean and to speak Korean at home. The Korean language just comes naturally to me even now.

Duk, my husband, joined Christian Endeavor (a study group at the Korean Christian Church). He did not have a lot of time; but when any elderly person needed to have letters translated, letters written in English by their children who lived on the Mainland, he would make time to help them. My children were brought up knowing that helping other people was the thing to do.

Could you tell me more about Christian Endeavor?

In those days, church was not only Sunday service, but it was a place where people met. Christian Endeavor was a young people's group that met in the evenings. My husband, Duk, was always in charge of that. That was when we went to Christian Endeavor. My children grew up knowing that Sunday was always a family time. We would go riding or do some activity, but all had to be back by six o'clock. Duke, who also took care of the children's choir, was a Sunday school teacher and president of the church congregation. He was very, very active in other Korean community affairs; plus he was the president of the Wahiawa Community Association. He was very active in the general community—not only for Koreans. So he was a very, very busy man. People admired him for that. In 1970 he passed away from lung cancer, which is very ironic because he did not smoke, never drank, and was a very good church man. I always used to tell people that, yes, he was only fifty-five. I guess he finished his work down here, and God needed him more up there.

As soon as he passed away, I could have sold the business and not have to worry too much. But I remodeled the store and worked at it until I retired in about 1980. All of my children, all went to college because they knew that they all had to go to college. And this is how the children were brought up, knowing that they had to go to college. All four of them have college degrees. I give my husband a lot of credit

Mary Moon Han at her remodeled store, circa 1980.

because no matter how busy he was, he spent time with the children. Today I'm really proud of all of them.

Of course, everyone knows that my oldest son, Ronald, is Chief Justice of the Supreme Court of Hawaii. My second son is an attorney on the island of Kauai, and my daughter is a speech therapist, married to an optometrist. She works for him. And my youngest son works for the City and County, as a manager of the open market. So they're all doing fine. Now I can retire, but still I try to keep the Korean culture, the Korean background and teach them at home. We still attend the same church. Our church just celebrated its eightieth anniversary a couple of months ago.

We had a club called the Taeguk Club. It was formed in the 1930s as an athletic club in Wahiawa. It was all male, and gradually they invited women to join. It became a cultural club. At one time, it was a huge club, but since then, it's been cut down to like two, three families. We try to keep it going because we feel that we don't want to lose it. Our husbands started this club in the 1930s, and we still wanted to be here to help, culturally. But over the years, the club did not meet monthly. Now we do meet whenever we feel it's necessary, at least three, four times a year. Lately, we've just elected a young man, originally from Korea. His name is Peter Choi. He settled down in our town because he has a business in Wahiawa. So we feel that the club may carry on into the future.

What did you say was the goal of the Taeguk Club way back in the beginning?

Way back in the beginning, it was started as an athletic club. The members were all men. They used to participate in baseball, basketball, and volleyball competitions. Very active. And then gradually, when the young men got married, their wives were invited to join. We changed the constitution to become a little more cultural and humanitarian for Korea. Whenever there were floods in Korea, we sent money to the orphanages in Korea. We sent food, clothing whenever it flooded. Every year it seems Korea has floods. Duk was active in other local American clubs or organizations, but his heart was always in Korean activities for Korea. We always had clothing drives. We always sent whatever money we could to Korean orphanages. We adopted an orphanage.

When were these activities?

In the 1930s, 1940s. We started the Taeguk Club when some of us were in high school. Our parents were so strict, they wouldn't let us out. The only time we could go out was when we attended the church services or the Korean youth club or the choir. In those days we had lots of members.

Were these members from Wahiawa?

Yes. But there was a very talented member, Donald Yong Gak Kang, who was more like a leader of youth groups in Honolulu. He was a Methodist. It did not matter to him if we were Rhee's followers. He helped us form our group, too. He is well known for the formation of young Korean leaderships everywhere. So he would come by to help us establish the club. The membership of the Taeguk Club was mostly from Wahiawa. However, as time passed by, we had members from Honolulu because they were originally from Wahiawa and then moved away. They still felt attached to us. The highways from Honolulu improved, and we all had cars, so they could come to Wahiawa easily.

How different is the Taeguk Club from the Korean American Club? And is the Korean American Club also based in Wahiawa?

The Korean American Club was more businesslike because it owned a building. Our parents belonged to it. The forefathers had the foresight to buy property to put up a community building. The founder was Mr. Cloud Owen, Philo Owen's father, one of the most well-known families in Wahiawa. But they were not Korean Christian Church members. Mr. Owen ran a grocery store for a long time. He had many sons, and he was very active in everything. We were very young when the Korean American Club began in 1923. Mr. Owen started a membership for the club, and one of the activities was to handle burial site maintenance. The club owned a truck, and he would take all of us to visit all the members' graves and put flowers on them. He would cook whenever we had a meeting. He would do the cooking when we had parties at the clubhouse. The Korean American Club members were from all over, even from Waialua and Honolulu. In the beginning the club initial membership fee was minimal. Now to join the club, there is a $100 initiation fee. The Korean American Club was more business-like, but they tried to keep the Korean culture alive by teaching us Korean things and getting us together to play. We played volleyball. I remember being very athletic because of that club.

As far as the Taeguk Club is concerned, it was more cultural and fellowship. We had parades, wearing Korean clothes. The members were very active in the established local community, whenever they needed help with Korean things.

Were there other differences, for example, in the age group that joined the clubs?

Yes. The Korean American Club got started by our parents, and then we took it over as they passed away. But the Korean Taeguk Club was started by our husbands. Ages and interests were different between the two clubs. Those people in the Korean American Club were more businessmen: They had money. But the Taeguk Club was for cultural reasons and fellowship. Like I said, it was an athletic club for the younger set.

So would you say that the Korean American Club members were more on the wealthy side?

I think so, because most of them had businesses, or they had a good job. And to me, they were older, they were more settled, whereas the Taeguk Club had younger people, just graduated from high school, just getting started in business, and so now, our children joined as members.

What year did you say the Taeguk Club began?

I think the Taeguk Club started in the 1930s.

Do you think the Korean American Club and the Taeguk Club had any connections with the Korean Liberation Movement?

The Taeguk Club was not interested in the Liberation Movement and the Korean American Club, too. I think the churches were more involved. The church that I went to —the Wahiawa Korean Christian Church—the members were the followers of Syngman Rhee, the first president of Korea. He was the founder. So naturally whenever he needed money, we raised money to help him, whenever he came to Wahiawa. We always had him over for a gathering. As far as the Taeguk Club was concerned, we were not interested in the Liberation Movement. Individually, the members may have been, but not as a club. Neither was the Korean American Club. I think in those days the churches were more deeply involved in the Korean Independence Movement.

You said that the Korean Christian Church in Wahiawa just recently celebrated its eightieth anniversary. So it's a little bit younger, by just a few months, than the Korean Christian Church in Honolulu.

Yes, I think so, because Dr. Syngman Rhee founded Liliha Church first, and then the country churches came after. We just recently changed our church's name to the Wahiawa United Church of Christ because we have so many intermarriages. Now a non-Korean person can join the Church no matter what nationality. So we felt we should change the name in the late 1980s.

What's the membership now?

We have about forty to thirty very active members. It's not large. But it's like a family church. We have different nationalities. We have some Filipinos and in fact, there are Japanese. So that's what we wanted; we wanted people from the community to come and feel that they could worship with us and so this is now our makeup of people, all different and a lot of intermarriages.

Tell us about the development of the Korean Christian Church in the younger days, when it was flourishing in the 1930s.

Oh, yes. That was when we were growing up. When you think about it, it was the only meeting place for our parents, and so it was like political plus worshiping. If they wanted to get together, it was at the church. At that time, most of them didn't have automobiles and some were far away in Honolulu. This was our meeting place and we grew up socially and politically in the same place of worship. I remember they used to have meetings during the week and on Sundays, for worship. So the church was used for many purposes.

What was the relationship with Koreans from the Korean Methodist Church, which was located near the Wahiawa shopping area? You all called it "down church" and yours "up church"?

Yes, we all went to either "up" or "down" church. It's so funny. Even now, we just refer to the churches as "down church" and "up church." When you say "down church," it's the Methodist Church. In school, we are all good friends and we got together, but then, when Sunday came, the Methodists went to their church and we came to our church. Sometimes, because we didn't have that many members as time went on, we tried to join together. We even talked about maybe we should join together, but it was funny, it just stayed that way. Maybe our next generation will just forget all about "down church" and "up church," but somehow, even at our age, it still is "down church" and "up church." Socially, we're friends, we're all good friends. It's just that we just don't go to each other's church. I guess it is because one group was anti-Syngman Rhee and one group was for Syngman Rhee. I think that was the basic reason; religiously, it's the same thing, we worship the same God and same everything. But to me . . . well, I guess maybe it's like the pilgrims in the olden days, when maybe they used the church politically. I think the same thing was just carried on.

Tell us about Syngman Rhee. What do you know about him and what was his relationship with Wahiawa? How did he get himself involved in church activities?

Well, as a young child, I always knew about Dr. Syngman Rhee. I remember my parents, even Duk, used to talk about him. They said we always have to help collect money for Rhee for the Independence Movement. This is how we grew up in our home; whenever we had extra money and if Rhee needed to have it to go to Washington, D.C., to fight for our independence, we all donated no matter how poor we were. I remember, it was Duk who said to his dad when he was young: "How come we give money to Dr. Rhee? We can't even have butter on the table except only once a week and yet you give money to him." The thing that was really funny to me was that he questioned his father, but Duk grew up helping Dr. Rhee all his life, even to adulthood.

Duk was American, but his heart was for Korea. And so, as we grew up and whenever March First came around, we'd all be dressed in Korean clothes and our parents would celebrate. I remember in those days we had to go to Honolulu because they would have a big meeting and everybody dressed in Korean dress. That is how we celebrated March First 1919. That was supposedly Independence Day.

At our church, Rev. Park Dong Whan, one of our first ministers, said he was involved in the Independence Movement in Korea. We could see the burns that he suffered on that day. They had put him in jail because he was active in the Korean Movement on March First. When he was put in jail, he was burned on his hands.

Yes, I will remember Dr. Syngman Rhee, always. Whenever he came to Hawaii, he would visit us in Wahiawa, too. We would invite him, and sometimes we had big, huge spontaneous parties. Rhee was always blowing on his fingers. I used to ask my dad, why is he doing that? My father said that Rhee was tortured by the Japanese. They put sticks or something under his fingernails and burned the sticks. Because of that, he blew his fingers still. And he always had twitches on his face—all this from all his suffering—and so we . . . the Korean Christian Church, which he founded—naturally, we backed him up whenever he needed money. We supported the poor Korean people, too. Everybody was poor in those days. Even many poor Koreans would save their money and helped Rhee's Independence Movement . . . even after the war in 1945 ended and Rhee became our first president.

Another thing I remember, in 1959 President Rhee invited many of his backers, anyone who wanted to go, to Korea. Eighty-one persons went from here. There were Methodist people, too. Yes, because it was open to anyone, but naturally most of the ones who went were the Korean Christian Church people, but I remember the Methodist reverend's family and his wife were there; they went with us, and that's the time they adopted a little daughter because they had two sons only. So they adopted a daughter in Korea.

I think people who really know about Dr. Syngman Rhee's history, whether Methodist or Christian Church members, they know he did something for our country.

As we grew up, we knew Dr. Rhee lived on Wilhelmina Rise. We used to visit him there, when we could. My brother-in-law, Seon Joo Choi, was a very active supporter. He was very active politically, and he was one of the founders of the Korean Christian Church in Wahiawa. As we grew up, that's all we knew about Dr. Syngman Rhee. We knew his background from what we heard from our parents; that's how much we knew.

Tell us more about your brother-in-law, Mr. Seon Joo Choi.
Seon Joo Choi had so much foresight. He was married to my older sister. He bought properties; he was the first to open a bowling ally in Wahiawa. He was very active at church, plus at the Dongji Hoi, which was the club that was formed to help Dr. Syngman Rhee. Seon Joo had only an eighth-grade education, but he was the only one among my parents and my older sister who could read and write English. He knew how to sew, how to run a business, and he bought a huge property, business property, in the middle of Wahiawa Shopping Center, which up to today, his sons are managing. This property contains everything they have businesswise: the Speed World Burger, Dot's Drive-In, and other shops that they own. Smithy Choi is his son and Anthony Choi is his grandson; they handle the properties. Smithy was a successful, well-known businessman, very active in many of the Korean clubs: the Taeguk Club, the Dongji Hoi, and the Korean American Club.

Where did Mr. Seon Joo Choi come from and when did he arrive in Hawaii?
From Pyongyang Do. He must have come in 1903 or maybe a little after because I remember my father saying that after he came here, he saw this young man who never drank, never gambled. Choi knew

my dad had a daughter in Korea and he wanted to meet her. As far as exactly what date my mother and my sister came, I have no idea.

Let's talk about Dongji Hoi. What do you know about it?

All I know of Dongji Hoi, when my parents and my brother-in-law were active in it, is that the main purpose was to help Dr. Syngman Rhee get independence for Korea. So no matter how poor we were, we always paid dues or when Rhee needed extra help. I remember my parents helping. I was very young at that time, so all I can remember as a child is that Dongji Hoi was Dr. Syngman Rhee's organization. My parents became members of Dongji Hoi early after it was established.

Right now, the purpose of Dongji Hoi is mostly scholarships for Korean children who are going to Korea. The interesting part of it is that most of the ones who are getting the university scholarships are the new immigrants' children [those who came to Hawaii in the 1990s]. They are so bright. But lately, we began giving to local Korean kids and our main purpose is helping them culturally, too. Most recently, there are not that much cultural activities. I think right now our activities are mostly to help children get scholarships. We still have Dongji Hoi.

One interesting thing that I remember about Dr. Syngman Rhee is that he established the Korean Christian Institute, and when they sold the property, half of the money went to the Inha College in Incheon, Korea. That's why its name is "In" for Incheon and "Ha" for Hawaii; they joined them to make it "Inha."

Were there many exchanges between the Wahiawa Korean Christian Church and Honolulu Christian Church? Did the two have very strong ties?

Yes, I remember whenever it was March First or some event, the Honolulu Korean Christian Church would be the one to initiate things because they were a larger group. We would attend, and even now, whenever they have something, we try to help them. I remember at one time their church in Honolulu didn't have a minister, and Rev. Richard Kim, who was our minister, felt that they needed him, so they asked our permission to ask him to be their minister. Naturally, we felt we're sister churches, and if they needed our help, we could go along, so he went over there. We had a lot of ministers, and because we were such a small church, we let him go to the Honolulu Korean Christian Church.

In the beginning, the ministers came directly from Korea so our church was like a training place. They would come here, learn the culture, learn maybe better English, and then, as soon as they wanted to better themselves and get more salary, they would move on to a bigger church in the city. If you come to our church, you would see all the ministers' photos that we had over the years. We felt that it was sort of our duty to help the new Korean ministers. We felt good that at least they got their training over here. Once they know the ropes they move on; after all, they all have to make a living. We are such a small church; we can't pay them too much.

After a while, we began to realize we were losing our younger people at church—even our own children—because they couldn't understand the Korean language; whereas, we older persons sat through the Korean sermons and the services, but the younger children, they wouldn't. Once the youngsters went to college and came back, they wouldn't come back to our church.

This is why we thought we'd change the name to the United Church of Christ and have services for other, mixed blood, parishioners. But it still was hard to get a minister. We tried to get them, especially when the immigrant Koreans started coming to our church, but somehow the cultural difference—a foreigner is so different, we just couldn't get along, you know. We Korean Americans had to have our own services.

The other nationalities had their own services, too, in the same building, but at different times. We rented the church building to them for a minimal monthly amount so that they could have their own church service after our church service. It's like doing missionary work. We feel that if they need our help, we give them some help. So that's the difference now. We don't have the word "Korean" in our church name, but basically we are Korean. We have the Korean flag on the podium beside the American flag and the Hawaiian flag to show that the church is for everyone.

What about the Korean Christian Institute (KCI)? Do you know anything about it or the students who attended the school?

Yes. I didn't go to the KCI, but I remember Duk telling me that he was there for a while because they were from Big Island, and they had no way to go to high school on that island. Dr. Syngman Rhee would go around the countryside and whoever wanted to go to school, he would bring them to Honolulu. Because Duk's mother died when he was very young, I remember he said he had to go to the Korean Christian Institute at one point for a short while. He remembered how poor they were at the Korean Christian Institute and how bad and negligible the food was there but then, he was grateful at least that he had a place to stay for little while, while his father was getting settled in the city of Honolulu.

What year do you think it was?
Oh, gee. I have really no idea how long ago that was because he said he was very young when that happened. And I remember Gertrude Lee saying she had gone there to KCI, and so many others had gone to KCI, and some went to the Susannah Wesley Home. I think the Wesley Home was a Methodist Church Mission. Quite a few other Korean children also went to the Korean Christian Institute.

Tell me what you know about Duk's family.
Well, I know he was in some place in Hilo and Honokaa [towns on the Big Island]. He was born in Honokaa, and he said he remembers his mother, who died very young . . . she was only twenty-six years old.

Could you give me Duk's father's and mother's whole names?
His father's name was Chong Hurn Moon and his mother's last name was Park. In those days, women kept their maiden names, so, as far as her first name, I'm not too sure.

How did she come?
She was a picture bride.

What year?
I don't know what year.

Was Duk the oldest?
Duk was the oldest and Dan Moon was two years younger.

Duk was born in 1915, so his mother must have come in 1914 or 1915, the same year my mother arrived.

Later, Beatrice was born. When she got married, she became a Kim. She died when she was only about forty-six years old.

Did Duk's father came to Hawaii alone?

Yes, he must have come here as a bachelor like most of them.

Before 1905?

Before 1905. So he was on the sugar plantation, I suppose, on the Big Island, Hawaii. And his wife came as a picture bride. She died so very young. Duk told me that she always went to church. He remembers going with her even in those days, and sometimes in the evenings, too. He would be holding her dress and walking everywhere with her; then, one day, he said she wasn't there. He asked his dad where his mom was; he said in the hospital. Duk never saw her after that.

So how many children were there in that family?

Four. All two years apart. Duk, Dan, and then came Beatrice, and then came the younger son, Thomas, whom they called Dike. All two years apart. Two birthdays were in April and two birthdays were in May, so strictly every two years. They had a very sad life because of losing their mother so young. They had a grandmother on the Pyo side, the maternal side. Duk and Jacob Pyo were first cousins. Jacob Pyo's mother and Duk Moon's mother were sisters, so their grandmother was on both sides. Duke and Jacob, Mable and Helen were first cousins. The oldest in the Pyo family was Helen Pyo Park. We all lived in Wahiawa and belonged to the same church.

Jacob's mother used to come and help take care of the Moon children once in a while, but mostly Duk's father raised them himself, especially when they were in Wahiawa and he opened a tailor shop in Schofield.

I guess among your generation you all married Koreans so that's why everybody is related.

That's right. Especially in Wahiawa the saying goes, better be careful because you could be speaking badly about their relatives.

In Honolulu, the younger set of your generation married Koreans.

No, all of my four children married outsiders, non-Koreans. That's why it's so ironic because Duk was such a patriotic Korean, a true Korean Korean, but then all his children married different nationalities.

That generation is slightly older than you, right? Weren't some of them born in Korea? When they came to America, they were called "1.5" just like your sister, who was born in Korea. They were all within the second generation, but very different.

Yes. During my time, I think, we were marrying only Koreans, so much so that all the Koreans became related. But later, the younger set of the second generation, who were born here after the 1920s, began to intermarry. That's why when my sister, Ruth, married Mack, a Caucasian, my father wouldn't give her away. So Duk had to give her away at the marriage ceremony. After they got married, our father began liking Mack so much that he couldn't do enough for his son-in-law because Mack was so nice, so very nice. Sadly, Mack died very young. Mack was only forty-one years old when he died. So Ruth had a rough time . . . widowed so young in her late thirties. She had a rough life.

Let's talk more about the second generation, your generation.

I remember going to Leilehua High School. We mostly hung around with Korean people because in those days we'd go to church, Korean language school, and somehow we just got directed to Korean friends only and married Koreans. But Bessie Lee, who moved away from Wahiawa after high school graduation and whom I haven't seen for years and years, married a Caucasian because she worked among them at the University of Hawaii. She was one of my best friends, when we were seniors in high school.

It was because of the Korean Student Alliance, too, which gave us the opportunity to hang around with Koreans our age, no matter what church we attended. Donald Yong Gak Kang formed the Korean Student Alliance. We always had meetings during school time, lunch time, or after school. All the Korean girls would sit around together, having lunch, or just chitchatting in those days. Yet, on the side, I did have some Japanese friends, too. But most of our friends—either in church, club work—we always hung around with Korean guys and gals. When the general non-Korean community wanted Korean entertainment, even though a few of us didn't know how to do Korean dancing or anything Korean, we'd dance because we had Korean dresses.

So nothing political like the Korean Independence Movement seeped into your relationships?

No, not in school—no politics—that to me, that was great. Once in a while, on Sundays, some speaker would say something at our own church, but after that, it didn't mean anything. Maybe for somebody older than us, but I didn't think so for our age group.

Who intermarried between the churches? Didn't it make a difference?

No, it didn't. It really didn't. Whether we were from "down church" or "up church," nothing like that affected us. When you think back, it was good to have friends from either side. Even though whatever our parents instilled in us, we still could be friends.

What about the war? How did it effect Wahiawa and your generation?

Well, when the Second World War came—I'll never forget that it was a Sunday—and my husband, Duk, got up early with our son, Ronald. Ronald was a few months old and Duk woke me up and said, "Mary, look at that. They're really having real maneuvers. They're practicing for real because I even see a plane with red paint on it, just like a Japanese plane." We really thought it was a maneuver because in those days, there were rumors that there would be a war. Then one of my neighbors living on Olive Avenue and one of my friends came running up and said, "This is a real war. Somebody got shot across the street on Kamehameha Highway." It was one of my Japanese friends that I knew that got shot because he went out to the corner of Olive Avenue and Kamehameha Highway. It was at a shoe store called Bailey Shoe Store. He was out there on the street and he happened to just lean forward to look up and a bullet got him.

Profile of
Mary Lee Moon Han

Mary Lee Moon Han was born 1918 in Waialua, Oahu, in a family of ardent followers of Dr. Syngman Rhee. They were founding members of Rhee's church in Wahiawa, the Wahiawa Korean Christian Church.

Mary married into the Moon family of Wahiawa, who were, with equal intensity, dedicated to Dr. Rhee. Both sets of parents, the Moon and the Lee families, were outstanding leaders in the Korean community in Wahiawa. (Mary married Joseph Han late in life, after her husband, Duke Moon, died.)

The Moon family is highly esteemed in Hawaii because Mary's son, Ronald Moon, became Chief Justice of the Supreme Court of Hawaii, the first Korean to achieve a high position statewide. This achievement is a reflection of the Moon family's dedication to community life.

Without a planned agenda, Mary's informal discussion of the Lee and Moon families' histories in Wahiawa led to the discussion of the unique place of the legacy of Rhee's affect on second-generation Koreans in Wahiawa during the most vulnerable time of the Independence Movement. Wahiawa remained Rhee's stronghold for his advancement in the political struggle to retain power throughout his entire life

in Hawaii and Washington, D. C. Wahiawa had the strongest component of Rhee's organization: the Dongji Hoi.

Mary Moon Han's casual description of the past greatly elucidated the many tiers of political development among the second generation. We can consider Mary a member of the second decade of the second generation. This differentiation of the decades among second-generation Koreans is important for understanding their perception of the Korean settlement in Hawaii. Other than Mary herself, this particular set of the second generation began to withdraw from deep participation in the Independence Movement, even before Korea was liberated. They were unlike the older second generation, who were ten years or more older. Within the second generation, there were so many drastic changes, politically, within one decade that we cannot evaluate the entire second generation as one entity and its affect on our major interest: the Korean Independence Movement in Hawaii.

From Mary Moon Han's discussion we can come to understand part of the reasons for the attachment between the Wahiawa second-generation children of the 1910s with Dr. Rhee. Many of the Wahiawa second-generation youngsters were the first in large numbers to benefit from Rhee's establishment of the Korean Christian Institute (KCI). The KCI allowed them or a sibling or a relative to stay in Honolulu for their education. During those early days, travel to Honolulu was long and tedious, making it more feasible to stay at the KCI dormitory.

The idolizing of Rhee among young Koreans began in 1914, when the first girls' dormitory began under Rhee's efforts. Thus most of these Wahiawa youngsters remained grateful and loyal to Rhee for many years, thereafter. One of the long-lasting dedicated youngsters starting from her KCI attendance was Gertrude Lee of Wahiawa, who became a wealthy businesswoman. She was a major Korean figure even years later in Hawaii in support of InHa University in Incheon, Korea. This discussion of the second generation begs further examination at another time. Suffice it to say that Gertrude Lee was always among the strong supporters of Rhee.

Gertrude Lee, a graduate of Dr. Rhee's Korean Christian Institute, became a wealthy woman. She supported Dr. Rhee's causes.

Mary Moon Han's interview is filled with valuable pertinent historic profiles of second-generation Koreans in the transition from being involved in their parents' emersion in the Korean Independence Movement and the youngsters' thoughts of breaking away from their parents' preoccupation. We must keep in mind the tiers of the second generation when trying to understand Mary Moon Han's references to the "second generation."

In 1959 Gertrude Lee (shown holding Rhee's hand) was warmly welcomed by President Rhee in Korea.

42

Interview with Dr. Thomas S. Min on his Mother, Mollie Hong Min

Mollie Hong Min   Dr. Thomas S. Min

I'm Dr. Thomas S. Min and I'm happy to narrate my mother's personal history. My mother, Mollie Hong Min, began writing her autobiography when she was in her eighties. She finally had time to sit down and write about herself. We found her handwritten story in a loose-leaf notebook after her death.

Mollie Hong Min, circa 1909.

My mother, Mollie Hong Min, was born in Pyongyang, Korea, on October 18, 1887. She described Pyongyang as a beautiful city that was completely surrounded by a large wall. There were two large rivers which ran on either side of the city, one on the east side called Tuman Gang, which flowed towards Seoul, and the other, Bok Dan Gang, which ran toward Manchuria. The city was protected by very high stone walls, and there were four large gates which were opened in the morning and closed in the evening by the government guards. Her parents lived in a large and beautiful house in the city, while Grandfather and Father lived in the country during the summer months to look after the farms on his land.

Mollie Hong Min's
parents: In Taik Hong,
father; Marjorie Hong,
mother, and brother,
Chi Pom Hong.

While growing up in the city, she lived with her mother and grandparents
in that very large and beautiful house, and she described the home as having
many servants. Her brother, Chi Pom Hong, was three years older. Her father
and grandfather were gone throughout most of the year, during the farm
season, because her grandfather owned a very large farmland, many miles off
from the city. The work was done by tenant farmers there, and they grew
many products which were brought into the city to be sold. When the late fall
weather began, her grandfather and her father came back and lived in the city
with the rest of the family.

My mother—this was not mentioned in her autobiography—told me
later about a humorous but sad period of this stage in her life. During the
winter months, when her grandfather and her father were back living with
them in the city, every evening after dinner they would leave the house and
go to a nearby tea house where all the wealthy Korean males gathered—no
females there supposedly, or theoretically, but *kyesangs* [female entertainers]
came to sing songs and create verses and poems and so on. In actuality, the
men did considerable drinking there. My mother told me that every night,
her grandfather and her father drank so much at the tea house that they were
brought home in two wheelbarrows and dumped on the front lawn. Then a
servant had to come out and carry them into their bedrooms and put them
to bed.

Mollie's mother and grandmother finally got sick and tired of this, so they packed up the two children and they took them way up in the hills to a Buddhist ladies' priest temple in Hwanghae Do, as I said, because of her father's and grandfather's excess drinking. Her mother and grandmother left word behind that they would not return until the men stopped drinking. Well, they stayed there for several weeks, and then a messenger arrived at the temple with a letter from her grandfather saying that they will reduce their amount of drinking. Grandmother sent back a letter saying that they would not return until they stopped their drinking completely. They waited there for a whole year, and finally, a messenger arrived with the message that they had stopped drinking and would never drink again. So grandmother and mother happily packed up their things and went back home with the children, and thereafter, they had a good life and everyone was happy.

During the early period in Pyongyang, I would say in the late 1880s, two missionary families came to the city to start churches, schools, and hospitals. They were Dr. William Noble with his wife, and Dr. Hall with his wife. They set up religious groups to teach Christianity. They set up a girls' school and a doctor's office and worked very hard for the Korean people. Dr. Noble was a physician. He set up a medical clinic where they gave free medical care to anyone that was willing to not be treated by herbal doctors. They worked very hard for the Korean people. Years later, Dr. Hall was killed by a very bad man. So Mrs. Hall went back to America and returned soon afterwards as a doctor with her two little children, a daughter and a son. There was a tragedy again, when her daughter died of an illness. Then her son went to America and also came back as a doctor

My mother's brother, Chi Pom, became a Christian and took her to Sunday school every Sunday. Chi Pom became very involved with the missionaries early on. Mollie also attended a girls' school that was teaching U.S. history, geography, arithmetic, and so on. Mrs. Hall found out that Mollie could read and write English well. She had been tutored in the English language by a private tutor at home. So, at the age of thirteen, Mollie became an English teacher at this missionary school.

Chi Pom Hong continued with his Christian faith. He became very, very strongly caring for his Christian faith, and in July of 1903, Dr. Noble induced Chi Pom to go to Hawaii as a Christian missionary for the Korean immigrants who had arrived in Hawaii during the past year. Dr. Noble also strongly suggested that Mollie go with him and attend English schools in

Rev. Chi Pom Hong and wife, Agyon Kim Hong, circa 1910.

Hawaii. Since the rest of the family did not want to remain behind without the children, their parents sold their large home in the city and went with them. The farmlands were given to the poor tenant farmers that had worked on those lands. The family got on a small boat that rowed down to the first southern port, which was Nampo. Sailing on a small boat was the only way to row down to Nampo. That took three days and three nights. Then they got on a larger boat and again slowly rowed down to Incheon. Finally, it reached Busan, and there they got on a larger boat that crossed over to Japan. There in Japan, they got on a large ship, named the SS *Coptic*. It took several weeks to reach Hawaii. They finally reached Honolulu on October 15, 1903, where they started a new life.

In Hawaii, Chi Pom Hong was placed in charge of the Korean Methodist community as a lay minister, and Mollie went to join the Kawaiahao Seminary for Girls, which was made up of a student body of white [Caucasian] and elite Hawaiian girls. Because of her Christian faith, they took her in without charging tuition.

Then Bishop Edmund Hughes, who was the head of the Methodist Church throughout the west coast of the Mainland and Hawaii and came to Hawaii on several occasions for conferences, met Mollie. When she graduated from Kawaiahao School, the bishop appointed her to go to San Francisco to attend the Methodist Deacon Theological College. The Methodist Women's English Board paid Mollie Hong's tuition until she graduated. She was the only Oriental and most likely the only Korean student at the Deacon School. During her years in college, many churches and organizations in San Francisco and California asked her to speak about the Christian movement in Korea. She became well known and respected. Mollie graduated from the Deacon School in 1913.

After her graduation, Bishop Hughes suggested that Mollie marry a Korean and made an arrangement for Mollie to meet Rev. Chan Ho Min. Chan Ho Min liked the arrangement. They were married on June 4, 1913, at Bishop Hughes' home, where numerous guests were invited.

Chan Ho Min had been sent to Hawaii as a young man to help the ministry for Korean immigrants in 1905. He was ordained before going to Hawaii and became the first official pastor of the Korean Methodist Mission Church in Honolulu in 1905. At that time Bishop Hughes had gotten to know Chan Ho quite well in Hawaii. The bishop also met with Chan Ho when Chan Ho was in Los Angeles to further his education at the University of Southern California in 1911, to further study divinity to become an elder. Although Rev. Chan Ho Min lived in Hawaii at the same time when Mollie was there, they were not formally introduced. He was very much older than Mollie. (He had been previously married in Korea. This part of his background is not clear, whether his wife died or they were divorced.)

After they married, they both went back to Los Angeles, where Chan Ho Min continued his schooling at USC for three years. My father in the end received three degrees: a bachelor of arts, a bachelor of divinity, and a master of arts.

About my father's background: Rev. Chan Ho Min was born in Pyongsan, Hwang Hae Province, on October 21, 1878, the son of Hyung Chan Min and Matilda Sur Min. I don't know why a lot of these Korean immigrant people—even that far back in the 1800s—had American names like Matilda and Mollie. I don't know from where she got that name, Mollie. Maybe it was because they were Christians. That could be it. My father graduated from the Methodist Mission College Pae Jae in Seoul at the same time with Dr. Syngman Rhee. They became lifelong friends from that time onward. My father was ordained a minister prior to coming to

Rev. Chan Ho Min, circa 1909.

47

Honolulu, Hawaii. He arrived in Hawaii on August 8, 1905. Mollie left Hawaii in 1909. In 1911, Chan Ho left Hawaii and went to Los Angeles to attend USC.

After my parents married, they lived in a tiny upstairs apartment in Los Angeles. Mollie took up nursing courses at the Methodist Hospital and took special courses at the University of Southern California. She received a USC Resident Teacher's appointment. When World War I started, Mollie joined the Red Cross in Los Angeles as a volunteer despite the fact that her first child, Paul, was born on June 10, 1914.

When Chan Ho continued his studies at USC even after they were married, they needed some livelihood to care for the growing family. So Mollie bought a larger house that was near Santa Monica, a farm outside of the busy city of Los Angeles. Mollie began raising produce, chickens, turkeys, and rabbits, which were sold to restaurants, and she was able to continue sending Chan Ho to USC until he received his degree in divinity, and, finally, his master's degree in divinity, also. At that time, two more children were born in California: Thomas, on January 4, 1917, and Philip, on September 7, 1919.

Min Family grows: Mollie; Rev. Min; standing, Thomas; lower child, Paul; infant, Philip, circa 1919.

Her parents and Chi Pom and his family from Hawaii came to live with the the Min side of the family at the farm. The extended family lived there for several years.

When my father completed his studies and received his degree in divinity, Dr. Syngman Rhee asked him to return to Hawaii with his family to become the minister of the first Korean Christian Church, which Rhee had formally begun in 1918. So the Min family left California and arrived back in Hawaii in December 1919. There my father became the pastor of Rhee's Korean Christian Church. My father was also the principal of the Korean Christian Institute (KCI), established by Rhee, which was where some Korean children of immigrants went to live while their parents worked in sugar fields throughout Hawaii. My father also worked there to teach these Korean children. Because money was quite short, my mother, Mollie, began to take in sewing, which she continued to do for many years.

The first Hawaii home that the family lived in was in Kaimuki, on Third Avenue. This house was rented and paid for by the Korean Christian Church. One reason for the subsidy was that my father's salary was only about thirty dollars a month. He did not have enough money to pay the rent. A few years later, Mollie bought a house in Kaimuki on Sierra Drive, which was a good, large house with many rooms. We lived there very comfortably. Since there was a large backyard, my mother built another large two-story, four-bedroom, two-bathroom house at the cost of only $5,000 at the time. Somehow she was able to borrow money from the mortgage department of the Bank of Hawaii because she knew the head of the mortgage department. He was willing to lend her money quite often. Actually, she was able to continue the mortgage payments as long as she was alive. Subsequently, she bought an even larger house in the front of Diamond Head that was called Crater Road, and it was quite a large house. We lived there for another few years. Then she bought a house in Makiki on Anapuni Street. The property contained another house in the front of our house. There was a cottage in the back that was rented to tenants. Then she bought another house up in Makiki Heights, a large, beautiful house, which again she also rented after we moved out and she moved us back to Anapuni Street. There she built a twelve-bedroom apartment, which was always filled with tenants.

All of this took considerable work and effort on her part. This made her quite tired, I'm sure. But still she looked after her children's well-being. For example, when I went away in 1939 to medical school in Philadelphia,

Jefferson Medical College, she wrote to me and said that she would come out and look after me during my second year to make sure that I was studying well and not working too hard. She had heard that during my first year I was working in a boarding house as a waiter to get free room and board and that made her unhappy. She brought my youngest brother, Andrew, along with her to visit me. They got on a bus in LA, I believe, and rode all the way across the country to New York City, where I met them. We stayed in the city for a few days. The New York World's Fair was going on at that time, so we saw that, among other things, in the city. Then we went back to Philadelphia just before school started. She found us a very nice apartment in West Philadelphia, and I was again able to eat good Korean food with kimchi.

Within a few weeks after she arrived in Philadelphia, she went around the West Philadelphia area and found this little factory that was making ladies' hairpins of some sort. She went in to talk to the owner. At that moment they were having their daily afternoon prayer meeting, so she joined in and gave a long prayer. The owner was so impressed that he hired her right away and she worked there for the rest of the summer and led the prayer meetings every day during the weekdays.

At the end of the school year, my brother Paul had ordered a Plymouth car from a car dealer. We were supposed to pick it up in Detroit. So we took a bus to Detroit and got the Plymouth and drove toward the west coast, stopping at many places, including South Dakota to view the statues of the early presidents at Mount Rushmore. We also drove down to Yellowstone Park and saw Old Faithful, and we continued on to Reno. Then, crossing the Sierra Nevada mountains with snow on top, we got out of the car to make snowballs. Andrew and I threw balls at each other. And finally, we ended up in Los Angeles, where the car was shipped out. I saw both of them, Mother and Paul, get on a ship before I had to return to Philadelphia to continue my studies. I believe the ship was either the *Lurline* or the *Matsonia*.

I graduated from Jefferson Medical College in 1942 and entered an internship for a year; then I was drafted into the U.S. Army as a medical officer. My first post was down in Charleston, South Carolina, in a large army hospital, and I was surprised to see my mother come to South Carolina to see me without advance notice again. This was in early 1943, when she came there. I wondered how she was able to get to the U S. continent from Hawaii. There were no airplanes for common citizens and no passenger ships crossing the Pacific Ocean at that time because of the on-going World War II. Only military ships crossed the Pacific. However, my mother, Mollie was able to come to the Mainland because she was very focused on getting her goals, and for some reason, she wanted to look after me again. So she tried to join the WACs [the Women's Army Corps]. The WAC administration board in Hawaii interviewed her, and they said she was too old. [She was fifty-five years old at that time.] She created such a fuss when she was rejected that they actually reported her complaint to authorities in Washington, D. C. The authorities sent for her and paid her way to Washington D.C. She traveled first by naval vessel, and then cross-country by U.S. Air Force airplane, all paid by the military, I guess.

Mollie met the general of the WACs in Washington, D.C., and again, the general said she was too old. The WAC army general—female, of course—had a long talk with her and personally said again that she was too old. The general said that she wished that Mollie was younger because she would have made a very good soldier, but that she really was too old.

At that time, after she was rejected, I received a telephone call at the hospital from my mother. I didn't know that she was in Washington, D.C. She said that she was on her way to Charleston by train to see me. So I immediately looked for a hotel room and met her when she came in. A day and a half later—she said she was there for a week—she came to the hospital and met all the other doctors there and the nurses. They all made her happy by saying how well I took care of the ill soldiers and so on, so then she was happy to go on home. She was able to take a train to Los Angeles to see some friends of hers. After she was there for a week, I got a call from her good friend in Los Angeles, saying that my mother was in the hospital. I immediately asked for leave and I was able to catch a military flight to the west coast. I found her in a small hospital there.

Apparently, as soon as she had reached LA, she developed a urinary infection, and the doctor gave her sulfur pills, which she should have taken with large amounts of water. Apparently, he did not mention to take extra fluids, so the sulfur crystallized in her kidneys and they went into a shutdown. When I got there, she was receiving IV fluids, and fortunately, the kidneys opened up and she was discharged after that. So I stayed with her for a few days and I had to fly back. She stayed with her friends in LA for a few more days then flew back home.

During the subsequent years, she kept herself very busy with several projects, even though she was talking care of all her rental units, etc. I forgot to mention when my father passed away. My father, Rev. Chan Ho Min, died on

Left to right: Mollie, Francesca, and Syngman Rhee at Rev. Min's gravesite, circa 1954.

February 5, 1954. My mother continued her volunteer work in Hawaii.

She was so active. I was amazed at all that she did: She was with the Pan-Pacific Association, the Southeast Asia Women's Association, the YWCA, and the Red Cross. She was sent to Manila in 1954 to attend the Pan-Pacific Conference. She was sent also to the 1955 World Brotherhood Conference in Belgium. And she went to the Southeast Asia Women's Association Conference in Australia in 1957.

In 1958, she wanted to see the whole world one final time, so she wrote to all the World Brotherhood associations in all the countries for which she'd kept addresses. She left by plane, first landing in Japan, where she was met by members of the World Brotherhood Conference. She stayed in one of their homes for about two weeks and saw a lot of Japan. Then she went to India, where again she was met by members there, and she stayed there another two weeks. She told me briefly that she tried to visit Jerusalem and Egypt, but her flight was to land in

Mollie Min receiving certificate award for work with the Red Cross, circa 1960.

52

Jordan at a major airport, where she had much difficulty. When I learned of this, I wrote to my classmate, a Dr. Zukowsky, who was working as a doctor for a large oil company, flying all over for the company, from one oil well to another. I wrote to him and said that my mother would be arriving in Jordan at a major airport and I was wondering if he could meet her and give her some assistance during that part of her travels. Later on, I found out that somehow he contacted the major airlines and told them that Mollie Hong Min would be arriving one of these days and to let him know when. I learned that he was informed of the exact time she was arriving and he went to the airport and picked her up and took her to his home.

My mother told me that Dr. Zukowsky lived in a beautiful villa with several servants, and she was really treated very well. He helped her visit Jerusalem, which she had always wanted to see. Also, he helped her to go on to Egypt, where she met the World Brotherhood Organization there, and they helped her visit the pyramids, among other things. I remember, from one of those trips, there's a picture of her riding a camel. She continued on through Europe, to France, Paris, London; finally she returned to the United States and went

Mollie Min sitting (center) with Senator Dan Inoyue and Red Cross workers, circa 1970.

directly to California and Los Angeles, where again she stayed with her good friends there for several weeks; then she returned home after three months of a round-the-world trip that none of us would ever dream of taking.

In May 1963, she became an honorary board member of the YWCA. She had also been a volunteer worker for the Red Cross since 1914, while she was on the Mainland. She became a Gray Lady for the Tripler General Hospital for several years. In 1973 she received the Award of Merit from the Republic of Korea for her dedicated work in the Korean community and also for the huge amount of work and time that she spent during the Korean War collecting clothing to send to Korea. The last few years of her life were spent peacefully at the Maluhia Hospital when she became too feeble to do much walking and so on.

I know very, very little of the politics among Koreans here in Hawaii, what went on in the community here. But I know when my father was active in the school established by Dr. Rhee, there were some interesting stories that I heard. One of my very good friends, Dr. Timothy Wee, and many of the people of that generation, had parents who were working in the pineapple fields, so they put their children in the Korean Christian Institute (KCI), where my father was the superintendent. I remember there was quite a large school building there. It had an upstairs floor, a second floor, one half of the building was for boys and the other half was for girls.

They had a baseball team and the ladies formed an orchestra. Then somehow, my father, I don't know who arranged this, the boy's baseball team and the orchestra were invited to go to Korea and play against a baseball team in Korea. Well, Timothy was a, kind of a—well, I don't know—a horrible boy at that age. I think he was about sixteen to seventeen years old at that time. He was very playful and naughty at times, I guess, so my father actually kicked him out of the KCI. But he was the best player of the baseball team. So when the team was invited to go to Korea to play at the championship games, my father asked Timothy to come back to the KCI. Timothy did come back when he found out that the only reason they wanted him back was that they were going to Korea to play in the baseball championship game. They went to Korea, and they had a good time. The girls' orchestra went along, too. I remember Timothy telling me some funny stories about that trip. I remember his story about Gertrude Lee's mother, cooking this huge five-gallon batch of *jang-jorim* and making tons of rice. All they ate was rice and *jang-jorim!* But they had a good time in Korea, they agreed on that.

As I said, in 1919, after Dr. Syngman Rhee asked Chan Ho to become the first pastor of his new church, the Korean Christian Church, my father came to Hawaii. Also my father became the superintendent of the Korean Christian Institute. Two more Min children were born in Hawaii: Jesse on April 6, 1921, and Andrew on August 29, 1923. Both Mollie and Chan Ho taught Korean to the students at KCI. Simultaneously, Mollie became active in the Korean Women's Society. Finding it difficult to raise a family of seven on a minister's salary, Mollie Min took in sewing on the side to bring in extra money. She had high hopes for her children and worked hard to achieve their ambitions.

In 1929 or 1930 Chan Ho resigned from the Korean Christian Church. Mollie moved the family to Schofield Barracks, and they ran a laundry, catering to soldiers. The family lived there for six years. When both of the older boys were attending the university, the family moved back to Honolulu. In Honolulu, Mollie ran various enterprises, including a boarding house for university students called the McDonald Hotel in 1939. We lived in the building, also. Finally, she converted that property in Punahou into rental apartment units and bought another property for our home.

I mentioned that on May 9, 1963, Mollie was elected to become an honorary board member of the YWCA. Because Mollie dealt with the public so much, she was always dressed immaculately and always had an attractive appearance. From the time she signed up as a volunteer worker for the Red Cross in 1914, she continued to give her time year after year, to the Red Cross and took every course offered except life-saving. She became a qualified surgical instructor. She was highly recognized for her fifty-eight years of dedicated volunteer work for the American Red Cross.

Some of Mollie Min's dreams came true when her older boys graduated from college: Paul with an aeronautical engineering degree and Thomas with a medical degree. World War II ended the plans of Philip and Jesse, who had been attending the University of Hawaii. Philip preferred to marry early and became an appliance salesman and Jesse preferred to work for the federal government at Pearl Harbor. Andrew also went into federal work after graduating from high school.

As I mentioned earlier, in 1973 Mollie Min received the Award of Merit. I wished I had kept that large medal that they gave her, but we buried it with her when she passed away. It was a beautiful thing. It came from the Republic of Korea for her dedicated work in the Korean community. Mollie Min continued her very active daily schedule of running the business of apartment rentals and doing volunteer work for the Red Cross on a weekly basis until she was well over eighty years old. She regretfully gave up her volunteer work when she became hard of hearing. Mollie Min's death on November 9, 1979, ended the era of a truly remarkable woman, devoted wife, and mother. Her busy schedules never kept her from being a loving mother to her children. She was an aggressive, determined woman and, like other women of her time, a devout Christian. Her capacity to help her fellow man regardless of race was well-known and appreciated.

What specifically was the award your mother received from the Korean government?
It's called "Of Merit," something like that. Came on a huge medal. It looked like it was gold. I don't know if it was pure gold.

Did your father visit Korea anytime after he left in 1905?
My father left Korea in 1905, shortly after my mother did, and he never did return to Korea until shortly before his death. He suffered a stroke and was unable to speak. My mother, knowing that he would appreciate seeing his country once more, did take him to Korea in the 1950s. Shortly after that visit, he went into Maluhia Nursing Home, where he died after three years.

My mother, when she was eighty, let's see, when she was about eighty-four or five, it's hard to remember those things, she suddenly developed mental confusion, and in those days, there were no instruments like now. They couldn't scan and use MRI and what not, so neurologists could only say she probably had multiple strokes . . . she was not paralyzed, but she had difficulty speaking. Now we can have better diagnoses of causes of mental confusion. She also went to Maluhia Nursing Home, and she was there for eight years until she passed away.

Did you say that your father was in a ministry school with Dr. Syngman Rhee?
My father graduated from the same school with Rhee, so apparently Rhee was thinking about going into ministry, too. I remember the first time seeing Rhee, shortly after my father came back to Hawaii in 1919. I've known Dr. Syngman Rhee personally all my life.

Didn't he give you a medal personally sometime after World War II when he was the President of Korea? What was that all about?

Not really a medal, but I did get something from Rhee. When he was in Washington with Mrs. Rhee, they had what they called an embassy, but it wasn't recognized at that time because there was no Korean government at that time. He stayed in that "embassy," and once he drove up to New York or near somewhere I was. On the way he stopped in Philadelphia to see me. Fortunately, it was a Friday afternoon, so he went into the dean's office at my university and asked the dean if he could take me down to Washington for the weekend. The dean said, "Of course." So I was called to the dean's office. And there was Syngman Rhee.

We got into his car and he drove to Washington, and it was the most nervous drive I ever had. When he kept driving, he'd drive with one hand and he'd blow on the fingers on the other hand, and sometimes he'd blow on two hands while still driving the car and it would go ... I said, "Wait, wait, wait, don't do that." Then finally I asked him to let me drive, and finally he did, thank goodness. I asked him why he blew on his fingertips. He said that when he was in the Japanese prison, they used to torture him by placing burning bamboo sticks under his fingernails. I guess that was very painful and it probably damaged some nerves permanently. It was quite a habit with him. He just kept blowing there, from time to time, when he was driving, and sometimes he'd blow two hands at the same time.

How old were you?

I was—let's see, I think I was a junior in medical school. I went to medical school a little younger than most of the others—I was, let's see, I was about twenty-one years old or so at that time. It must have been in the '30s. I remember that I was assigned to a general hospital down south and stopped in South Carolina. I wanted to go overseas so badly, especially to the South Pacific because I understood that those of Korean ancestry who could speak Korean would eventually end up in Korea to help the troops. I thought then I could interpret for them and what not. So I found that the only way to go in that direction was to attend Walter Reed, where they had two-month courses on tropical diseases. The troops in the South Pacific were coming down with malaria and all these parasite diseases. No doctor in the United States or the army knew anything about parasites and tropical diseases. They had this course at Walter Reed. So finally the general hospital in which I was in let me go to Walter Reed to take this course. I did spend two months there. While I was there, I looked up Dr. Rhee and he invited me to an "embassy" party. There was still not a real embassy but they were able to invite a lot of non-top consuls. Rhee asked me to invite and bring along several of my fellow officers. I did—a good party was going on then.

What about your father? You said he left the Korean Christian Church. Was there anything about that?

Well, the Korean Methodist Church was the only religion for the Koreans in Hawaii, and Syngman Rhee decided to form a separate church which is now called the Korean Christian Church. My father was the first minister of that church. He was a minister for years there. I remember growing up as a little child, and we'd be driving from Kaimuki down to Rhee's church .The first church building was a small wooden building. It got bigger until finally we have the present church now.

When we drove to the church on Sundays—we would be driving a Model T—four of the children would be singing Christian songs that my mother had taught us. Then we would go to Sunday school, then after Sunday school, all the other children would go home. We Min children had to stay there for not only Sunday school, but for the whole sermon afterwards, which was a long deal for a Sunday, while all the other kids went home. My father preached there for a good many years up to the early 1930s.

Tell me a more about what you know of your father's work at the Korean Christian Church.

Well, apparently my father was the first Korean pastor for the Korean Christian Church because of Dr. Syngman Rhee's efforts to have him come back to Hawaii. And he remained a pastor for many years. I remember, we were very young. Apparently, they had a good congregation for many years. Then I think about ten years after Rhee began his church, it seemed to split into two groups, as far as I know. There was the other group, who was trying to bring Rev. Kingsley Lyu into the church. Things got pretty bad, I remember, right in Rhee's church. Once the two groups, sitting apart on both side of the aisle, got into an argument during church hours and got into a fist fight. Even the younger people of the church. The police came and took a couple dozen of the young people that were brawling there to the police station. It was quite an embarrassing thing for the church. So when these things got to a point, my father decided to resign. He did resign, in what year I forget.

I believe he left the Honolulu Korean Christian Church when we moved out to Wahiawa in 1932. It was at that time because I entered Leilehua High School when I was fifteen years old, in the tenth grade. So that must have been 1932.

In Wahiawa can you tell us what your family did, what kind of work?

We stayed in Wahiawa Town just for a very short time until my mother and father found that there was a laundry shop up for sale in the Schofield Barracks area, which they took over. To be close to our shop we moved to Castner Village, right on the edge of Schofield Barracks, and did laundry for the military people there for the next several years. We lived and worked there, and I recall it was very hard work. Even at the age of fifteen, I helped with the laundry and delivery of clothes to Schofield Barracks and to the officers' homes.

Finally, in 1938, we moved back to Honolulu. At that time my father was quite elderly, and he retired from work, but my mother continued doing work chiefly as a landlady for various buildings that she owned and rented out.

Do you remember attending Korean school?

Yes, my father opened up a Korean school, a little school at a public school, open after the regular school hours. I believe it was an elementary school that he was able to rent, and my mother taught Korean there, also. There were other teachers that taught Korean there, and quite a few young Korean boys went to that school. That was before 1932. I remember I was only about ten years old when I went to that school for a couple of years. Then, after that, I forgot all my Korean until I began practicing medicine and met all these new immigrants from Korea, who knew no English at all. So I had to relearn Korean.

You once told me you attended Aliiolani School when it was a Korean school.

No, the KCI at Aliiolani was a boarding place for all the immigrants' children who needed it because their parents worked in the fields, the cane fields and pineapple fields. I did not stay there. Later on, when the school population grew smaller, then the KCI was moved to some place in Kalihi. The public school government took over the area and Aliiolani School became an elementary public school, I remember, up to the sixth grade.

After that boarding school closed, what happened?

KCI moved to a smaller place in Kalihi because, as the early immigrants stopped working in the fields and built up their own businesses in town, they bought homes where their children could live at home and go to public schools throughout Hawaii. So the Korean Christian Institute became smaller and smaller and finally closed. I don't know what date, but probably not too long after they moved out of Aliiolani.

Did you feel any different from the local people? After all, you were born on the Mainland.

No, because I was just a little kid. I was born on January 4, 1917, and I was only two years old when I moved to Hawaii. I always felt that Hawaii was my home. The only difference probably I had was that when my mother was being cared for during her second pregnancy with me, she thought so highly of her doctor—actually, he was not an obstetrician. They didn't have obstetricians during those days. They were all general practitioners who delivered babies. She liked him. His name was Dr. Sweet. I don't even know his first name. But when I was born—she made my middle name "Sweet," so I was Thomas Sweet Min. That created a problem when I was growing up in public schools in the second and third grade. When the teachers called out our names and they called my name, "Thomas Sweet Min," all the kids would shout "Whooooo" and whistle, and so on. I used to get into fights sometimes because they were calling me sissy all the time. But I think that was good for me in a way because it made me study harder than the other kids. I read more because they didn't select me to join their baseball games and football games and things like that.

So I had more time on my hands and on the way home, I stopped by the library and took home books. I read ten times more than any other kid in school and that was nice. So I think that helped me mentally, in a way, to be called a sissy.

Who were your friends when you were in high school?

Well, there are a lot of names: Namyong Chung is still my good friend. We practically grew up together from that time on when my family moved to Wahiawa. He was living in Waialua at that time. We went to college together, and then we went into the army at the same time. He is a veterinarian.

Did you experience any prejudice anywhere?

No, there was no prejudice at that time. Possibly, there was a little prejudice at Leilehua High School. It wasn't real prejudice. At that time, the military did not have their own public schools, so their children came to Leilehua School, a local school for Wahiawa. I remember about half a dozen Caucasian kids, boys and girls, attending our class. They were nice kids, and we tried to be nice to them, but sometimes, they—well, we never got very close to them like our own Oriental pals.

Tell us about the organizations during that time, Korean organizations.

I don't remember any organization. There was a small Korean Christian Church that I attended every Sunday. I was even in the choir. I think the chief reason I was in the choir was that every Thursday night there was choir practice and that was where we could meet girls and get dates. But I don't remember any organizations. I was never knowledgeable about Korean organizations throughout my whole growing-up period. Even when I got older, I did not know much about the Korean organizations. When I graduated from the university, I joined the Korea University Club and that was the only Korean organization I ever belonged to.

61

You don't know about Delta Frat?

I had some friends in Delta Frat, and frequently I was invited to their meetings and so on. But I know very little about that society except that it was more of a social organization than the Korean University Club, which tried to be a little bit more educational.

What are your general thoughts about Dr. Rhee?

I first knew Syngman Rhee when I as a little kid, when we were living in the first house on Third Avenue shortly after we came from the Mainland. I remember I was, I think, only about four years old and the Korean Church, they came over and helped chop down some—I remember—two huge mango trees in the backyard. Someone climbed up and cut down these large branches, and Syngman Rhee was there, helping to get rid of a log by pulling it out to the front of the house for the rubbish truck to pick up. I remember he had this large log that he dropped on himself. I was running around him, and then he suddenly tripped and the log fell on my leg and cracked a bone in my leg. In those days, we didn't really go to the doctor's often, but apparently, a small bone was cracked. I could walk around, but it was quite painful for about a month.

When we grew up, I lived up on Sierra Avenue. Syngman Rhee had a home way on top of Wilhelmina Rise. He had a Korean man living there with him who did the cooking and cleaning for him. He frequently asked my parents to send us boys up to his house on weekends to stay overnight with him. I remember being driven up to his place way up on Wilhelmina Rise and having dinner with him. He had a large bed and the three of us would sleep in one bed. He would impress us because he had a rifle. It was not a shotgun and I was amazed looking at it. When I grew up, I tried to do the same thing, but it was impossible. I think it was not a shotgun, but a shot bullet; he could actually shoot birds, flying in the air, with his bullet; that's an almost impossible thing to do. The bird would fall down and be dead.

The next time I met him was when I was in medical school. They had like an informal embassy in Washington, D.C., with a nice, beautiful home. Mrs. Rhee used to make Korean food, even kimchi. Once in a while, as I said, Syngman Rhee would drive back to D.C. after attending some conference in New York City and he would stop by my school. He would go to the Dean's Office. It usually was on a Friday afternoon.

Back home in Hawaii, the other kids that I knew there were good friends like Unsik Kang and Namyong Chung. We as children were never closely associated with most of the Korean organizations. We just knew they were separate and had different ideas. We, the second generation, really didn't know too much about that. I was gone from Hawaii for so many years. For one thing, I was at medical school, and then immediately after that, I joined the army. In those days, when you left Hawaii to go to school, you didn't come back until you finished school. So I was gone four years. After I

Mollie Min and son Dr. Thomas Min, circa 1946.

finished college, I started my internship in Pennsylvania, and when I finished that, I was drafted into the army; I was in the army for three and a half years. So I didn't get back home from the time I left, in 1939, until 1946.

4

Interview with Inez K. Pai

My name is Inez Baeksoon Kong Pai. I was born here in Hawaii, actually in Wahiawa, on February 4, 1919.

My father was Kong Chi Soon. He came from Yunan, Hwanghaedo, in the years between 1903 and 1905, I'm not sure. He worked for a while, two or three years, on the plantation on the Big Island. He took lessons while he was on the plantation on how to become a tailor. He had heard that the military base at Schofield Barracks was hiring and employing people who could make uniforms for the soldiers, who were, apparently, preparing for the First World War. So eventually he got a concession and moved to the island of Oahu. Finally, he got a tailoring concession at Schofield Barracks.

My mother came from Korea, during the same period as my father, but they did not know each other at that time. My mother was twenty-seven years old when she came from Hongchun, Kangwon Do. She came as a widow, and through the help of missionaries, she came to Hawaii. From the very beginning, she didn't work on the plantation but worked in the homes of well-known families, at the plantation bosses' homes, where she learned how to cook all kinds of American foods.

My father was thirty-four years old when he came. By the time he met and married my mother in 1925, she was thirty-eight years old, and my father was forty-five years old. A year later, my brother, John, was born, in 1916, and I came along in 1919.

My father even had a certificate from the "New York Cutting School," I remember it. He sewed so well. This was, of course, prior to marrying my

Chi Soon Kong, father; Sook Chin Ahn Kong, mother.

mother. My father even recalled that they had a tremendous earthquake sometime in 1913, when he was going through all the plantations in the islands and taking orders for suits or clothing that he would bring home to sew. But by 1919 the military decided to do away with all those tailoring concessions and all other concessions which were going on there inside the military base. What were they going to do? This was after I was born.

Chi Soon Kong, circa 1905.

They gave up that tailoring concession and mom and dad bought a mom-and-pop grocery store on King Street in the city of Honolulu, which is where Aala Park is now. That's between Beretania and Liliha Streets in Chinatown. Of course, this is a very different place now. They had a big concession there. I must have been two or three years old. Mother and Father thought that was not the best place to raise children. So we got a farm. They decided to farm up here on Maunaloa Heights, where I'm presently living. The land I'm

John and Inez Kong, circa 1923.

living on right now is the same land that my parents developed. We went through all kinds of things to make a living.

At first, they were going to make candy, I still remember: *yeut*. They called it *yeut*. They cooked this barley malt and then they made this candy and took it into town in a little four-wheeled cart and tried to peddle it. But it didn't make a living. I still remember how mother and father would pull the candy to make these nuggets of *yeut*. If you go to Korea, they sell it on the streets. But Mother and Father didn't make money on that, too. So they changed businesses so many times. The other thing was they decided to become chicken farmers. So the whole house was filled with egg mechanical hatchers downstairs. I still remember, turning on the electricity and trying to hatch the eggs mechanically. Well, that was all right except that the problem was that the chickens would eat each other, they would pick on each other. The chickens didn't thrive so we tried making money on eggs. I ate so many eggs when we couldn't sell them. So that didn't work out. It was a lot of work.

So my mother thought—I don't know whereever she got the idea—of raising carnations to sell to the lei sellers on Maunakea Street at the Oahu Market. I still remember; such memories I am having now since I'm starting to talk about it. They would bundle up in the carts after harvesting the flowers to sell. At the same time we were cultivating around fifty acres, both sides of Wilhelmina Rise. Of course, now it's a different landscape. On the Ewa side of Wilhelmina Rise,

Inez Kong with parents in 1919.

Sook Chin Ahn and Chi Soon Kong at their mom-and-pop grocery store in Chinatown, Honolulu, circa 1923.

I still remember we planted corn, watermelon—we had a lot of watermelon—and on the Koko Head side of Wilhelmina Rise, near where Kahala Heights is, we had carnation fields. Acres and acres of carnations. We also raised tomatoes, cucumbers. Mother and Father would pack my brother and me in the four-wheeled cart and take us downtown with all the vegetables and flowers. They would wrap us up in a little bundle on the sidewalk, then they would go around selling their flowers. My father would drive and my mother would do the marketing. When we were all through with the wholesale houses selling our cucumbers, tomatoes, corn, etc., in Chinatown, we would go to Palama Market, where more recent immigrants lived. Nowadays, they call the area Palama Settlement.

At that time there was a whole settlement of Korean families living at Palama Settlement. Many second-generation Koreans remember that place even today. I still remember Subok Kim's, Clara Kim's, parents living there. They had about ten children in the family. My mother knew them well and so it was her philosophy that if we sell all these vegetables and we can't do

67

anything with them after, she would for 25 cents a bag, a paper bag, fill it up with tomatoes and cucumbers and sell it for a very reasonable price to them. And then we'd go back to Maunakea Street and do our marketing. One of the biggest treats in Chinatown, after the hard work, I remember, was when she would take us to the chopsuey house and order a bowl of rice and a bowl of soup, vegetable soup. We never ordered anything else.

As I said, I was born in February 1919. It must be remembered that March 1, 1919, is a very historical day because tens of thousands of Koreans rose up on March First in Korea to declare independence from Japan. We who lived in Hawaii heard about it between that time and April. I was about two, three months old. In those days, there were no such things as cars or buses, so my father took my brother on his back and sometimes he walked a little bit because he was only about three years old. And my mother carried me. Imagine, we walked all the way out from Wahiawa to Honolulu [18 miles] to participate in the mass meeting of Koreans that was held. I don't know if it was in the KNA building. I was, naturally, too young to know that. But at that time there was a Korean National Association, very active in the work for Korean independence. Eventually, the KNA split; I don't know details of the split, but my father was a supporter of Syngman Rhee. I remember the Korean National Association building on Liliha Street very vividly. It was a tall, two-story building with white trimming. They would have these meetings, and I was present one time when the women, both of KNA and Dongji Hoi, got mad at each other and started to beat each other up. That's the kind of remembrance I have of that occasion.

So we were operating this carnation farm. Like my father, Syngman Rhee was born in Eun An Hwanghae Do, but in 1875. My father was five years older. Syngman Rhee wanted the Koreans to get together and sort of form a community and do the work for Korean independence. This is as I know it and I saw it. The *Korea Pacific Weekly* printing press was brought up here. My mother and my father helped him set that up. My mother always took care of him. She was sort of a caregiver to Syngman Rhee, the times he spent here. I remember him very vividly because he would carry me on his back and play with me when I was growing up. He had a beautiful house. At that time, we just had a farmhouse, but his was beautiful to my eyes. His home here was right below ours. We were neighbors so I was always running in and out of his house, and he would call me, " Beksoona, Beksoona 나 하고 놀자, come play with me." Really, so I grew up that way, very close. He worked very hard to establish the

Korean Christian Institute in Kalihi and also the Korean Christian Church on School Street, that wooden building. I still remember Syngman Rhee very fondly. He was sort of like another father to me. I don't know any of the details of the differences he had with the community then. Eventually, I found out by studying the story and history.

I remember very vividly when the Korean National Association was near Liliha Street. I remember the building; I can picture it, two stories. It had a central stairway going up to the second floor. There must have been a basement downstairs, and it had a long hallway. I remember that this was at the time when KNA was breaking up because Syngman Rhee wanted his own way. He had his own political philosophy or personal political drive for power or whatever it was; he decided to break away. What I recall, I still remember, is he felt the Koreans should not be under any kind of a mission board which belonged to the Methodist Mission. He wanted to be independent. The person I remember who was sort of his enemy was a man by the name of Rev. Fry. I remember Fry because, well, it's a name you remember, Fry.

My father and my mother were very close to him; as a matter of fact, I practically lived at the Korean Christian Church, which Syngman Rhee eventually founded on School Street. It was a wooden building on sort of a marshland place. I remember going to Sunday school, teaching Sunday school later, going to Wednesday prayer meetings. Imagine, living way out here in the mountains of Kaimuki. We'd go to prayer meetings on Wednesday nights, then Friday night we had choir. I also at times played the piano as a substitute pianist. I was very active in the Christian Endeavor. I became president. I think I surprised a lot of people because I was so active.

In public school, when I was in the eighth grade, I surprised everybody by winning the Territorial Oratorical Contest. And the following year, I was student body president. When I think about it, I just can't believe I was so active. I remember I served at McKinley High School in what we called the Girls' Reserve. I was the only one who served two years in a row as President of the Girls' Reserve. I remember being chairman of the McKinley Carnival Festival that collected enough funds to build that swimming pool. That swimming pool, gosh, I can't believe it. We were so young, and yet we worked hard and didn't sleep for three or four days. Just didn't sleep, we worked so hard on the carnival. I can't believe I ran a carnival. Eventually, I became brave enough to run a lot of things like when the Korean War broke out, the bazaars and the relief drives. Oh, we made thousands and thousands of dollars. We made

Inez Kong (Pai), accompished writer, poet, and orator, becomes president of Liliuokalani School.

daegu and kimchi to sell. At one point, I think we sent $13,000 to Korean charities in Korea.

Anyway, I graduated from McKinley High School, and I went to the University of Hawaii for a short while. Then I went off to the Mainland. I went to Los Angeles City College and got involved in Korean affairs. Oh, in the meantime, the most fantastic thing in my life—actually, a turning point—was what my mother did in 1935. In 1935, I was a junior at McKinley High School, the largest public high school in Hawaii. At that time, I had my eye on running for student body vice president. But my mother said—I really had an extraordinary mother—I mean, her life is a story on its own—anyway, she said, "I don't want my children to grow up being nothing, not realizing their Korean heritage." So she went to McKinley High School to talk to the principal in May of 1935. School normally ended in June, but she told the principal that she was taking me and my brother to Korea before school ended. We were going through Japan to travel in Asia. She said, "I want my kids to know who they are." I guess in today's words, she meant that she wanted us to realize our identity. She said in Korean, "You must know who you are; if you don't you are nothing 여기서 기르면 아무것도 안돼. You are not a person 사람 안돼."

So, the most dramatic period of my life, there I was in 1935, sixteen years old, going to Korea. We went by ship on the *President Coolidge*, I still remember. I still have pictures of that experience, too. I do. We went to Yokohama, and then we went to Kobe. We got off at Kobe. My mother wanted us to see Nara, Kyoto, so we saw all those beautiful temples; I still remember how awesome it was, how beautiful Japan was in those days. Then we went on to Shimonoseki, and we took a ferry, an overnight ferry, to Korea. It was a fantastic experience.

We didn't fly. Everything was by train and this was in 1935, at the height of Japan's expansion. Japan had already gobbled up Manchuria in 1931. My mother was very active in the Korean Independence Movement in North China, so we were considered like spies, you know, and we were followed all around in Japan and in Korea.

Then, imagine, getting into Busan! I've always compared that scene to a beautiful, modern Japan. I had been in Yokohama, but I hadn't seen Tokyo. I saw Kyoto and Nara, all those beautiful places. Then to land in Busan! To see the beggars on the street. I had never seen scenes like those in Busan. You would see poor people begging and in rags. You would see people who were beggars but didn't have their minds, who were obviously insane, mentally very ill, dragging themselves around. I never forgot a woman who was in rags; the dress she was wearing was bloody. She probably was menstruating or something like that, but nobody was caring for her and she was lying around like that. Huh! Can you imagine a sixteen-year-old girl—me—seeing all that?

The trip to Korea was a turning point in my life. I was young and very impressionable, most struck by the way Koreans were at the time being oppressed by the Japanese. I saw so much starvation and hardship on the part of Koreans and the loss of their freedom. So I decided then that my life's work would be to work for the independence of Korea. I would do everything in my power to help in trying to work for the independence

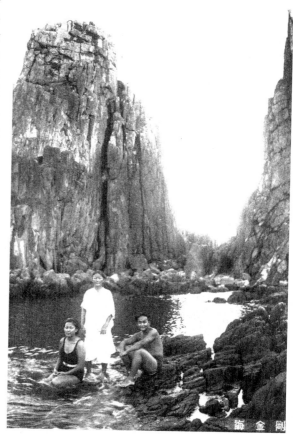

The trip to Korea, 1935; Inez, mother, and John. Background: Kum Gang San.

71

of Korea. It was something like a fantasy because this was 1935, when Japan was at the height of her powers. So it was a dream to do something. I decided to pursue this dream.

We returned to Hawaii in September. We came home late so my school year had started, badly. I couldn't run for student body president. However, somehow, I ended up vice president of the senior class. After McKinley, I went to Los Angeles City College, and it was when I was at Los Angeles City College that Pearl Harbor was struck. That's when I wrote to Syngman Rhee, who was the director of the Korean Commission in Washington. I still have his letter. I had been thinking of going to Berkeley, to matriculate to Berkeley, but Pearl Harbor was bombed and that changed my decision. Imagine, being happy about Pearl Harbor. I knew that because of the attack, this was the beginning of Korea's independence.

So I went off to Washington, D.C. There I worked for Dr. Rhee as his gofer. At the same time, I registered to go to George Washington University. I was going to school, but after hours I was doing all sorts of political things. Also, because of my speech-making abilities, I went around to various colleges making speeches. I have pictures of myself at Bucknell University, and that's the only one I remember, but whereever anyone spoke about Koreans, I was

Inez and collegues on the way to Washington, D.C., 1941.

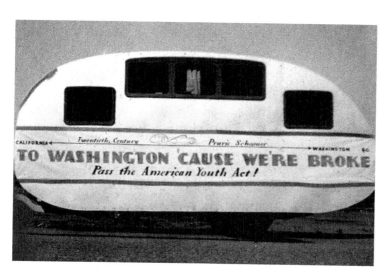

Inez goes offf to Washington, D.C., 1941.

there to speak up for Korea's independence. Eventually, I ended up getting very much involved in the Korean Independence Movement.

At the same time, I got to know all these leaders who were sent from the different Korean organizations on the continental United States and Hawaii, such people like Jacob Dunn—I got to know Jacob quite well—and there was another man who worked for Syngman Rhee, who became minister of transportation later in Syngman Rhee's government, when he became president. The other big man I knew was Warren Kim, who was very informed and knowledgeable about Korean affairs. There were only a handful of us Koreans in Washington, D.C., at that time. My husband, Edward Eui Whan Pai, was in the U.S. Office of Censorship then. That's where, at that point, I began to break with Syngman Rhee. I was studying, majoring in poly science, and I must have been a really kind of headstrong person because I didn't agree with Rhee. My personal experience with Syngman Rhee is really another dramatic story because he told me, "I don't want you to associate with those people." They were the people I just mentioned, previously.

He also mentioned Kil Su Han. Kil Su Han was a very nice person. You must remember that I was only twenty-three, twenty-two years old in 1941 or 1942. These men were in their forties and fifties, so I was sort of like a kid. And Rhee again told me, "Don't associate with those people, they're communists and traitors," and so forth. I have to tell you this story because very few people know this, you know. So Rhee really said: "I don't want you to be associating with them." I don't know if I should be saying this, but I have to tell the truth.

At that time, when the war was going on, he wrote a letter to my mother, saying, "Inez is associating with very undesirable people; in fact, they're communists." He was talking about Warren Kim and Jacob Dunn and Kil Su Han. In my situation, no way were they communists, traitors. They were working for the same thing: Korea's independence. It was my personal conscience that rose and rebelled. But the point that got me so angry was that he would tell my mother, write a letter to my mother saying I was associating with undesirable people such as them. So in my impulsive anger, I called Dr. Rhee. Here I was in Washington, going in and out of his office everyday. There were other incidents which turned me against him and I really turned.

On top of that, my husband, Edward Eui Whan Pai, was working for the U.S. Censorship. He was reading all of Rhee's letters. Ed was in censorship of all foreigners' communications. He was a great follower of Syngman Rhee until he found out all the terrible things he was telling the Korean people, you know, in the United States. Also lying to the Korean Provisional Government in Chungking at the time when Kim Ku and Kim Kyu Shik were there.

So when Syngman Rhee said that I shouldn't associate with people like them, I thought to myself, no, that's not true. They're not communists. I know something about communism because that was my subject in college. So we all kept associating with each other because there was only one Chinese restaurant where all the Koreans would go. It was called Wings Café. It's famous, famous, because all the Koreans would go there. So we'd all eat together. We all became friends.

One day, I don't know whose idea it was, the KNA people selected me as a courier. This was in December 1942. Also I had applied to become a member of a troop of Korean women who were being recruited to go to Kuk Min Hur. Right after the war, they didn't have the WACs as we do now, and they didn't have the WAVES [Women Appointed for Voluntary Emergency Service], but they were picking Asian women—Chinese or Korean, not Japanese—to go to Kuk Min Hur to man the office from which, at that time, that famous General Stillwell was flying over the Burma Road. Oh, that was so exciting. So I applied with the help of the people whom I got to know on the American side, who were the "Flying Tigers." They were in and out of Washington and I met them. We socialized a bit and I said I wanted to register. One of the men's names was, as I recall now, John Davis. He was very well known in those days.

74

Anyway, I applied with the goal that I would be one of their recruitment of nine women. Of course, I had to go through a security check. In the meantime, they sent me to Canada, Monte Blanc, where the powers of the war were. The allied powers were getting together in Monte Dome. I carried a petition because they were going to discuss Korean trusteeship. The KNA was against it, Syngman Rhee was against it. It was the KNA who sent me to protest it with the recommendation of a bunch of my friends: Kil Soo Han, Jacob Dunn, and Warren Kim, who submitted my name to the KNA. I think Kil Soo had a lot more to do with that.

Anyway, they sent me up there. It was winter, December. There was snow all over, from Montreal up to Monte Blanc. It was one of the most exclusive ski resorts, the largest on that side of the world. So I still remember going on the Tunable: I call it the Tunable Train, the little rickety train that went to the lodge. When I got there, I was like an intruder. Who is this person? This is a kid. So one group wanted to send me right back, but they couldn't send me back. The train wasn't going back right away, they had to keep me there. And the other group said, "Well, just let her stay. She can go back when the train comes back. In time, she can go back."

I never forgot my defender. He was very famous: Admiral Yarnell. He was the head of the navy during the war. He came to my defense and said, "We can't personally blame her." Even though I stayed, I was not allowed to attend any of the sessions. I had to sign a letter saying that I was just there to perform … I think I still have that letter. So all these men got together, and they allowed me to stay there. They sent me back the next day. So when I went back, which was around early December, I had to report to all these Koreans who had sent me to Canada.

I still remember, Ed was sitting there. When I first met Ed, we had gotten into a verbal quarrel. It was in the late summer of 1942, when I first met Edward Eui Whan Pai. He had come to Washington to work in the Office of Censorship. Previous to that, he had come when the war broke out. This was in 1942. Only four months earlier, he had been working in New Hampshire—Manchester—in a brokerage firm. When the war broke out, he came down to Boston to join the army because he felt this was a wonderful opportunity to participate in Korean independence. And when they found out that he could read, write, and talk Japanese, they were amazed, pleasantly amazed. They didn't recruit him into the army. They said they needed him much more urgently as an interpreter. So they sent him out to Missoula, Montana, straight from Boston.

75

Edward Pai was from Kimhae, Korea. He was born in 1904 and had come to America under the sponsorship of George McCune's father. Incidentally the McCune's family is well known in Korean missionary history. Edward Pai came back to America because, although he had finished his studies at Pusan Commercial College, he knew he didn't have a future in Korea under the Japanese. He wanted to return to America, I'm not sure when. Maybe it was in 1925 or 1927. And he went to the University of Dubuque. Also he finished his studies at New York University. He got his BA from Dubuque and got his MA in international finance at NYU. He graduated from New York University in 1937. He was going to go to Shanghai and open up a shoe factory with a friend who is very, very famous now. He happens to be the founder of McCann Shoe Store. Two young fellows, imagine, Tom McCann and he were going out to Shanghai. Can you see these two young fellows, 1937, going to a foreign country, not knowing what was going to happen in September 1937? Shanghai was bombed, you see. They couldn't go to China. So they decided to stay home.

Anyway, Ed Pai somehow got into stock brokerage work in 1937. This was in Manchester, New Hampshire. He was working there, and then eventually, in 1941, the war broke out and Ed came out to his new life, which I have already explained. Anyway, when he was in censorship, he began to read all those letters that Syngman Rhee was writing to and receiving from Chungking. Ed became very disillusioned with Syngman Rhee. One of the things was Rhee was writing letters to Koreans in the U.S. saying that the Korean Provisional Government was going to get recognized. This was something that was going on between Syngman Rhee and Cordell Hull, who was Secretary of State at that time. Of course, the significant part of Cordell Hull's letter back to Syngman Rhee was that the U.S. could not and would not recognize the Korean Provisional Government without the consent of the people who were being governed. We could not have a government outside the country which had not ruled the country be recognized as the legitimate government. However, Syungman Rhee was writing letters on the contrary. [The contrary information given to the Korean community by Rhee had a political impact on strategy plans.] Ed Pai realized that he was lying to the Korean people and all the time collecting money from them. He needed money and so forth.

Meanwhile, Ed and I had nothing to do with each other. As a matter of fact, the first time we met in late summer of 1942, he thought I was some sassy Korean woman, a Korean girl who thought she knew so much. That was his impression of me. And I thought he was just a stuffy fuddy-duddy because he said to me, "You need to just continue going to school a little more so that you can grow up a little more." I took great offense and we never spoke to each other for some time. But we always saw each other at the restaurant because we always ate Asian food at the Wing Café. Anyway, Edward broke away from Rhee. He had admired, respected, and almost worshiped Syngman Rhee before he broke away from him.

I broke away from Syngman Rhee in his office after that quarrel I had with him. I told him, "You should not get angry with me; they're not communists." Actually, you don't argue like that with Syngman Rhee. However, when he wrote to my mother and said I was associating with that kind of people, I got so angry. I called him up on the phone, and I said, "I know in your eyes I am doing things that you don't agree with, but why do you have to call my mother? Why do you have to call my mother and complain to her that I am not behaving myself according to the way you want? I think that's a terrible thing for you to do." That was the kind of thing that broke me away from Syngman Rhee. Of course, he regarded me as just one of the traitors, communists. That's where the break began. However, I had another very dramatic encounter and break with him.

Rhee was very anti-communist. That was because he had by that time married Francesca. She's Austrian. They had both traveled, and now I realize why he became so anti-communist. I didn't realize it at that time. He saw Russia when it was really, really in a very bad situation in 1935. He went to Geneva also in 1935. It was there he met Francesca. He came back so anti-communist. Of course, he was a very religious person and Confucian at heart. He used his powers in a very classical Confucian way . . . in a bad way. The negative side of Confucianism is that there is no real democracy. You have to accept, obey, respect your father; you have to obey and respect your state; all these five principles of Confucianism. He literally believed it. If he is the sovereign or the father of the house, he expects to be listened to, and if you are not listened to, it is not idealistic at all. If you don't obey him then, you're persona non grata. That was his way of doing things. That was the reason for his eventual downfall. When I took a newspaper clipping about the Yeon Ahn incident to Rhee, I think the communists were already there in China. I said to him that this article is about KOPOGO President Kim [Kim Ku], leader of the Koreans. He said, "This doesn't mean anything," and he threw it out, I mean he threw it away! In my simple mind, I thought well a Korean is a Korean. Kim Ku is fighting for Korean independence, right?

77

I wasn't a communist, but I certainly was leftist. So we broke up over that. When we were in Korea, I was always afraid that when Syngman Rhee came to power, we would have to leave Korea. We couldn't stay. I was in the United Nations Commission. That's another story because I was teaching at a school when I got to Korea. I was teaching school at Seoul National and at the Women's Medical College, Sudo Medical College. The Americans were so admired by the Koreans, so admired. Eventually, that feeling changed after Syngman Rhee got elected.

Rhee wasn't doing very much for the people, and he was doing some policies that were going so badly. For instance—I could give many examples—anybody who opposed him in some way, he, himself, personally, did not cause that person's downfall, but he had them somehow . . . We knew, personally knew, people who were very powerful in the political parties who were eliminated by a third person. Certainly, a supporter of Rhee eliminated them, and he [the person who carried out his wishes] didn't get punished. Kim Ku's assassinator was allowed to live. His name was Ahn, I think. We all think that he was killed because . . . what Syngman Rhee did . . . his modus operandi was that he never went out to kill someone himself, but he said "Umm, ah . . . that guy, that guy 저런저런," like that. That was enough. And the people who just adored him went out and found ways to get rid of that person.

It was that year, 1942, December, which was such a momentous month. I can remember it so vividly because that's when Hitler and the German army were turned back. They called the place at the time Stalingrad, then Leningrad, and now it's St. Petersburg. That was the turning point of the war, and that's December 12, 1942. I had just came back from Canada. In other words, we had already had the Midway Battle, May 1942. We had reached a turning point in the Pacific War. The European War had a turning point in December 1942. You see, I lived those days from day to day. We lived in a time that we couldn't have butter, we couldn't have meat; we used to wear silk stocking, then no silk stockings. You know, we went through the war and through the deprivation and rationed things. Anyway, that was the turning point.

We had this dinner, and there was Ed Pai, sitting there, watching me. I don't know what thoughts went through his mind. It was a few days after when he asked me for a date. I was so excited because he was one of the Korean men that I had met who was appealing, although I had this big argument with him. He seemed serious, and he also was nice looking. He was a gentleman, really a gentleman, not like some of these guys you might date. They

Edward Eui Whan Pai and Inez marry in
Washington, D.C., circa 1941.

just want to proposition you, like
most of the Korean men that I met,
people like . . . They were too old or
I wasn't interested in them in any
way other than working together
in this Independence Movement or
whatever. Ed Pai was someone that
I found rather attractive. So he called
me and we dated. I was living at the
International House Dormitory on
New Hampshire Avenue. Boy, we really got interested in each other. We
were seeing each other for dinner
at the Wing Café practically every
evening. Then he'd come back to the
International House, and we'd play
ping pong down in the basement.
Eventually, he got so tired that he
said, "I think you have to marry me."

In the meantime, I told you I had
applied to go to Kuk Min. The first
thing, when I came to Washington, was to apply to Kuk Min. That was also
when Philip Ahn's sister, Ahn Chang Ho's daughter, was in Washington. This
was after I was married. She went into the WAVES, the women's navy. Anyway,
the permit came through and I was checked for security. There was another
crazy thing I was doing. I was going to Maryland every week to fly, you know,
an airplane. I had started flying, taking lessons in a piper cub. They called it a
piper cub . . . small airplanes. I also had been taking lessons in dueling, nine
hours a week.

Since I was going to Kuk Min, I wanted to learn how to fly. Oh, I was crazy.
Anyway, I used to go down there. Ed just couldn't figure me out. The approval
to go to Kuk Min came through. So, in the meantime, I was dating Ed. He
took me on Christmas Eve to this most fashionable restaurant in Washington,
the Balalaika. I'll never forget it. I never tasted such things as frog legs earlier.
It was delicious. I had a bottle of wine and all that. He treated me like a queen,
trying to sweep me off my feet or something. Anyway, I liked him. It wasn't
too long before I felt that I really fell in love with him. Anyway, this Kuk Min

John Kong, only sibling of Inez, was an active counselor for her.

approval thing came through in February. So I went to Ed and asked him, "What do you think?" He said, "Well, that's a decision you'll have to make. I think that you're going to be graduating in a short while. You should maybe get your degree first, but I want you to make that decision all on your own. Don't expect me to advise you." He didn't ever say he loved me or anything. However, we were attracted to each other, right? Whew, I had to go through such connections on account of that.

At that time, telephone line connections were made with Hawaii. I called up Honolulu and talked with my brother and I talked with my mother. My brother was just furious. Not really furious, but he couldn't figure me out.

He said, "What are you doing with yourself? When are you graduating?" I said, "Well, I'm due to graduate in June [1943]." He said, "OK, if you really want to go, but why don't you at least finish your degree?" That seemed reasonable enough. I didn't know what was going to happen. It was very exciting because I had been selected. I have all the newspaper clippings, too.

My life went in so many different ways. I've done so many different, crazy things since the time I was in Los Angeles, just before going to Washington, D. C. Not crazy, really, but when I think about it, in 1938 I went to represent LACC [Los Angeles City College] at the National Youth Congress in Washington D.C. Five of us, from UCLA in Pomona, from USC and LACC. I represented Los Angeles City College. They selected me as a delegate. Professors got together and they asked me if I would go, and I said, "Sure." So we took a trailer and went to Washington, D.C., with a car and a trailer. I have all those pictures. In 1939 I was selected by LACC to represent LACC at the Japanese-American Youth Conference in Tokyo. We had to have the approval of the committee in Japan. They turned me down. They said it was because I was not an "Occidental American." That was the reason they gave, but I think it was when they found out my Korean background. So I couldn't go, but I have newspaper articles on that. That's what happened that let me go to Washington, D. C.

Regarding Edward Eui Whan Pai

Inez and Edward Pai returned to Korea after World War II ended in 1946. When Dr. Syngman Rhee was elected President of Korea in 1948, they left Korea and lived in Hawaii until Rhee was impeached in 1960. Mr. and Mrs. Pai returned to Korea that same year after Rhee's impeachment. Edward Pai then became President of the Bank of Korea. Shortly after Chung Hee Pak was elected President of Korea, Pak appointed Edward Pai Ambassador to Japan. Mr. Pai presided over the normalization of Korea-Japan relations negotiations. Subsequently, he was made Ambassador to Argentina and Ambassador to England.

5

Interview with Agnes Pahk Kwon, Wife of Manuel Kwon

My name is Agnes Pahk Kwon. I was asked by Roberta Chang to recall some of my memories of childhood and my life before and after I got married.

My father's name was Pahk Duk Soon and my mother's name was Martha Han. I was born in 1913. I come from a family of mostly girls; there were twelve in our family, but the number of surviving children was eight girls and one boy. I'm second to the last. We lived our early years in Ewa Plantation and my father was one of the first to come to Hawaii with a family, three children. This means that the first three children were born in Korea.

Duk Soon and Martha Pahk, circa 1920.
Greta Kwon Uyeki Album.

When we lived in Ewa, my father was not like the laborers in the sugar fields because he was put in charge of cooking for the laborers in the fields. He was given a *gok sang* [kitchen], like a restaurant, where he provided meals for the single men when they came home from work.

Duk Soon and Martha Hahn Pahk family, left to right: Wallace, Duk Soon, Annie, Agnes (sitting), Nora, Rose, Hazel, Martha, and Stella, circa 1918.

My father knew how to cook for a large number of people because when he was in Korea some missionary families instructed him on how to cook for a big group of people. The single men did not live in houses with kitchens.

So, when I was a child, we spent much of our time—our leisure time—helping in the preparation of vegetables, like stringing the beans and cleaning the onions, stuff like that, which we enjoyed doing very much. My father and mother got up at about three o'clock in the morning to prepare food for the men's lunch pails to take to work. My memory is not too good about the early days, but at the time of the First World War, I was old enough to know that there was a great need for food. Because my father was trained in the business of providing food, he had a whole room full of food goods, such as rice, stacked full to the ceiling. Because he had a Christian background, he really helped a lot of Koreans in those times of need.

I know that during the time when he was the cook, we were very busy. I believe he must have been paid by the plantation to do this work. I'm not sure.

But then we didn't have a real need for food, you know. We were such a minority. We Koreans clung together. We had a church, a Korean church. The first Korean minister was Mr. Won Myung Chung. He was Willa Chung's husband. He was really not an ordained minister, but he was like a leader, and we all went to Sunday school under his instruction. We went to church, and we had Korean classes after public school. Because of this closeness with each other, we developed a great friendship among us Koreans.

It continued that way even after we left Ewa Plantation because of the Korean Methodist Church. It was not just a Methodist church. It was a Korean church. When we moved to Honolulu, I can recall very happy days because as children, we didn't see the things happening in the world. I have very happy memories in Ewa.

The sad thing was that my mother died when I was five years old. My father continued to take care of the kitchen with the help of my older sisters. I was still very young when my sisters were already teenagers. My oldest sister, Louisa, married Shi Dae Han. They moved to California. I hardly saw her because she moved away before I was a year old. My second oldest sister, Lily, became the wife of Tai Sung Lee, who was a youth worker at the YMCA. He was very close to the Korean people.

My third sister, Nora Pahk Chai, was one of the leading nurses at the Queen's Hospital. She was first Korean to become the supervisor of nurses at that hospital for many years. These three sisters have all died. My next sister, who is surviving today, is Rose, the first in the family to marry a Caucasian. She's living in San Francisco with her children. And my other sister, Alice, who is living in Hawaii, is the widow of Hyun Woo Lee, who was a chemist with the Hawaiian Sugar Plantation Company.

My sister Hazel is next; she is married to Rev. Euicho Chung, pastor of the Methodist Church at Fort Church. They had an interesting life because they went to Hilo and then in the later years, they established the Good Will Industries in Hawaii. Hazel and Euicho went to the Mainland to head the San Francisco Good Will Association there first, before they established a branch in Hawaii. [The Chungs' life story is told by Hazel separately.]

My brother, Wallace, is the only brother I have. After my parents died, Wallace was sent to Los Angeles to be with my older sister's family because he was still very young. But he came back to Hawaii to live in Hilo because he was appointed manager of a hotel in Hilo. There he met Pearl Choi, whom he married, and they have, I think, four girls and one boy.

Because we lost our parents when we were very young, my youngest sister, Stella, was sent to our older sisters' families. Stella didn't have any chance to further her education. She lost her husband about ten years ago. Her name is Stella Baptist.

Your brother-in-law, Tai Sung Lee, is in our Hawaii history profiles. He was really an outstanding Korean community figure. Could you tell us what you remember about him?

Because we were such a minority, the Koreans clung together. Tai Sung Lee, who was, at that time, a YMCA worker, was very concerned about Koreans. And so he organized little groups of students and tried to help those who didn't have jobs.

Because we were very close and we had no welfare or anything, I was one of those who was sent to live with my sister Lily and Tai Sung Lee. They happened to have a daughter about my age, whose name was Daisy Lee. Daisy is right now living in California. She used to be the organist for the church. She was a very talented pianist. I forget when Tai Sung died, but after he died, there was a continuation of his work by Donald Yong Gak Kang. Donald took over the work that they began together.

Tell us about what you remember about Donald Kang.

He was a teacher. And he was very active with the student movement, too. I believe it was during his time that Donald put out a school annual for Korean high school students. My graduation from the School of Nursing in 1934 is in that book. We had this annual of all the graduates of Korean ancestry for several years. The annual kept us closely connected to each other.

What did your mother die of and when?

I think she died of cancer. She died when I was about five years old, in 1919. That's what my older sister said, that she died of cancer. So it was my father who really raised the younger children.

Your father became ill when you were about thirteen. How old was he then?

He was about sixty-five, I think, in 1923. He had some gall bladder trouble. In those days, all people thought that once you went to the hospital, you're dead. So he'd go to a doctor, but he never wanted to go to the hospital. Through the grapevine, he found out that if you went to a masseuse, you would do better and would recover. But then his gall bladder erupted when he was at the masseuse, and following that, he died a few days later. At that time, my sister Nora was in training at Queen's, and she was very angry because our father listened to the women who directed him to go to the masseuse instead of going to the hospital to be treated.

Anyway, he died, and so that's why we younger children were sent to different homes among our sisters to be taken care of. I went to my sister Lily. My sister Hazel was already kind of engaged and Alice was kind of engaged. My sister Stella, the youngest in the family, lived with my sister Rose. So this was how we all stayed connected as a family.

When my father was living, I was still in high school and was living with Lily, the older sister with whom I was very close. I went to McKinley High School, but she was at Roosevelt High School. When my father died, I was there and saw everything, and I made up my

Burial place of Duk Soon Pahk and wife Martha Pahk surrounded by noted persons in the Korean community.

Agnes Pahk graduation
photograph, 1934.
Katherine Kwon,
Manuel Kwon's sister.

mind at that time that I would be never ignorant about sickness again.
I wanted to know why he died. So, at that time, I volunteered to be a
nurse like my sister Lily. I wanted to know about ideal health methods.
It was from then that I was health minded. Because we didn't have
money at that time and I was too young to be a nurse, I stayed out of
school for one year after graduating from high school.

However, I was not behind in school level because I had skipped
two grades in elementary school, pushing me on to a higher grade
level—and that's another part of my history. My sister Nora was a
teacher. I was living with her at that time, so I could see how she taught
her classes. There were two grade classes in one room. When I was in
the first grade, I would be listening to what was happening in the second grade. When the time came for promotion, they skipped me to the
third grade, so I missed second grade. I think that happened to me in
the fifth grade, too. So I skipped two grades. Having graduated within
a short time, I was too young to go to the nursing school. So I had to
stay out another year to become qualified to go to Queen's Hospital.
The school age for entrance was age eighteen and it was cut off in
September. Since I was born in November, I was not yet eighteen for
entrance, so I had to wait. When I graduated from Queen's, I was still
very young, not even twenty-one. I was always the youngest, also the
smallest in stature, of the students in the class. I always had this complex
that I had to be better because I was so small. I studied harder to be
equal with everybody else. I felt much pressure because of these feelings, and partly because of my feeling of wanting to be my own boss.

Manuel Kwon, second from right, visiting Korea to meet his parental extended family, circa 1929.

Before I graduated from Queen's Hospital, I met Manuel Kwon on a blind date, well, not really a blind date because he was at the university and he called the School of Nurses' home. I didn't know who this fresh guy was. He called and wanted to talk to anybody, and I happened to be on the phone. He asked me to go to a certain dance party. He said that he was a Maui boy. I told the other girls in my nursing class that he called for a date, and they said, "Go with him. He is really a nice guy and he's smart." So this is how I met my future husband, on this blind date. Ever since then, it's been history.

We got married. Before we got married, Manuel was already teaching in Hana, Maui, and there was opening in Hana for a nurse, so he applied for me. And because Maui people all know each other, he told the commissioners or whoever was in power there, that we were planning to get married, and he told them that I had to have this job at Hana Hospital. It was a two-nurse hospital, a country hospital, where we nurses did everything. I got the job and became an expert overnight because we had to do everything. I recall the times when there was an emergency, big accidents. I would call Manuel because there was no other emergency help. He would always rush over to help me, but then he was horrified to see the mess that was all around due to the accident—all that blood, broken legs, and broken heads! I could see

Manuel Kwon's maternal family; standing right, his mother, Maria Gonzales.

Manuel Kwon's father.

that he could hardly stomach it. Dr. Harold Patterson was the doctor there. On other occasions, Dr. Patterson would call on Manuel to help the surgeons. I recall one time Dr. Patterson had to amputate a leg. He called Manny, and after he amputated the leg, he turned around and gave the leg to Manny. As Manuel was holding the leg and didn't know what do with it, his face became pale white.

There were many, many happy occasions in Hana. It is a beautiful town, more so during those early years in Hawaii because Hana was something like Kahuku, a little, isolated area. If there was a wedding, everybody in town went to the wedding. In a small place like Hana, the teachers and nurses had special treatment when they went to the movies. They had a set place for them in the theatre. You knew your seat when you went to the movies. People played tennis a lot there, too, because it was a good place to play tennis. Everybody played tennis. I did enjoy Hana. Today, when I think about tennis, I remember that we had wonderful times there.

Before I got married to Manny, my sister used to tell me never intermarry, and my husband is part-Spanish and part-Korean. That put a fear in me. There was an opportunity for me to go Chicago to take a post-graduate course in obstetrics; it gave me a chance to think it over about Manny. I went to Chicago and he remained in Hawaii, getting his final teaching degree in education. I thought if we survived the separation then we'd get married. We survived and married after I returned to Hawaii.

We had many, many interesting happenings after we moved to Honolulu. He became a full-time certified teacher at Central Intermediate School, and I was certified in nursing.

How many children do you have?

We have four children, one boy and three girls. My two older children are teachers and my son is in Samoa. He's with a Korean group, I believe, who are fishermen. He's connected with the Korean fishery thing there. And my youngest, Greta, is the only one living in Hawaii. She's my real backbone for whatever I need. She's very willing to do whatever I need. I'm very fortunate to have her with us here.

Could you go back and tell us about Manuel as a teacher at Central Intermediate School and what happened next?

In 1941 he volunteered to go into military service. When he enlisted, I didn't know what it meant. Later, I resented it very much because he left me with three children. I had to take care of these three children by myself. And because everything in the armed forces was so hush-hush, he was sent to Fort Benning, Georgia, without my knowledge. They took him away because everything was blacked out.

Was this during the war?

Yes, the war.

What year did he leave?

1942. And so I decided I wasn't going to stay on the island. I was going to move to the Mainland, too. So he arranged that I go there with our three children. My oldest was about six years old. I, being born in Hawaii, was ignorant about simple things that Mainlanders do. For instance, in Hawaii shoes were worn only on Sundays. I and the three children got very sick on the ship to the Mainland. I was a very poor traveler. My son also got very sick. I think we were on the USS *President Tyler,* which was an army transport.

The three children were Melvin, Laura, and Irene. Greta was not born yet. She was born after the war. And as I said, Melvin was very seasick, and I got seasick; I wanted to die. The first three days, I wanted to die, but after the third day, I got a little better after I got some fresh air and we all recovered.

Then we had this long train ride to Fort Benning, but we were given a place outside of it because it was overcrowded at that time. We were put on a train again, and this train took about three days to get to Georgia. As I mentioned before, our kids did not wear shoes in Hawaii unless it was a special occasion, so half the time they were leaving their shoes under the chairs or on other people chairs. One day we had to get off the train to eat lunch because they did not have dining cars in those days. So we had to get out of the train, eat, and dash back to the train. I remember one time, this porter ran up to us to give us one of the children's brand new coats which one of them had left behind on the train. My daughter told the porter, "My mother told me to keep my coat clean and your hands are dirty." The children didn't know what a black person was. I was so embarrassed, but I didn't say anything. That was their first experience with black people. I felt bad because everyone on the train was very good to us. When they knew I was rushing with meals for the kids, they helped me get food for them to finish on the train. They helped us a whole lot.

My husband had put this woman in charge of taking us to our hotel, which they had found for us. When got there, it was so heartwarming. The woman brought blankets and brought flowers to us; I thought Hawaii was the Land of Aloha, but they were even warmer than we were. We were just nothing, and yet they were so good to us. When Sunday came around, this woman who took care of us came to pick up our kids to go to Sunday school. She was so wonderful. They called her Sister Louise. Throughout the years we kept in contact with her until she died few years ago. She used to write to us every Christmas. I think she was a great strength and source of warmth for people like us. Another thing, because we were Oriental—we weren't black, weren't white—people didn't understand what we were because they didn't have Orientals in the South in those days. People would stop us on the street and ask us to say something because they didn't know what strange animals we were.

What year was this?

1942? 1943? In Hawaii, I can remember, there was shortage of toilet paper and Kleenex. But where we were, the factories making those things were in that area. They had counters full of Kleenex and toilet paper. We just hoarded them because back in Hawaii we were so used to hoarding goods like these. It felt very strange to have more than one box of Kleenex, and people all crowding around us to wait on us because we were different. Sometimes I think we were an education for them, and they were an education for us. We had never seen anything there that we were familiar with in Hawaii. I loved the things I saw. I was a little scared because I'd never seen so many black people in my whole life.

The white people would walk out of the store when a black girl came in. I didn't know they had such great prejudices. I've never felt that before, and it made me feel hurt even though they treated me as a white. I was so used to mixtures of people in Hawaii, where I don't think we have these extreme racial prejudices. After we left Fort Benning, we went back to San Francisco. Manny bought a car and we drove across from Georgia to San Francisco, where he was going to the University of California to take Mandarin-language classes because he was going to be sent to China as a liaison officer with the Chinese army. We stayed in the U.S. It happened that my mother-in-law had a place in San Francisco, and she had a downstairs apartment, so we lived downstairs, and Manny was able to go to school from there. But after he was through with that, he was sent to the China–Burma theater. He was able to use his Chinese-language knowledge enough to carry on a conversation with the Chinese people there. He said that he had many happy and very unusual experiences while he was in China. He told me when he was dying for Chinese food, they would go to a Chinese restaurant in the community and they'd be sick later on. But he felt it was worth it because they enjoyed the food.

In the meantime, I was in California. A new law was imposed on all travelers going to Hawaii. You had to prove that you had a job waiting for you before you were allowed to buy a flight ticket to Hawaii. It did not matter even if you were locally born in Hawaii, even if you were a military veteran and a graduate nurse, because we did not have reciprocity in Hawaii with California at that time. So they didn't even consider me as a graduate nurse. Maybe it was because in Hawaii our standards were different. So I decided to go back to school again because if I had to stay in California for a long time, I didn't want to be unable to work if Manny didn't come back. So I went back to school at Blow Mountain, which was a ladies' finishing school. It happened they had advanced courses in nursing education. I took them.

One day I remembered a person by the name of Mother Rossie at a Catholic college. I went to her office. She asked me how I felt about the Japanese. I told her I had a very good friend who was Japanese and that I didn't have any prejudice against the Japanese. She asked me if I was afraid. I said, no, I wasn't afraid.

That was during the war, and I experienced many, many good things and bad things. I remember one day I was parking on the side of a hill, and then two women on the sidewalk said, "You better get out of here, you Jap," or something like that, very angrily. Because I was hot tempered myself, I got out of the car with my hands on hips and I said, "Don't you dare talk to me like that. My husband is fighting for you, and here you're talking to me like I'm a Jap. I'm not a Jap and, to begin with, if I were Japanese, I wouldn't be disloyal." So I was really angry. Another time, I was in the library with the kids, and a man stopped by us and said, "Who is this? Are these your children?" I said, "Yes," and he said, "I didn't know Filipinos that young." So we were called Filipinos and they called me a Jap. I said to myself, I'm learning a lot of things being there, all these different experiences.

Manuel came home on furlough in 1945, and just about the time he came home, the war ended. He had a choice of either continuing on and being promoted to another rank or getting out. He decided he had enough of the army. He got out. A problem developed. Here we were in California. What happened is that we found out we could not go back to Hawaii until we could prove that we were able to support ourselves. I had to write to Queen's Hospital, and he had to write to his former employers to secure a position before he applied to return to Hawaii.

I'm surprised. What do you mean? You could not come back to your place of birth?
The government in Hawaii did not want too many people coming to Hawaii, even former residents, that's why we resented it. The reason

was that there was shortage of food in Hawaii because shipments to Hawaii from the Mainland were restricted and the land in Hawaii to grow its own vegetables came under the control of the U.S. Military Command. Many people were coming back to Hawaii and military wives wanted to join their military husbands in Hawaii after the war. A regulation was put out that people who wanted to come to Hawaii had to prove that they could support themselves.

Because of our connections in Hawaii, we were able to come home to Hawaii, but it was not easy and it took much effort to get the clearance. I had my sister write to me about a job. Manny used his connections to get his job back. We even proved that we owned a house in Kaimuki. Incidentally, we had rented that house to Song Hae Lim and his wife, Lily Ahn Lim. They rented the house and we had to tell them to move out because we were coming home. What was nice was that they were paying our mortgage for us while we were away, so the house was being paid for.

When we finally came back, we got our jobs back. I did not go on a regular staff shift. I became what was called a floater nurse; they put me where I was needed, but I'd been out of nursing so long, it was a big strain on me. Manny was assigned to Central Intermediate School as a teacher. Then, a year later, he was offered many, many different positions at different schools throughout the island of Oahu.

Luckily, we had a house waiting for us. Many interesting things happened when we returned home. We were invited to different places for dinner. One night, after coming home from a party with the three children, we were so tired. Manny took the kids out from the car. We didn't check with each other, if all the kids were in the bedrooms. Next morning, we heard something coming from the garage: "Mommy, Mommy." We thought Lorna had fallen out from the second window, but she had slept in the car the whole night and we didn't know that. That is a fun thing to remember.

What happened to us next in settling back in Hawaii was that Manny was given certain seniority: He could apply for higher positions instead of being a teacher, so he became vice principal at Central Intermediate School. They even gave him credits for the years he was away during the war. He was later appointed principal of Kipapa School, which was a very small school. I had to make a decision what to do, rent a house again or what, so we decided to move to Wahiawa, just a few miles from Kipapa. That's where he became principal for maybe four or five years, then he was transferred to Mililani School, which is a little beyond Wahiawa. After that he went to Nanakuli School. That's another interesting story because Nanakuli Town is a Hawaiian community and the people were very different there. The Hawaiian people have a way to love people, they have a certain loyalty, and you have to understand their way of loving. We made many, many warm friendships while in Waihawa, also. I remember one morning, after I got up, I found some chickens at my back room door and some pineapples, sometimes pies. People would bring us things like that, they were so nice. And in Kipapa, they used to bring beautiful produce, lettuce and string beans. There we had many mango trees and all kind of the trees in our backyards. There were wonderful birds living there.

However, this was a time of a little trouble happening. My son and daughter were in the same classroom. My daughter got promoted, so she jumped a grade. That was bad for my son. He felt inferior because others thought that he had either flunked or done something wrong. But nothing was wrong with him. It was because in the rural areas the schools were small and the school had to combine two classes. That continued when we sent them to Mid-Pacific School in Honolulu, where they were still put into the same grade. That created hardship for him many times. Maybe this is the reason why he did not want to do certain things, because he felt he was not as good as the others. But he was fine, there was nothing wrong with him.

By this time, Manny had learned how to golf. He joined the Lion's Club and became active with them. Of course, he also joined PTA. He was very community-minded, which kept him very busy. I used to think that he had no time for us with our children because he was too busy with the community. I guess he had to go out to coach basketball to make extra money. In those days everybody needed extra income for so many things.

We went to Nanakuli to help out people there. The people in Nanakuli, as I said, were very soft and very warm, but you can see that they were some of the poorest people in the community, even though they're very giving. At the same time even the parents were like children; for instance, my husband and his vice principal had to go out in his jeep to pick up the kids to take them to school, but sometimes it was because the parents were irresponsible. Once he told me that he had to get funds to see that the kids had breakfast. Many kids didn't have breakfast when they came to school, so they had to give them free meals.

Manny used his connections with the military to get help for the children in various ways. One example was getting musical instruments from the military. Manny was able to get all these instruments, given free by the military. The well-known Mr. Hodoki started a band in poor Nanakuli because of Manny. It made Nanakuli really proud of their children's accomplishments. Up to that point, they had nothing to be proud of, there was just nothing.

Actually, Manny was not active in the Korean community when he was busy working at the schools full-time, particularly while we were in Hana, Kipapa, and Halemanu.

How about you? Were you active?

Actually, I was too busy raising the kids. I was busy with the children when they were all young. But then the only contact with Koreans was at the Methodist Church in Wahiawa because Euicho, my brother-in-law, was the pastor at the new building of the Korean Methodist Church on Keeaumoku Street.

Euicho Chung was married to my sister Hazel. At that time, there was no real building for the church. The Korean Methodist Church on Fort Street was exchanged for a temporary house in which Euicho's family lived upstairs and the church was downstairs. Finally, a new church was built at the present place on Keeaumoku Street in Honolulu.

As I said, we gave all our energies to our jobs, so we were not active in the church and in the Korean community—except for the Korean University Club and maybe, sometimes, the Lion's Club. Later, Manny joined the Korean Golf Club. He played a lot with Korean golfers. I think he was one of the founders of the Nanakuli Lion's Club. He was very active in all the community activities where he was principal.

What was the goal of the Korean University Club (KUC) at that time and what kind of activities did they have?

The KUC started in 1934 or '35, the year we graduated from college. I remember the club meeting at our house. We used to meet in different homes once a month throughout the years. We would get together to form some sort of activities to raise funds for scholarships for Korean students. The KUC was the first to start this idea of a scholarship fund. Of course, we did not do that well in the beginning. We had fashion shows and we had golf matches and other ways to raise money for the students. In the beginning, it was only for students from Hawaii, but we got more lenient and included Koreans from Korea in this scholarship program.

I believe it was about that time that they had the Friendship Mission to Korea. The Korean Community Council was asked by the U.S. Eighth Brigade to select four representatives to go to Korea for a "Friendship Tour" between Korean Americans and Koreans.

Would you explain what this friendship tour was?

Well, it was an exchange between the Korean government and Hawaiian Koreans. They wanted to exchange knowledge, information, and stuff between the two countries, between the two groups of Koreans. So they sent about four persons from Hawaii to Korea and four from Korea to Hawaii in exchange. We had to entertain the Koreans from Korea and the Koreans from here were entertained by the government in Korea.

This was in what year?

I believe it was in the late 1960s and early 1970s. I don't know how long it continued, but I'm sure it was at least about six years that the groups exchanged representatives.

President Syngman Rhee was ousted in 1960, so all these exchanges took place after he was president. Why do you think they took place after Syngman Rhee left and not before?

I think it had nothing to do with politics. It was an economic exchange—they would pick someone from the community. Manny was one of them as was Rosie Chang.

As far as Dr. Syngman Rhee is concerned, my earliest recollection was when I was a child: I would overhear people talking about this man who solicited funds from Koreans and many times they resented this. And that was Dr. Syngman Rhee who was out collecting money.

Did you know that? Well, anyhow, as I said I was not in contact with this political movement because I was so busy raising our kids and going to the Mainland and going to war and stuff like that, so I really don't know too much about the history.

I do know that there was friction between the Liliha Church and the Methodist Church on Keeaumoku Street. I never knew the real reason. To me, I feel the Korean University Club was able to bridge the gap between the young members from both churches. It lessened the animosity between the two groups. So I think that education is the door to the togetherness of people.

Manny was the president of so many Korean organizations. One of Manny's last presidencies of a Korean organization was the Korean Community Council, which was composed of representatives from all Korean organizations in Hawaii. They accomplished many projects for the Korean consulate. So you see, he was very concerned about Koreans and the Korean community.

6

Interview with Winifred Lee Namba on Her Mother, Nodie Kimhaekim Sohn

Nodie Kimhaekim Sohn   Winifred Lee Namba

My name is Winifred Lee Namba. I am to talk to you today about my mother, Nodie Kimhaekim Sohn. She was born in Hwanghae Do, Korea, in 1898 on October 29th. Her family migrated to Kimhae, Chollanam Do, the southern part of Korea. And from there, the family—consisting of my mother, her older sister, a younger sister, and a brother—had plans to immigrate to Hawaii in 1905. My mother's older sister, who was about to get married, said that her future husband had promised their father that he would immigrate with them to Hawaii and that was why my grandfather agreed to their marriage. But after the marriage, my sister's husband changed his mind and refused to go to Hawaii and remained in Korea with his new bride. My grandfather was furious, according to my mother.

However, there was nothing my grandfather could do because they were married. So they had to leave her behind. He went on with the plan to go to Hawaii with the rest of the family—my mother's brother, John Kimhaekim; Nodie, my mother; and a younger sister, Mary Kimhaekim. They arrived in Honolulu in 1905. Nodie was seven years old. Unfortunately, Mary died in Hawaii when she was nine years old, of small pox. My mother always said that Mary was the beauty in the family, and Nodie referred to herself as the "ugly duckling."

The earliest recollection I have of what my mother told me about herself was that she attended Kaahumanu School in Honolulu. It was a public school. My grandfather, after working a while on the sugar plantation, decided that it

Kimhaekim family; mother, Yoon Kuk Kim; father, Yoon Chong Kimhaekim; left, Mary; right, Nodie; second right, unidentified, circa 1900.

was not the life for him. So they left the plantation. My grandmother supported the family by being a seamstress and being a midwife. I was told that my grandfather was a very handsome man and he was quite an adventurer. He never really settled down anywhere. He was always off to somewhere. Then suddenly, my grandfather decided to leave Hawaii for somewhere in China to seek his fortunes without us. He died in Manchuria. I have no recollection of him at all. Later, my Uncle John moved to San Francisco and married there. He was like his father, going off on his own. So I never knew my uncle. That left only my mother and my grandmother here in Honolulu.

I remember my grandmother very well. She practically raised me until she died because my mother worked very hard, long hours, at the school that Dr. Rhee founded. My mother never really talked much about her own early experiences. She always tried to raise me as a "you were born in America, so you are an American citizen, so you learn all about America."

At age sixteen my mother became acquainted with Dr. Syngman Rhee, who became her mentor. After she graduated from Kaahumanu School, a public school that went up to the eighth grade level in Honolulu, Rhee arranged a scholarship for her at Wooster High School, far away on the U.S. continent in the state of Ohio, to finish high school. But there was no money for transportation. Rhee had even arranged a place for her to stay at Wooster High School, where she could work for room and board. The problem was to get to Ohio. Determined to get an education, my mother went to the piers every day for weeks, asking anyone who was going to be on board ship if they needed someone to help babysit on the ship because she had to get to Ohio, where her scholarship awaited her. A colonel and his wife who were going on

Yoon Chong Kimhaekim, Yoon Kuk Kim, Nodie Kimhaekim, circa 1914.

board ship to California then travel all the way to the East Coast by land, hired her and took her with them. As far as I can remember from what my mother told me, the colonel's family remained good friends with her.

Nodie went on to Wooster High School in 1916, so, by then, she was seventeen years old. When she got to Wooster, she worked for her room and board. After she graduated, she received a scholarship to Oberlin College in Ohio, where she also worked for her room and board. She graduated in 1922. After graduation and getting her bachelor of arts degree in political science, she returned to Hawaii to work for the Korean

YMCA Student Convention in Des Moines, Iowa, December 1919; Nodie Kimhaekim is standing, fourth from the left; William Pyung Won Lee is in front, third from the left.

Nodie Kimhaekim and mother, Yoon Kuk Kim, circa 1925.

Christian Institute (KCI) and, eventually, she became the superintendent of the KCI, which Dr. Syngman Rhee had founded. She was a very loyal supporter of Rhee, and she believed strongly in the independence of Korea. She spent months lecturing on the Mainland, trying to raise money to help the Korean cause.

In 1927, my mother married my father, William Pyung Won Lee, in Chicago. Very shortly thereafter, the marriage was annulled. From what I understand, the reason for the annulment was because they were on different sides of the political fence. She was a strong supporter of Dr. Rhee, and I assume my father was not. But after she came home, she found out she was pregnant with me. So she had me: I was born on August 31, 1928, in Honolulu.

It was a very difficult year for my mother because my grandmother, meanwhile, had gone to San Francisco to take care of my Uncle John, who was dying of cancer. After hearing about my mother's pregnancy with me, my grandmother hurriedly came back to Hawaii and took care of my birth. My uncle died a month before I was born in 1928. And my grandmother brought his body for burial in Hawaii. His wife had asked her to bury him in Hawaii. That is one reason why, although his family remained in San Francisco, his body is buried here in Honolulu.

Then, Nodie, my mother, returned to work at the Korean Christian Institute and continued as superintendent in 1925 until 1935. Dr. Syngman Rhee had gone to Austria in 1931 or 1932. He returned with a bride, Francesca Donner, from Austria. When Rhee returned, Nodie left KCI because Rhee

Sohn and Nodie family together; left to right, front: Nodie, Eva, Syung Woon Sohn; back: Peter, Winifred, Abraham.

took over as superintendent and he and his wife lived on the compound of KCI.

My mother then went to work for the Kim Furniture Store for five years. She became a very close friend of Mrs. Kim. In 1935, a year after my mother started working there, my mother became more acquainted with Syung Woon Sohn and they married. He had two children from his first marriage, Abraham and Eva. Eva, the younger child, was four years older than me. Their mother had died. Abraham and Eva were students at the KCI. That is where Nodie, my mother, and Mr. Sohn met for the first time. I was there at KCI, also. The classes were very small and we were all thrown together—just like a little classroom where the fourth, fifth, and sixth graders are all put together in one room. We had lessons together. Other than that, my memories of KCI are pretty hazy. I'm sorry.

I remember both Mrs. Rhee and Dr. Rhee at that time because I was a little bit older then, but I was a day student, so I would just go to KCI for classes and come back home. I remember one thing about Dr. Rhee. He used to love to have his head scratched with a comb. And several of us had the assignment to scratch his head every afternoon. I was one of them who had to scratch his head. We hated it. I remember another thing about Dr. Rhee: When he used to talk to us in school, he had the very nervous affliction of blowing on his fingers. We were told it was from the torture he suffered in prison. I don't think he ever got over that torture because whenever he talked, he always blew on his fingers. That's what I remember about him.

While you were at KCI, what did your mother do?

Well, I guess, she ran the school—KCI. She was the superintendent. There was a boys' dormitory and a girls' dormitory. And there was the school building in the middle and the kitchen or cafeteria. There were, I remember, one, two, three, four buildings. The teachers always stayed in the boys' dormitory to supervise the boys. My mother sometimes stayed in the girls' dormitory and she supervised the girls.

I remember when Dr. Rhee came back with Mrs. Rhee, from Austria, they stayed in the girls' dormitory. At that time, I did not stay in the dorm anymore. I stayed with my mother and my grandmother about half a mile from KCI. My mother had bought a house in Kalihi, and so that's where we stayed before she married Mr. Sohn. After my mother married Syung Woon Sohn, we became a family and he and his children lived with us in Kalihi Valley. At their wedding, Mrs. Kim of the Kim's Furniture Store was my mother's maid of honor and her daughter, Daisy, and I were flower girls. I was good friends with Daisy. I knew the whole family. We would get together quite often for holidays and things like that. We were very close to each other because we were all Dr. Rhee's followers.

In 1940, my mother left the Kim Furniture Store and worked with my stepfather, who was a shoe repairman. He had shoe repair shops in Schofield Military Barracks, Wheeler Field, Wahiawa, and at the naval housing during the war.

Eva was four years older than I, and Abraham was six years older. So at that time, Abraham went to McKinley High School and my sister Eva went to St. Andrews Priory after she graduated from KCI. I went to Roosevelt High School. After my graduation, I went off to college in Michigan.

When the war ended, my mother and father went to Korea at the time when Dr. Rhee had become President of the Republic of Korea. They came back very excited because now Korea was an independent nation. Upon their return to Hawaii, my parents opened what they called the Kalihi Gift Shop, bringing in goods from Korea for the first time. During this time, she and my stepfather remained very active in the Korean community. There were a lot of Korean organizations for which my mother chaired, many of them.

Meanwhile, I was at Michigan State University. It was there that I met and married my husband, Dr. Ryujin Namba, who received his doctorate in microbiology. While there in Michigan in 1952, my mother asked me to come back to Honolulu quickly to meet with her because she was going to Korea at Dr. Syngman Rhee's request. He had asked her to become a member of his cabinet: Director of the Department of Procurement. She was not sure how long she would be there. She was not sure if she would come back to the U.S. So my husband and I hurriedly came home from Michigan in 1953 to see her off.

It was at this time of her departure that my mother told me that no matter what others said about our family's past, I must know that she was my real biological mother, not adopted. All those years I was not sure because of the rumors.

Then, when my mother went back to Korea, my stepfather followed her and they purchased a home in Korea. They called it Chongun Dong. That's when my mother was formally appointed to Dr. Rhee's cabinet. She had to come home to Hawaii every two years to renew her U.S. immigration papers because she was still a citizen of Korea. Because she retained her Korean citizenship, it was one of the reasons why Dr. Rhee could appoint her to a Korean government position. But she did not want to lose her green card status in Hawaii, so she had to return every two years to Hawaii to re-establish her card. Then she could go back and forth to Korea without a problem.

Do you know anything more about Mr. Sohn? His background?

He was a very wonderful father to me. He was with my mother at the Korean Christian Church, very active in Dongji Hoe. They were both very strong followers of Dr. Rhee because during the war Dr. Rhee was in Washington D.C., working very hard, trying to get independence for Korea. During this period, someone else took over KCI. Mrs. Mary Lee, the wife of Won Soon Lee, I think it was.

After some time in Korea my father, Mr. Sohn, who had gone with my mother to Korea, started to fail in health, so he returned home to Honolulu. When his health was pretty bad, my mother returned to Hawaii to take care of him. After my mother came back to Honolulu to take care of my father, she retired from the Korean government and she retired from all Korean activities in Honolulu, except she attended church services. My stepfather died in 1960, and my mother followed him in death twelve years later, in 1972.

When Dr. Rhee was here in Hawaii after being ousted from Korea in 1960, did your mother keep in touch with him?

Yes, I chauffeured my mother to go and visit with the two of them, Dr. & Mrs. Rhee. Then my husband, Dr. Namba, and I left in 1963 for Bangkok, where he had an assignment to do some kind of research on microbiology. My husband was still with the University of Hawaii, and we continued to go back and forth on contract to several parts of the world, especially the Far East. When my mother was in Korea, we visited with her several times. The last time, in 1965 or 1966, we were passing through Korea, after Dr. Rhee had passed away, and it was finally agreed by President Chung Hee Park that Rhee could be buried in Korea. My mother was in Korea at that time, and she was very busy and active in helping with Rhee's funeral arrangements. They had flown his body to Korea to be buried there. We did not have a chance to see her at the airport, but she sent an official person to look after us when we arrived in Korea. We didn't know that Rhee had passed away. That's why there so much commotion at the airport when we arrived at the same time as Rhee's body arrived. So she didn't meet us there, but we were able to go to his wake and look at the casket and all that. And we met with Mrs. Rhee there, too.

So you knew Mrs. Rhee as well?

Yes. After the funeral, Mrs. Rhee went back to Austria. We were in Iran on sabbatical then. On our way through Austria, we met Mrs. Rhee in Vienna. Even at that time, when we called her up, she would say that we'll meet, but she didn't want to meet in the lobby because she was still afraid of communists. So she came up to our hotel room.

Do you remember the time that Syngman Rhee came to Hawaii for a visit, after he became President of Korea? I have a picture of you with him when you were an adult. I've heard stories about how emotional it was when the two of you saw

each other for the first time after he became president and you had become an adult. Some have said that there was a deep emotional exchange between you two, especially the way he looked at you and solemnly nodded.

Yes, because as I said, my mother and father were very strong supporters of him. Whenever he came to Hawaii and they had receptions or anything like that for Rhee, my father, Mr. Sohn, especially insisted I come along. So I would go.

Did you ever have special meetings with him?

Not really, no. I just met him with the rest of the group. But that was mainly because I took my mother several times to see him. And my mother was very close with Mrs. Rhee.

You are aware of people's rumors about you and Dr. Rhee, aren't you?

Oh, yes. Ever since I was little. I was always teased about . . . that he was my father. And for a long time, I thought that I was adopted by my mother. My mother had claimed that I was the daughter of a very good friend of hers. Finally, after I married and before my mother went to Korea, my mother did tell me that I was her biological child. And she also told me that my father . . . the reason why they separated was

Winifred Namba shaking hands with Dr. Syngman Rhee, 1954.

Dr. Syngman Rhee with Mollie Min (standing, far left); Francesca Rhee (with lei); and Winifred Namba (sitting next to Rhee) at the Korean Christian Church, 1954.

because they were on different sides of the political fence. She knew that it would just never work. So, shortly after they married, the marriage was annulled. She said she was so upset, she tore up the marriage certificate. Of course, at that time, she did not know I was on the way . . . that she was pregnant with me. She told me that she was very happy that she did have me and I'm glad she did.

So she then told you way after you were married.
After I was married, uh-huh. She was going to go to Korea to work there indefinitely, so she sent for me. She felt at that time that she probably was never coming back to Hawaii, but after she got there, I think she changed her mind and decided not to give up her green card. And I'm glad she didn't because we had many very nice years together and she was able to enjoy her grandchildren.

Do you know why she waited to tell you until after you were married?
Probably because the marriage was annulled. So, as far as the Korean community and the world knew, she was never married. Back in those years, it would have been very difficult to have said that I had a child with no husband to show for it.

She was a brave woman.
She was, she really was.

Why is your name Winifred?
Well, she told me that I was named after my father, whose name was William, and that if females are named after someone who is called William, then her name should be Winifred.

Did she ever offer to introduce you to him?
Yes, she did at one time. That's why I firmly believe that the rumors about Dr. Rhee being my father are not true. It was about 1958, 1959, when my mother was living with me, the phone rang. I picked up the phone and there was a man asking for Nodie, so I called my mother, and she talked on the phone. After she hung up, she asked me, "Do you know who that was?" I said, "No." And she said, "That was your father. He was in town and so he called to see how everything was." And she said that she was going to have lunch with him before he flew off. She said, "Would you like to meet him?" I said, "I'm not interested in meeting him." So that's why I firmly believe that that was my father.

What happened at the airport? You mentioned something about the airport.
When he was about to leave, my mother asked me again, "Are you sure you don't want to meet your father?" I said, "No," and she said, "He's leaving today and we can go to the airport and say goodbye." But I said that I did not want to go to the airport.

So his name was William Lee?
Uh-huh.

You have no idea where he came from?
No, but she did say something, that he was an attorney and that he was not in good health. This was when she asked if I wanted to meet him. That he had problems with his heart or something like that. That he had married and I think she said he had a son and a daughter. So, somewhere, I've got a half-brother and a half-sister.

You mentioned once that your mother and he met in Chicago?
The reason why I said that is once I told my mother that I was staying at the Drake Hotel in Chicago. It was a time when I was in college; during the Christmas break, my husband and I went to stay at the Drake Hotel. My mother made the comment to me, "When you told me you were at the Drake Hotel, I should have told you that's where your father and I spent our honeymoon."

Winifred Lee Namba (middle) and daughters Ann Namba Cassidy (left) and Nodie Namba Hadar (right).

Profile of
Nodie Kimhaekim Sohn

Winifred Lee Namba, daughter of Nodie Kimhaekim Sohn, was born on August 31, 1928. Mrs. Namba has lived in the shadow of two famous persons in her life: her mother, Nodie Kimhaekim Sohn, and her daughter, Anne Namba. Both latter persons are well known in Hawaii. In essence, this interview focused on her mother, Nodie Kimhaekim Sohn.

Nodie Kimhaekim Sohn will always be a noted historic figure in the early establishment of Koreans in Hawaii. She is particularly remembered as an outstanding, faithful follower of Dr. Syngman Rhee and all that Rhee stood for: Rhee's church, school and political activities. Nodie at age sixteen was under the guidance of Dr. Syngman Rhee in 1914, which afforded her a higher education and personal accomplishments. The relationship lasted to the end of Dr. Rhee's life in 1965. Through this friendship, Nodie became Director of the Procurement Ministry in Korea when Dr. Syngman Rhee became President of the Korean Republic. In this presentation of her life story, the discrepancy of the birth of her child, Winifred Namba, should be definitively resolved.

Winifred Namba is the mother of Hawaii's foremost well-known fashion designer, Anne Namba. Anne Namba's acclaimed fashion designs reflect her mother, Winifred Namba, who can be described as a refined and elegant person.

7

Interview with Sarah Kim Lee

My father's name is Kim Kook Kyung and my mother's name is Emma Cho Kim. They arrived together in Hawaii in June 1904 with my sister, who was about nine or ten months old. They may have gone to Ewa Village and from there, they moved around the island of Oahu. They settled, I think, in Waialua, on the northern side of Oahu, for a short time. Then they moved to Castner Village, which is outside of Schofield Military Barracks and Wahiawa Town, up to around 1925. Since then, we have lived in Wahiawa all of our lives.

Tell us about their arrival from Korea. You said they brought their young baby, your sister.

My mother told me that my sister was one of the few babies on board the ship, and a Chinese woman, who was a cook on the ship, loved to take my sister and play with her. When she came back to my mother with the child, she always brought extra food for my mother and father.

When my parents left Korea, they did not tell my mother's family about going to Hawaii. So, when her parents found out about it, her father rushed down to Incheon Port with a pair of Korean booties that he wanted to give her for my sister. When my grandfather got there, the ship had already left. So he gave them to someone else who was going to Hawaii. My mother got them later on. And so, my parents moved around, and they lived in a placed called Won Luk Camp . . . that's a pineapple camp in the back of Halemanu, where I was born.

Kook Kyung and Emma Cho Kim family, circa 1935; left to right, front row: Bessie Shin, Sarah Pil Soon Kim, Philip Shin, Robert Kim, Emma Cho Kim, Nora Shin, Kook Kyung Kim, Margaret Kim, Nancy Kim Shin, David Shin, Nellie Shin, Daisy Shin; back row: Ching Do Kim, Mary Shin, Harold Yon Do Kim, Millicent Chinogi Park Kim, Sung Do Kim, Elsie Yang Kim, Won Do Kim, Ruth Shin, Chun Do Kim, Kyung Do Kim, Esther Shin.

When I was three years old, we moved to Kunia, another pineapple camp, and we lived there a year. Later on, when I was about five years old, we move to Wahiawa, where we have been living ever since. My parents wanted to have a place close to an elementary school so that I would be able to walk to school. My father worked at the Schofield Military Base for the army, which was near Wahiawa.

Then later on, he worked at the nursery [growing plants] in upper Wahiawa. Many years later, after World War II, in 1948, he left for Korea to do missionary work. He wanted to start a church in Korea. Meanwhile, my mother stayed at home in Hawaii. When he got to Korea, he contacted Syngman Rhee's office. He had been a strong and faithful follower of Dr. Rhee in Hawaii. So Rhee remembered him. Rhee's office people in Korea, after he had become President of Korea, were instructed by Rhee in whichever city that my father was going

Kook Kyung Kim, circa 1940s.

to go to assist my father in anything he was going to do. The staff would guide him and take him around. When the Korean War started, my father had to go to Pusan. When he was in Pusan in 1951, he caught pneumonia. Meanwhile, he had met my mother's niece on the streets of Pusan and moved in with her, and then his pneumonia got worse. The day he was dying, he told his niece, "Don't go anywhere, just stay here," and he passed away. My father worked with the Korean veterans, so they helped to have his funeral in Korea. He was cremated and in 1952 a woman who worked with him brought his ashes back to us. He's buried now at Nuuanu with my mother.

You told me that he called on President Syngman Rhee when he went to Korea because they knew each other very well, and your father was Rhee's ardent follower in Hawaii. Could you tell us a little bit more about their relationship?

Well, I know that my father worked for him. I mean, he helped by going out to collect money, donations, to support Syngman Rhee in the early days when Dr. Rhee was living in Hawaii. After working in the pineapple fields each day, my father would come home and go out to Honolulu and go around to different churches and different places to collect donations. He worked with Dongji Hoi. He did a lot for Dongji Hoi, Dr. Rhee's organization. I remember seeing receipts for the burial grounds that Rhee set up for a new organization called . . . I cannot remember the name of the organization. My mother said that he was very busy doing church work for Syngman Rhee. So he was very close to Rhee in that way. I believe I have a book that Syngman Rhee sent him on the conference they had in 1946 in Washington D.C., regarding what they were going do in Korea, after Korea was liberated.

Was your father at that conference?

No, he wasn't. Syngman Rhee sent him the book, which he signed, about this conference. I have the book.

How about your mother? Was she active in the Korean Christian Church?

Well, I know that she went to church with the church Ladies' Society. But I don't think she was as active as my father was. My father would go to church on a Wednesday evening . . . perennial meeting . . . and he sometimes would be the only one with the minister there: Rev. Richard Kim. There was no one else sometimes.

Your parents were very close followers of Syngman Rhee and the Korean Christian Church in Wahiawa then?

Yes.

Could you tell us about any special events that happened?

Yes, there was an unforgettable event in 1923. My brother, who was attending the Korean Christian Institute, was selected to be on the baseball team to tour Korea; this was arranged by Dr. Rhee. My oldest brother, Won Do Kim, was on that baseball team. My father also went on that trip. They went to raise money for the KCI. My brother became a hero because when the team was playing their last game in Seoul, there was a condition that if they won, they could stay in Korea to have another game to win the final championship; if they lost, they would have to take a boat to Japan to play there. They wanted to win so that they could go on to challenge the last team in Korea the next day. That would make our team eligible to compete in the final championship game over all Koreans—if they won that game. In that game, my brother hit a home run, and so they were able to stay for the last game the next day. It just so happened that on that day, when they were supposed to have gone to Japan if they lost, Japan had a big earthquake. I remember they were all so glad that they won not only the Korean championship, but also my brother saved their lives because the earthquake hit the stadium where they would have had to play in Japan. They said that the manager of the team just hugged my brother even more when they heard the news of the earthquake.

The KCI baseball team and girls' orchestra visiting Inchon Naeri Church, the site from which the first immigrants came to Hawaii, 1923.

My goodness! Tell us more about this brother. Was he very active in other activities? And tell us about the Korean Christian Institute, which was responsible for taking the baseball team to Korea in 1923.

Well, my sister also went to KCI. She said that she used to work at Dr. Rhee's home to help serve meals and do things like that. And she said that Dr. Rhee liked her very much. But she had to leave and discontinue working there because she was having headaches, you know, migraine headaches. Although my mother wanted her to go on to school, she got married instead, when she was about eighteen years old, to Phillip Shin, who was working in a Waipahu store. After they got married, they started a tailoring business in Schofield Barracks. They also worked in the medical section of Schofield Barracks, but their major work was their tailor shop there for many years. After their tailor shop work, my sister tried a little bit working at a restaurant at Fort Shafter, and then she retired from it.

So what about her husband? Tell us about him and his family.
I only know that he and his father came from Korea, and he was an only child, so he wanted a big family. They had seven daughters and one son. And he educated the seven children very well.

How old was your sister when she died?
She was, I think, ninety-two years old.

How about your other sisters and brothers? How many were there in your family?
Well, my sister was the oldest one, and there were six boys, and then I was born—the last one—the *mak nae*. My brother Ching Do is ten years older than me, and he is the *mak nae* of the boys. My brothers all love to play golf and go fishing. Only one brother fished, but five of them were golfers. They would get together and play golf.

So there were two girls and six boys. Ching Do is well known in the Korean community. Can you tell us a little bit more about him?
I guess he was well known since high school, where he played sports well. After high school, he went to the University of Hawaii. I think he was recruited by one of the university board members to play football. He played as a guard.

Tell us what you know about leaders in the community. Who do you think were the leaders? Of course, you feel Dr. Rhee was a leader. So tell me about him, start with him.
Well, I don't know too much about Dr. Rhee except what few things I've heard from my parents. I know that we had the March First Celebration at our church every year. We would all say *"Man Sei"* at the church. Most of the people at the Wahiawa Korean Christian Church were followers of Dr. Rhee.

What activities do you remember at the Korean Christian Church?
Our life was centered around the church. We went to Sunday school and we had different holidays: Christmas, Easter, and then, of course,

Easter Sunday, April 17, 1960
Wahiawa Korean Christian Church

March First. In high school, we did different things that weren't so close to the church, but I know that we had Christian Endeavor for the young people. And many of us were in that activity.

What was Christian Endeavor?
Christian Endeavor was a society of young teenagers. They carried on activities when they did different things, like going on outings.

Did you have any close relationship with the Korean Christian Church in Honolulu on Liliha Street?
No, when I was young, not too much. But as an adult, I've gone to their activities more frequently.

What about the Methodist Church in Wahiawa?
No, we were friends with the girls and boys that were members of the Methodist Church, but we did not do too many things together that I can remember. We were good friends, though.

What about other leaders in the church? Who would you say were the leaders?

We had Ji Han Park, Ji Na Park.

When was that?

In the 1940s he led the young people. Then we had Duk Moon. He was very active. He was a leader for us in my younger days, when I was in Sunday school.

What kind of organizations, Korean organizations, did you belong to?

Four or five years ago, I joined Dongji Hoi. Before that there really wasn't anything.

What do you do in Dongji Hoi now?

We support the scholarships that they have for Korean members, the youths. That's one of the big things that they do.

So Dongji Hoi, you joined five years ago. Did you hear anything about Dongji Hoi earlier?

Oh, yes, when I was a youngster, my father was active in it.

What do you remember him saying?

I didn't talk to him about that because of the language. I mean, he spoke more Korean. I never talked to my parents about those things. Whatever I heard or know about the family comes from my mother, more than my father.

So what did you hear about Dongji Hoi or any other Korean events when they were living?

The only thing that I can remember is the March First Independence Celebration. At church, I remember one thing, and that is, when they said that my father was going to the pulpit to pray, I thought of sliding under the seat. His prayers were long, and they would start out in a monotone and then increase in volume and then I would be very uncomfortable because I didn't understand the language he was using. I mean, he was speaking in Korean, but it didn't mean anything to me.

The discomfort was that his prayers were so long. That's one thing I remember about my father in church. He always carried a Bible, an English and Korean version. He tried to learn English through that Bible. He would stop anyone, including his grandchildren, to find out how to pronounce a certain English word. He'd stop all of us, all of us, not only his sons, but me also. But mostly he'd ask the grandchildren.

That's a cute story. Tell us more stories like that.
No, I can't remember. I don't remember anything more.

What kind of food did you eat? Was your mother the cook? Who was the cook in the family?
My mother was the cook, and she made very good kimchi. So did my sister. My sister was a good cook; people liked her kimchi. Rev. Richard Kim said that my mother's kimchi was one of the best he ever had. My mother used to cook for him during the war, when he was working at Wheeler Field. He would come over and have supper at our house, and we would be there, waiting on him.

You mentioned once about Onyong Camp, where many Koreans lived, although the camp was established for the Chinese. Could you tell us a little more about this camp and what years did you live there?
Gee, that camp was there quite a while ago. It must have been in the 1920s or so, up to maybe the 1940s ... no, '50s. It was a poor area, I guess, when they demolished it. There were quite a few Koreans living there, and my girlfriends, two of them, lived there. In fact, my sister lived in that camp, and so did my oldest brother. Later, my sister and brother bought properties elsewhere, and they built houses in nicer places in Wahiawa.

Could you describe Onyong a little bit more?
It was in the middle of upper Wahiawa on Kalani and Cane Streets. It was around the center of those streets. They had duplex homes there. The rent was very cheap. I guess that area was owned by the Territory of Hawaii. [Hawaii was a territory before it became a state in 1950.]

All the homes there . . . my brother, my sister and my brother-in-law after they married, they lived in houses there years ago, where the toilet was inside the house. Other houses, the toilet was outside and the washroom was outside. My brother and my sister had a garage and had an enclosed yard. Indoor plumbing was a new thing in those days.

Would you say that most of those living in Onyong Camp went to the Korean Christian Church?
No, not all.

Was it a mixture of other ethnic groups?
Yes, they had lots of Hawaiians, Filipinos, Portuguese living in that camp . . . in that housing area.

Was it in the 1950s that the camp was torn down?
Must have been in the 1950s. They were pioneers, new immigrants. They had a number of boarders working at the nearby companies, and after a while, they demolished it.

What do you do know about the relationship between the Wahiawa Korean Methodist Church and the Korean Christian Church? They have certain names for the two churches?
We used to say "down church" and "up church." The Methodist Church was in the lower part of Wahiawa, so it was the "down church." And Wahiawa, the Korean Christian Church, was in the upper part of the Wahiawa, which is the reason we called it "up church." That's only a nickname.

Which was larger?
Well, I think the Methodist Church was. I don't know really because at one time we had many of the Korean families centered around it. The Wahiawa Korean Christian Church eventually had many of the older ones. When the first generation passed on, the children were very few; I mean, I would say that only twenty or so of us were active in the "up church," the Wahiawa Korean Christian Church.

I'm surprised to hear that your father went to Korea with the Korean Christian Institute baseball team. Can you tell us a little bit more about it?

I guess my father went along with the group because he wanted to show my brother around Korea and have my brother meet his family, our grandparents. When I asked my brother Won Do what he learned about our grandmother, he said he could not remember; he couldn't remember the relatives at all.

Any personal things that your father might have mentioned?

No, I didn't talk too much with him. Because he spoke all in Korean, and our communication was not that close. Even with my mother, I would overhear them saying things. When my father was in Korea, I know that she called him long distance on the telephone. She said that our father was in Kyung Joo, Kim Ga. That's where his ancestors came from: Kyung Joo, Kim Ga. My brothers didn't even bother with them. I mean, they weren't interested in relatives there until they got older, when one of their sons was going to marry a Korean girl. Then he had to find out about the family background.

Tell me about your trip to Korea.

Well, when I went to Korea in 1959, I took my mother because she wanted to see her niece and to thank her for taking care of my father, who was living in Korea, setting up an orphanage. And my fourth brother also was working in Korea. So, when my brother said that we could go and stay with him, we went out there and we met all of my mother's nieces, her sisters, and I met my cousins on my father's side. There were about five girls and one son. We had a good time. It was nice to meet them.

What was your brother doing there?

He was working for a game company that had pinball machines and things in the NCO clubs.

So this group that you went with, were they sponsored by the Korean Christian Church?

No, my mother and I just went on our own. We stayed two months. That was in the summer, June and July.

122

Which reminds me, the trip that your mother took in 1936 and the one that your father took with the baseball team, did they ever talk about how they went there or on what kind of passport?
You know, they never said anything. But then, just thinking about it, I am curious about what kind of passport they had—if they had any, even my mother, I don't remember. I guess she didn't have any passport that I can remember. They were Korean citizens. They never became naturalized. So I don't think my mother had a passport at all. She also went in 1937. And that was when I was about ten years old. I wondered why she didn't take me, but she said, "No, you would not be happy being there." I think it was because of the facilities they had there. I wanted to go because I had a cousin that was about my age in Seoul.

What do you remember of Lee Won Soon.
I knew Lee Won Soon had a big business in New York City because when I went to school in New York, my niece and I stayed with his family. Velma Pyun Kim was there. When I got to New York, we called Velma and she told us to come and stay with them before we left for a different destination. So, every vacation break I had, I would go down and visit with them. Lee Won Soon had this big business, I mean he had this business, in lower New York. He bought properties in different places. Then he moved to Los Angeles, then back to New York. And then, I guess he went to Korea after WWII. That's where he stayed for a long period of time.

Were you aware of any activities he was doing?
No, the only thing that I know is that he worked with the Olympics. That's about it. I was not interested in politics and whatever they had going on.

Tell us about your brother's wife, Elsie Yang. Their son, Dr. Robert Kim, has always been proud of your father, his grandfather. But tell us about Elsie's parents, the Yang family. Her parents were very refined and quiet.
Elsie was my oldest brother's wife. Elsie would have family get-togethers at her son's home, my nephew Bob Kim's place, for Christmas. Her mother and father lived close to our house. And I remember that her father was always an active man, moving around. Other than that, I don't know what kind of politics, what activities they did.

123

Profile of the Kook Kyung Kim Family

Kook Kyung Kim was one of the fortunate Korean fathers to have produced six sons who all became accomplished men. Mr. Kim belonged to a close-knit group of supporters of Dr. Syngman Rhee in the small town of Wahiawa. Its remoteness from Honolulu in the early days and Rhee's frequent visits there intensified the comradeship in the Wahiawa Dongji Hoi. This Dongji Hoi has been described was the most loyal branch in support of Rhee within the Korean population in Hawaii.

The children of the Kim family were popular among their peers, especially Won Do, the hero of the phenomenal baseball trip to Korea in which Won Do and his father participated. Arranged by Dr. Rhee in 1923 in the midst of Japan's occupation of Korea, the trip is considered an extraordinary event by some historians of Korean history today. It was a great boon to Dr. Rhee's prestige in the eyes of young Koreans as well as his adult followers. Mr. Kim's children were among the first students to attend Rhee's school, where a close relationship between Mr. Kim's family and Rhee may have developed.

With assistance from President Rhee, Mr. Kim's dream of pursuing missionary work in Korea immediately after World War II was fulfilled—and came to an end, unexpectedly, when Mr. Kim died, ending his final days in his beloved Korea.

Kook Kyung Kim
and wife, Emma
Cho Kim; children:
Song Do, Won Do,
Kyung Do, Sooni
Yun Do, and Chun
Do, circa 1922.

Hung Yup and
Susannah Kwok
Yang family,
circa 1918.
Elise, first right.

8
The Story of Ha Soo Whang

Ha Soo Whang Mary Whang Choy

The Ha Soo Whang story is a documentary film. The following excerpts were taken from the film.

Narrator:
Sometime in the 1930s, when I first saw Ha Soo Whang, I was only three years old, but I knew she was a very special person in the Korean community. She was known as Whang Ha Soo because the Korean custom is to use the surname first. Her two nieces, Elizabeth and Mary Whang, lovingly called her "Komo."

Ha Soo Whang was unlike local Koreans in Hawaii. She always wore a hat and spoke with great confidence and authority. She was always among so many people. Ha Soo Whang was born in Korea and came to Hawaii, via California, sometime in 1919. The Korean community was fractionated by political turmoil at the time she arrived, the story of which is a novel in itself. So she came at a crucial time. It was Ha Soo Whang, the "YWCA woman," among a few other leaders such as Tai Sung Lee, the "YMCA man," and the gifted Donald Yong Gak Kang, who all together did extraordinary things to guide immigrants and their children through the turmoil of assimilation and acculturation.

But let's begin Ha Soo Whang's story from the beginning, as told by Mary Whang Choy, a niece of Ha Soo Whang.

Mary Whang Choy:

My aunt, Ha Soo Whang, was one of three siblings who came to America when they were adults. There were eight siblings all together: four daughters and four sons. But only three came to America. One of them was my father, Rev. Sa Sun Whang. Her parents (my grandparents) and other extended family members were living in Uiju in the northern part of Korea . . . right on the border of China and Pyongyang. The northern part was not North Korea then.

Ha Soo was the second to the youngest, the seventh child in a family of eight children. Their mother died and their father died when they were all very young children. The eldest sister became the head of the family. So my Aunt Ha Soo looked to her as another woman of great strength and courage and independence. Her older brother, Rev. Sa Yong Whang, was number three in the family. He was the first to leave Korea and come to America. From that point, he was very instrumental and responsible in bringing out many of his relatives to America. He brought my father, Rev. Sa Sun Whang, to America; that was when my father and mother left North Korea during the political turmoil there. They settled in San Francisco.

Rev. Sa Sun and Tai Sun Chang Whang and children: Mary, Paul, Elizabeth, circa 1920.

Following that, my Auntie Ha Soo, with the encouragement of Korean missionaries in Pyongyang, Korea, joined her brothers in America. The Whang family members were Presbyterian missionaries, basically. From Pyongyang, she went to Seoul, attended school there, and it was there she had the final encouragement to go to America. So, with the help of my Uncle Sa Yong, she, too, came to America and went to school first in California and

127

Rev. Sa Yong, first of the Whang family to come to America, circa 1917.

went on to Athens, Alabama, to attend the women's college there. They were the only three who came to America.

After Aunt Ha Soo got her degree, she came to Honolulu, where she was offered a position with the YMCA International Institute. But first, I do want to mention how she worked in Alabama and was very well received, very well loved. Still she never, at any time, lost her consciousness of being a Korean woman. A picture shows her with her beloved Korean flag wrapped around her skirt.

She came to Hawaii between 1919 and 1920, and a year later she was offered the position of vice president of social workers at the International Institute. In that year, in April, she went to San Francisco and brought me and my sister, Elizabeth, to Hawaii to care for us during a time of great bereavement for my father because our mother, his wife, had died. Aunt Ha Soo, we called her "Komo," brought us back to Hawaii with her so she could take care of us. Our brother, Paul, was left in San Francisco with our father.

Aunt Ha Soo was one of three ethnic social workers at the YMCA in Honolulu. She was the Korean social worker, and there was a Chinese woman, Mrs. Yi, who took care of the Chinese women, and Miss Kishimoto, who worked for the Japanese women. I would say they were the first ethnic social workers in Hawaii. They cared, they nurtured, they tried to meet the needs of the immigrant women who had come to Hawaii. Primarily, Aunt Ha Soo worked with women who were picture brides. She helped them adjust to the many, many problems that they faced . . . their domestic problems and often times abusive situations. She would act as a court interpreter: go to court and speak for them. She also would conduct classes to encourage cultural affinity with American society; that would be in the areas of English and homemaking

Ha Soo Whang displays her ethnicity at Athen's College for Women, Alabama, where she matriculated, circa 1919.

and, at the same time, expose them to American culture.

She also developed a great interest in Korean young people. In the early twenties, I would say in 1925 or 1926, the Hyung Jay Club was organized by Aunt Ha Soo. Youngsters, young Korean girls, from all the broad community of Hawaii—despite the political cleavage among their parents—came and joined this organization, which was primarily cultural. There we learned about the cultures of Hawaii and the old folk cultures of Korea.

Aunt Ha Soo would bring into the organization Korean men and women who had more recently immigrated to Hawaii and were experts in Korean folk music, Korean dancing. She would have them teach us the Korean folk cultures of our native country. From there, productions were produced. My Aunt Ha Soo would write a play, she would dramatize it, she would produce it, and she would bring in all the artists from Korea, the elderly people, to perform. We, the young women of the Korean community, would learn from the elderly and perform the dances depicting the old folktales of Korea for the local people in Hawaii . . . very dramatic productions. That was a wonderful era for all of us young people because we never lost sight—particularly my sister and me—we never lost sight of the fact that we were Koreans, and we had pride in our heritage. We credited my Aunt Ha Soo for her deep feelings for Korea, for carrying on the old culture, cultural ways, the music and the dance of Korea, and passing them on to our new generations, the Korean Americans. At the same time, she was still nurturing and caring for the women of Korea who came to Hawaii in need of guidance.

I always think of the very dramatic production at the Honolulu Academy of Arts. It was held in the central court with this huge arch. I have pictures here

Hyung Jay Club, Old Folks Korean Culture at University of Hawaii, 1930s.

Hyung Jay Club performing Korean dance at the old Honolulu Stadium, circa 1930s; left to right: Margaret Kim, Joyce Kim, Yealinae Kim, Sunbee Inn, Sarah Hong, Sarah Lee, Elizabeth Whang.

of the early productions that were put on at the YWCA on Richards Street. I have photos of some of the early productions of Korean dance and Korean stories that were produced by my auntie and the Hyung Jay Club. I have other photographs of the young women who learned to dance the Korean dances,

YWCA; front row,
left to right: (third)
Ha Soo Whang,
(last) Esther Park.

performing at some huge general community gathering. I have also another picture of a production that was put on at the YWCA in their hall, and other photos depicting some early customs of a wedding with a Korean bride and groom.

A few years later, there was this production at the Academy of Arts, which was, really, I think, one of the greatest productions at that time. It was held at the Honolulu Academy of Arts, depicting again the culture of Hawaii. We had Sarah Lee Young as a Korean bride. My sister, Elizabeth, and I showed off some costumes worn by Korean people for the Korean dance scenes. More members of the Hyung Jay Club, who also participated in that production, are in some of the photos that I have. The programs were so well received: The whole community, hundreds and hundreds of people were present. The color, the music, the dramatic presentation of these programs was well written. If you go back to the *Honolulu Star-Bulletin* or the *Honolulu Advertiser,* you would see many articles written about that very wonderful production by my auntie.

Personally, my Aunt Ha Soo was a tremendous influence on my life and my sister's life. She was a wonderful model for us. She reared us because we came here as very young children. I was five years old and my sister was eight. She reared us, she taught us, she educated us. We remained here in Hawaii throughout our lives, and we did not return to San Francisco to join my father

131

and brother. In the meantime, my father remarried. But our lives, my sister's and mine continued here with my Aunt Ha Soo, who was family, who was both mother and father to us. With her strong sense of self and her strong will of independence and courage, trying new things and being a forerunner of new attitudes, she was right there, and without her, I'm not sure where our lives would have gone. We look back and respect and admire her as a woman, a single woman who reared—literally, reared—a family of two young girls.

Her work with the International Institute began about 1922, and she worked there until 1939. At that point the YWCA decided that the International Institute was no longer viable. I'm not sure what the true reason was because they were the women who were offering great services to women of each of these ethnic communities. At any rate, the YWCA decided to close the International Institute. My auntie continued with the YWCA for about two years. Then she made another transition in her life: She retired. She was a very wise business woman and bought a place in Waikiki. Then she sold it and bought another place.

I think women at that time, very well-known Korean women in particular, were esteemed for their sense of business. In many cases, women, Korean women, were the ones who were financially responsible for their families and for educating their children. Evidently, my Aunt Ha Soo had that very wise streak of good business sense. She started buying properties in Waikiki, then she sold them and bought property on Dole Street across the University of Hawaii. There, my sister and I have many, many childhood memories. We went to University High School, right across the street from our house. She sold the property there and bought another place in Waikiki with a little apartment in the back, so she was able to take care

Elizabeth and Mary Whang, circa 1940s.

Ha Soo Whang
in 1974.

Ha Soo Whang with three generations of her clan; her grandniece Peggy Chow,
far left.

The Korean Methodist Board of Leaders, circa 1950. About half of them were not able to return to
Korea. Ha Soo Whang, in the middle with a hat; Rev. Chang Ho Ahn, sitting first right; Rev. Sa Yong
Whang, back row, fourth from the left; Dora Moon, front row, third from the left.

of herself financially. She never depended on anyone for financial help; in fact, she was a source of help to other people, other family members, or other people in the community. She was so compassionate. She was such a compassionate woman. Her self-interest never came into the picture. Her mind was always focused on the other. That is something I will never forget about her, her great compassion for people. But anyway, she lived very happily in her cottage in Waikiki with the little apartment in the back that gave her a little income. Therefore, she was able to live very fully.

During her last years, I would say her last ten years, she moved from the Waikiki area to the Punchbowl area and involved herself in condominiums. The last ten years of her life were spent there. Her health deteriorated, but she was still pretty alert. We needed to care for her, but she was able to stay at home. She had a short stay in the hospital and returned to her home. We were there when she passed away. So her life . . . she went very peacefully; she had a life of great, great fulfillment. She died, we think, at about ninety-two years of age, in 1984.

I did take a trip in 1989 to North Korea, to Pyongyang. A small family group, my brother and his wife, made this trip to the North with us. It was a very symbolic trip for me. Our little family unit of my brother and his wife, my own daughter here in Hawaii, and a niece in California—six of us made this journey to Pyongyang—to the home of my parents and my father's family. It was such a symbolic trip for me because my Komo—Ha Soo—my father, Sa Sun; and my uncle, Sa Yong; their lifelong wish was that someday they would be able to go back to their hometown, Uiju, which they never did. So my being there in Uijiu I felt was in some sense . . . I was there for them. I think it was a kind of closure for them and their love for their country, my being there.

9

Interview with Emily Kim Choi

My name is Emily Kim Choi. I was born in 1919 in Kohala, on the island of Hawaii.

My father was Hong Soon Kim from Pyung An Do and my mother, Young Chin Park, was from Pusan. My father came to Hawaii as a bachelor in 1910. He was recruited as a laborer to work in the pineapple fields. I suppose he didn't like the life of a bachelor because he soon asked to have someone act as a go-between to find him a wife. There was a friend of his who knew my mother and they started corresponding. My mother was a beautiful woman and she was thirteen years younger than my father. She arrived in 1913 as a picture bride and they were married in Honolulu. She always thought that she could further her education in Hawaii because that was what was promised her. But instead she got stuck on a plantation where my father was working and they struggled to make a living.

I'm the third child in a family of five children. We had four sisters and one brother. My eldest sister, Rachel, was born in 1914 on the Big Island; my second sister, Florence, was born in 1917, also on the Big Island; and then I was born as the middle child. Aida was born in 1921, and my brother, Joe, was born in 1923. As you can see we are all two years apart. My sister, Aida, passed away in 1995. She was the youngest in our family and we all miss her terribly.

My father was never cut out to be a plantation laborer and there were many times when he would cut out from work. He really hated it. So he would play hooky from work—not go to work. I remember my mother saying that he was a very poor provider. He would stay in his room and help other Koreans with

Hong Soon and Young Chin Park Kim family, circa 1924.
Children, left to right: Rachel, Emily, Joseph, Aida.

letter-writing because some of the Koreans could not read even Korean. He would read to them what they received from Korea. My father also taught young children the Korean language.

Whenever the family moved to a new place, my father looked for a place where there were jobs for women, too. So if they needed a cook in a certain camp, my mother said he would try to move there and if they needed a seamstress to make slippers or fix clothes, my father would get a job there for her. My mother helped out by sewing and cooking and doing things for the bachelors, that the bachelors couldn't do themselves.

For a while, my father homesteaded on the Big Island in Kohala, where I was born. And although they didn't make a good living there, we were able to survive. Later on, he heard that life was easier in Honolulu, so he gathered the family, and we all moved to Honolulu, where my father had a little grocery store on Liliha Street. My father started another business in Honolulu, the City Captial, because people told him that's where the money was. He started a loan business. He was a trusting soul and he gave too much monetary credit to many people who didn't pay him back. Naturally, he went broke. And so he had to close this business.

Then he heard that Wahiawa was a good place for families to be brought up and to make a living, so we moved to Wahiawa. In Wahiawa, we went into the laundry business. It was hard, backbreaking work for all of us, but we managed. My sister Rachel, being the eldest, learnt to drive when she was fifteen, I believe. And she could barely drive, but we bought an old Chevrolet. The first week after she got her license, we drove around the island. I wonder how we survived because we couldn't make the little white hill in Waialua. We practically had to lighten ourselves to get over that hill, but we had a lot of fun in spite of all the hard work we did.

Rachel became the driver of the car to pick up and deliver the laundry. She marked the different items of laundry, and she sorted them. My father and my mother did the washing. Florence, my second sister, also helped. I helped my sister Rachel do some of the marking and checking. And after the laundry was done, we pressed and put them in baskets. We would check the laundry again to see that all the pieces were there. Aida, being the youngest in the family, would do the cooking, simple things like rice and maybe soup. And she would hang up the laundry when it was time to hang up. My father helped out with the flat pieces, just as I did, and my sister Florence, who was pretty good at ironing and doing things, did the uniforms and the dresses, and the more difficult things. And I remember that they all worked far into the night, and my mother used to work until 2:00 or 2:30 in the morning to get the laundry ready to be delivered on the specified day. In those days, we used to do the bachelors' laundry, complete with uniforms, linens, clothing, everything you can think of, for $4 a month. And yet, there was competition among the Koreans to do the soldiers' laundry, and sometimes we would lose a customer because someone else would do it for $3.50 a month. Those sure were tough days.

We surely didn't have any time for homework. We used to work in the ironing room until about 9 o'clock. We were excused to go to our home, which was connected of course, and by that time we would be too tired to read or study, so naturally, most of the time, we would go straight to bed. We went to Wahiawa Elementary School, then to Leilehua Intermediate School, and then to Leilehua High School. After high school, I went to a business college in Honolulu, where I studied secretarial work. From there, I got my first job at Wahiawa Motors for $40 a month, which we considered was good pay at that time. But after about a year, I took a civil service exam and got a job at the Board of Water Supply for $105 a month, which was a real, real big salary at that time.

We were members of the Korean school at Wahiawa Korean Christian Church, but I think it was Rev. Park who taught us our elementary Korean. My father was also very instrumental in teaching us because he would reward us with candy or whatever he could get to encourage us to remember our *hanmunja* [Korean alphabet], and he would give us tests. I remember he gave us all ten handicaps. Rachel would have to know the most, Florence would have to know the second most, which was ten less than Rachel, and I, the third, would have twenty less than Rachel. So as long as we could write the *hanmunja* and tell my father what it was and how it was used, we would be credited for that many points.

When I was still very young, living in Wahiawa, most of my friends' parents had joined the Korean American Club, which at that time was "the thing" to join. The Korean American Club was quite prestigious in those days because you had to have a pretty large sum of money for the initiation fee. As long as you were Korean, I believe you could join the club if you paid the initiation fee. Most of my friends belonged to it. I remember Mary Lee, Beatrice Moon, and Anna Kim. Those are the ones who come to my mind now, but it had nothing to do with church affiliation. It was just an ethnic thing and I really envied them. They never flouted their connection with the club, but when they said, "I'm going down to take piano lessons," or "I'm going down to practice piano," I was very, very envious. I wished our parents could afford that, too. I remember they had a piano there, and I wanted my parents to join the club really badly because I wanted to go down and take piano lessons.

At that time, Mr. Owen was the manager of the store and he ran everything. He had a son who was called Philo (he was also known as George), but not the younger brother, who was also named Philo. He was nearer our age and we knew him well. I don't know how come they had the same name. But they were the "in people," meaning well-known, modernized Koreans because of their father, who was very stylish himself. As the founder of the Korean American Club, Mr. Owen made the club fancy. We were quite envious of those who were in the Korean American Club.

While we were living in Wahiawa, we used to go to church every Sunday, Korean Christian Church, and my mother would give us each a penny. And we would be so tempted to buy a piece of Oh Boy gum for one cent a stick, instead of giving it as an offering. But somehow we managed to hang on to it. Once in a while, my parents would give us two cents. And with one cent, I remember we would buy dumbbell candy: a lollipop with candy on both ends of the stick. It was coated with chocolate. Boy, was that ever good!

As we grew older, we went to Christian Endeavor meetings every Sunday. And after Christian Endeavor, we'd get together and wish that we could get a ride to Schofield Theatre, where we could watch some movies. The movies I think at that time were twenty cents. And we had to wait outside until all the

Clarence Choi, Emily Choi's husband.

GIs got in first and then we were allowed to go in and sit in the back. That was really a treat.

In 1943, Clarence Choi and I were married at Wahiawa Christian Church by the Rev. Richard Kim. Clarence's family also lived in Wahiawa, so we grew up together. His family is known for their strong ties with President Rhee. Clarence's brother was the one who financed Rhee's flight to Hawaii when he was deposed in 1960.

My parents were very strong members of the Korean Christian Church. I suppose they were Christians in Korea; at least my mother was. They continued going to church here, and my father was even a lay minister at times. My father was a very broad-minded person and he loved to read. He would read whatever he could, even opposing newspapers. By opposing, I mean views that were not Dongji Hoi views, but other views. My mother would ask him, "Why are you reading that paper?" Almost anything else outside of Dongji Hoi, according to my mother, was communist at the time. If you are not Dongji Hoi, then you are a communist. Or at least that was how it sounded to me at that time. My father would say, "Well, I have to read both sides of the question. Otherwise, how can I make a right decision?" Of course, all his decisions had already been made because he was always a staunch Dongji Hoi member.

Whenever Dr. Syngman Rhee came to Wahiawa, he was greeted with much excited feeling. We were really happy to see him. No matter how poor the family was, we would try to invite him to dinner and he would come over and have dinner with us. He was really down to earth. I remember when I was born, about two years old, the Korean Independence Movement had begun already, and all parents would feverishly teach their children, even very little children, about it. I remember standing on the table and my mother said I should raise both hands and say three times: *"Mansei, Mansei, Doklip Mansei."* Of course, I didn't know what it meant, but our parents told us the story that if you were an independence fighter and waved the Korean flag, they would cut off your hand which was carrying the flag, and if you changed hands to wave the flag with your other hand, they would cut off that hand. My mother told us all about the torture the Koreans had to endure that she had heard about going on right then in Korea. I don't know how true they were, but these were the stories that we grew up with.

I personally don't feel that strongly about President Rhee. I admired him because of our parents' devotion to him. I guess some of that must have rubbed off on us. As a matter of fact, I didn't join the Dongji Hoi until just last year because Clarence, my husband, belonged to it. I just went along with him to take him there, to accompany him. I heard about the good works the Dongji Hoi were doing—they were helping, for instance, by giving scholarships, ten scholarships each year, which grew and grew and grew. Now I think they are giving about fifteen scholarships to young college students. I think that's a real good project that they are working on. I think it's not for Korean independence that we are working for now, but it's working for the good of Koreans here.

I also joined the Taeguk Club after I married Clarence. The club started out as a men's club and it was a fun club for young adults; yet, it was a service club because we tried to help the community. Any time the Wahiawa community and the Korean community asked us for help in certain projects, we would send a small check or what we could afford. We also sent money to the orphanages in Korea. We did quite a bit of service work in Hawaii, too. Whenever a project came up and they needed help, they would write to us and we'd donate a few dollars. Our biggest project that I know of is the bathhouse that we helped purchase for an orphanage in Korea. From what I understand, the project in Korea is still going strong and with that project completed, the orphanage is self-supporting, mainly because of the bathhouse. The members of the Taeguk Club are second-generation Koreans, and some recently arrived first-generation Koreans such as Mrs. Sunni Song. She is married to Benny Song, an old-time second generation. Benny passed away. Mrs. Song is still living, but I understand she's not very healthy now.

Other than that, most of the young people in Wahiawa at that time joined the club for social activities. Even though membership decreased, we still have parties now and then, and there was always a lot of fun. Recently, we dwindled down drastically in the membership. We have just a few members now. It's just the same people that meet all the time. Now that we are old, we're not into fund raising. That activity dwindled quite a bit. We just meet at members' homes and have pot luck supper, and if there is any solicitation that we think is for a worthwhile cause, that is brought up at our meeting. We hardly do any-

Clarence and Emily Choi, second-generation descendants of the first wave, at the Korean Christian Church eightieth anniversary celebration, November 1998.

thing now. As for our children, we have a few third-generation Koreans like Ruth Mack's family. We tried to get some of our other youngsters interested, but they're just not interested. Ruth Mack's children are members. Maryann's son came for a while, but ours never did.

Tell us about your own life.
I worked for the Board of Water Supply, where I had a civil service job. I was very happy there. I have three beautiful daughters and three wonderful sons-in-law and three handsome grandsons. There's one that finished college, one who is finishing this year, and another still attending college. I don't have much to say about my life. I think it's such an average life. We've had a good life and have no complaints about it. Clarence has been a good husband and I've tried to be a good wife. We've been married fifty-five years since this past February.

10

Interview with Helen Sonia Sunoo

My name is Helen Sonia Shinn Sunoo. I was born in San Francisco in 1915. My mother came as a picture bride. She came in 1914, when she was seventeen years old. Friends introduced my parents through a picture bride arrangement. My mother agreed to being a picture bride because she did not like the pressure of living in a Japanese-controlled Korea.

My dad came from Pyongyang, Hwanghae-do. He first arrived in Hawaii in 1903. Later he moved on to San Francisco in about 1920, which he found very difficult. It happened that he settled in Sacramento first. Sacramento's summers are quite hot. So he chose San Francisco for his home. There, he decided to become a barber. He established himself for several years, and later

Helen's father, Mr. Shinn, was a barber in San Francisco.

he hired five barbers to work with him. They worked with him on a commission basis. The Filipino barbers were chosen because they were very artistic in hair cutting. He had Chinese barbers also, because it was in the Chinatown. He felt that he should be a friend with the Chinese.

In San Francisco, usually a shop is in the front, and there is a long hallway which often has five or six rooms and a toilet [along it]. There wasn't a bathroom at our place. Then my father managed to have one ordered. At first, it was a basic washtub. Later on, my dad ordered a stainless-steel bathtub, which was about five feet long and about three feet tall. Mother had a very unique idea. The bathtub was set up on a brick oven. The Chinese had this brick oven and they placed a wok on top in order to heat food and cook. My mother used it to make hot water. She would build a fire under a big wok with water and the water was heated on this brick oven. The water was very hot. My mother could use hot water anytime. It was not a common thing to do at that time.

Were there other Korean families in that area?

There were several Korean families. My parents lived on Jackson Street, where my father's barbershop was located. Many other Korean family homes were above Grant Avenue. They lived in the alley. There were three families that I can recall. The Kim family; the older son was Philip Kim. I don't remember his mother's name. He had two brothers and one sister. Another Kim family: his name was Dong Gyun. I cannot remember the full name of the family.

Did you form a community? An association?

No, we didn't form any kind of association. If there was a meeting and important things to discuss, we went to the Korean church. At that time, the Korean church was way down on Oak Street. There, we had a Korean printing press. It was a hand press. *Shinan Minbo* was the publication. Il Kyu Paik was the editor. The minister helped.

So the community was the church then?

Yes, the church welcomed Christians and anyone who came.

Were your parents affiliated with this church?

Yes, all the Koreans would come to that church. There was only one church at that time.

143

What was the name of it?

Southern Methodist. We continued to have this one church until later we built our own on Powell Street. There was some controversy about the sale of it later on under a new minister.

Tell me about this Methodist church way back in your youth. Was it purely Korean or a mixture of ethnic groups?

No, it was purely Korean.

How many families do you think went to the church?

My guess is that we had twenty-five families.

Spread out in the San Francisco area?

Yes, there wasn't any Korean Town or such to find jobs. The cleaning shops were scattered in American districts.

Did you identify yourself always as Korean or did you just blend into the Chinese community?

In Chinatown, as a family, we still identified ourselves as Koreans. My father was very patriotic to Korea. He said that we have got to remember we are Koreans. I remember he sat me in his barbershop because my mother sent me there. She was busy with the younger children. I was a chatterbox. My mother had three younger children. So I was often sent out to the barbershop. At the barbershop, my father would teach me the Korean alphabet. He even made me a notebook; he made it with used financial papers from the newspapers. He couldn't afford to buy me a tablet.

What other kinds of Korean activities do you remember?

Oh, I remember the most outstanding activity was March First; it is called *Sam Il Ku*. For years, Mr. Kim Dongwoo read the Declaration of Korean Independence out loud to us. It was the time when Mrs. Ha came from Colorado. She had a very lovely voice and she also taught Korean. Her daughter's godfather was very learned. He taught Mrs. Ha to read the Declaration of Korean Independence. I remember she read it to us for many years at this celebration. While she read, all the Korean children and everybody in the audience paid attention. And after she read it, everyone shouted *"Mansei!"* three times. That response was led by Kim Dongji at the Korean church. That's where everything was done on Independence Day. It was a special day. We would all be there, all the Koreans; no matter where we lived, we would come.

Do you remember what other kinds of occupations Korean families had?

Yes, around Chinatown, half a block down, the Shinn family had a coffee shop. Then the block that was across Jackson Street was Kearney Street, and there was a Korean by the name of Chun Deukgu who had a shoe repair shop. And next to the shoe repair shop, there was a laundry shop run by the Lee family.

When did you know them and when did these things happen?

It was about 1920. I would like to mention that on the opposite side [of the street] was Dora Yum Kim. Her parents had a restaurant there. And there was also a candy and tobacco shop.

What outstanding leader was there at that time?

Korean leaders? I wasn't into politics. I was just a kid. But I remember one thing happened. Kuk Min Hur was strong in San Francisco. Lee Dae Wi was the leader. Il Kyu Paik was another leader.

What kind of activities did they have? What were their interests?

I don't know. At that time, we kids played upstairs.

So you were not involved?

Yes, too young to be involved.

Tell us about yourself when you were growing up and when you went to college.

I went to San Francisco State College. I was interested in teaching high school. So I took several courses there. The day before graduation, the dean of women [students] called me and said, "Well, Helen, I am sorry to tell you, you will never be able to teach in California in the position of a secondary teacher. So you might as well think of something else.

Did you ever want to be something else?" I said, "No. Teaching was the only thing I wanted." She said, "Well, I have a scholarship for you." That brightened my spirit, the thought of a scholarship. "And what is that?" She said, "It's for cosmetology study." My heart sank. Tears rolled out my eyes. But then, what could I do? So I accepted it. Scholarship to cosmetology school to become a beauty operator!

Was this after high school?
It was after college.

After college? Can you describe again what happened?
After I graduated from college, I wasn't offered a school teaching job but a scholarship for cosmetology, to become a beauty operator. That was the offer that was made to me. So I had to become a beautician. Then I operated a beauty shop in Chinatown.

At the same time I also attended as many of the child development courses I could and enjoyed doing that. And by going to college I could make a living on the knoll. Then my advisor said, "Helen, you have enough [credits]. You'll need to get a master's degree." Later I enrolled in San Francisco State University. I had met all requirements except residence. They required one year of residency.

At that time I was married and I had two children. I told my husband about this requirement, and he said, "Oh, no. You don't have to get that degree. You don't need a doctor's degree because we will go back and live in Korea. And you can teach in Korea without a doctor's degree." That was my academic ideal, to teach in Korea. So I did not go to get my doctorate. That's what happened. Later my husband found a job. He was offered a teaching job in Missouri. In Missouri I was also offered a teaching job. This was at a college, so this was quite a jump that I had. I got a chance to teach both at a small college, and later on I was invited to teach at the University of Missouri.

What degree did you receive, and what did you teach?
Oh, I graduated in child development. I taught child psychology, adolescent psychology, and I taught educational psychology.

Did you make use of your degree in your work?

Yes. I was teaching what I learned in child development at the university, and they also offered me a job working at a home nursery, observing the children at different stages of childhood. They had a one-way window. I observed a dozen students behind this one-way viewing window. Different play areas had a microphone and we could observe children at different kinds of play, such as individual play or parallel play and all kinds of things. Children wouldn't know they were being observed, so they were very free. Then I had students from a nursing school come into my classes. They could also observe the young children's ways and how they solved problems.

Was life in the Midwest different from California?

Yes. I thought it was quite nice in Missouri. We, as Koreans, didn't meet with prejudice in the Midwest. They accepted us very well. I think we lived there for thirty years.

What happened to your parents? After you married, did they remain in San Francisco?

Yes. Mother remained in San Francisco until my father's death.

When did he die?

In 1950.

And your mother?

My mother passed away in about 1980.

How many were there in the family?

I am the oldest of four children. Three brothers and myself.

Tell us about them.

They are very close to each other, the two brothers especially. They have been close all their lives, David and Anthony. Anthony is the first son and an attorney. David is the second son; he married a girl in Honolulu. They settled in Honolulu and he became a policeman. He was a captain in the police force until he retired.

東京月見少年会
1937. 10. 3.

Dr. Harold Sunoo
(right, standing).

What about your children?
I have two sons.

Let's talk about the Korean National Association (KNA).
For a while, my father was president of the KNA. My mother didn't think much of it. She used to tease him and say, "There aren't many people so why don't you take turns being president?" However, she joined too, but . . . [Here Helen's husband, Dr. Harold Sunoo, interjects: "She was a chairman of the San Francisco branch also." Helen responds: "For a while."]

What about the general community? Were there other kinds of activities—besides Korean activities—you participated in? I know it's been a long time since you've been in San Francisco. You spent thirty years in Missouri. Do you recall any peers at that time? Any Koreans your age?
When we moved to the Midwest, my Korean friends were brand-new friends. They were mostly teaching in colleges or universities or they were doctors.

Mrs. Sunoo, you are well known for the many interviews you conducted among Koreans everywhere, the earliest stories about the lives of Koreans in America. Let's discuss the interviews. You conducted eighty interviews of Korean picture brides or Koreans in general, starting from many decades ago. Would you tell us about that?

Oh, my goodness. At that time, I wasn't . . . didn't know how to interview really. I let them tell me their life stories . . . [Dr. Sunoo interjects: "You left your job to do that project."]

You gave up your paid profession to interview these Koreans of the early days without a stipend? You gathered the memories of the first Koreans in America as a community. Is that what you did?

Yes. More on their own lives. I had to spend an awful lot time of time on each interview, writing down what they remembered. I did not know what a tape recorder was.

I told them that if they said something they did not want me to know then we could erase it. Oh, I spent hours. They did have confidence in me. They said, "Why do you want to know so much about me? I didn't know things well." "I am doing this because our children are very interested in history." Many of the interviewees would always say, "I led such a shameful life; I'm ashamed of myself." I said, "You established 'Koreanness' in us. You taught us how to be Koreans and what you have suffered as a Korean. You have done tremendous things for our lives in a foreign country."

What do you suppose they were ashamed of?

Oh, they were ashamed of their lives . . . the fact that they left their families. In those days, a good wife served her mother-in-law, but the women who came here had to be very independent. They thought independently, which was hard to do in those days. But I said to them, "You are admirable. You are very brave to have come, and then some of you suffered with the man you married." I think among the interviewees I found only two cases of divorce.

149

Only two cases of divorce?

When I asked them how they were treated when they were going to be picture brides, some said that the families that they joined as picture brides sometimes didn't accept them as their daughters. In spite of that, they came. They knew they would be damaged, I mean banished. But they came. When they came here, they got very disappointed. Most of the men couldn't afford a wife. Most of them said that as soon as they got married, they had to go out to the fields and work.

What kind of fields?

Those that came to California worked in rice fields and fruit farms, picking fruits.

These people whom you interviewed, you said all eighty of them were picture brides?

No. They weren't all picture brides. They weren't all women. There were men, too. My aim at that time was that they were all getting old and ready to die, so I wanted to know and find out about their lives for our future knowledge of our past.

When were these interviews done?

They were all done in 1975. I traveled all over the world, and I had to ask who knew what . . . from the Northwest, from California—most of them were from California. I found one in Denver. One in Chicago. [Dr. Sunoo: "Because of the urgency—they all were on the verge of dying—she quit her job to do this."]

Oh, my goodness.

At that time, I was about sixty years old, and I thought, my gosh, they're gonna die. Here I am today, older than they were, and I haven't finished.

But you've done it and it's waiting to be edited and so forth. That's wonderful. That's really great.

I saw the urgency of interviewing the early pioneers and I quit my job to complete this mission.

In total you interviewed how many?

I interviewed over ninety-nine Koreans or something like that. All over the United States. No one was sponsoring me at that time. It was through aid from friends and family.

There were both men and women?

I began interviewing picture brides, but the people I interviewed were men also.

What happened to the manuscript?

I have it.

Helen Sonia Sunoo and Dr. Harold Sunoo. Photo courtesy Eric Sueyoshi for *KoreAm Journal*.

11

Interview with Dora Yum Kim

I am Dora Yum Kim, second generation. My father, Yum Man Suk, came to San Francisco in 1904. I guess he must have stopped in Hawaii, and then he came to San Francisco, where he joined a group of Chinese men and went up to Washington state and worked on the railroad tracks. After his contract there was finished, he came back to San Francisco. My mother, Han Shin Kim, came over in 1920 as a picture bride. And I was born in 1921.

Where were you born?

I was born in Manteca, California. Apparently, my parents went down to the southern part of California to see if they could do farm work. They decided to come back to San Francisco, and on their way back to San Francisco, they dropped in Manteca to see their relatives, and that's where I was born. We moved on to San Francisco and have been in San Francisco ever since.

Tell us about life in San Francisco.

Well, we all lived in Chinatown because we weren't accepted anywhere else. People don't realize that because now there are Asians all over the city, not only in Chinatown, but all the other districts like Visitacion Valley and Richmond District. They are just all over.

My father's first business was a cigar store on the corner of Pacific and Columbus Avenues. Then, about a year later, he moved down to Jackson Street, which is the border line of Chinatown. He had a

Man Suk Yum, San Francisco, circa 1918.

Picture bride, Han Shin Kim.

Picture brides; Dora Yum Kim's mother in middle, Han Shin Kim.

Man Suk Yum family: George, Man Suk Yum, Han Shin Yum, Henry, Dora, circa 1937.

24-hour restaurant and my mother worked there, and we did, too, when we grew up. We lived in an apartment on Jackson Street for many years. Then, in the '30s, he decided to buy a house, one block from Powell Street, which was the west border line of Chinatown. I believe he was the first Asian to buy property on Mason Street. When he first bought it, the Korean community said, "Oh, he's gonna *manghae,* he's gonna go broke." After quite a while, they found out that he was doing pretty well because they saw that he bought a building with four flats and sold two for double the price. Then he bought six apartments on George Street, sold that, and bought fourteen units on the corner of Broadway and Jones. At that time it was so funny. We got a letter from the Nob Hill Association which said, "Would you please come and join us to keep Chinamen from moving up here?" I should have kept that letter. I couldn't believe it.

How many children are in your family? How many sisters and brothers?

I'm the oldest and then came my brother George and my youngest brother, Henry, who was born in 1928. And when he grew up, George joined the U.S. Army during the Korean War. He didn't want to go, but he was drafted and he went down to Fort Ord, California, took leadership training, then he took a test. A sergeant said he passed everything and that he would be good in anything he did. So they sent him to Officer's Candidate School in Oklahoma. He graduated with hundreds of Caucasians; he was the only Asian face in the graduation picture. And that picture is in Korea right now at the Independence Hall. The researchers there came here and took the picture and said they would make a copy and send it back, but I never got it back.

Tell us a little bit more about Korean incidents when you were a child going to grade school. Were you involved and was your father involved in Korean organizations?

Oh, definitely. We had a Korean Methodist Church on Powell Street in San Francisco. That's where everything started. Patriot Ahn Changho—that's where he started his independence movement. The Koreans in San Francisco were really on to the Independence Movement. You know that Japan took over Korea and tried to eliminate Korea from the

Oak Street, First Korean Church in San Francisco. Rev. Sa Sun Whang, left with child Mary, circa 1915.

map. They compelled the Koreans to speak Japanese. The Koreans were stubborn enough to keep their own language on top of the Japanese they had to learn.

You don't remember the Korean Methodist Church on Oak Street?

That's the church where my parents were married on May 1, 1920. I have a picture of that and the building is still there. It's changed but I remember that building.

By the time you were growing up, were you at the Powell Street church?

No, I was at Oak Street first. I don't know how they did it but the Korean Methodist Church got some money from a wealthy woman or something like that. And the church on Powell Street was built in 1930. Then we had a succession of ministers and Rev. Sa Sun Whang was the longest minister there—for twenty-five years. His son, Paul, is still alive. His age is seventy years old now, but he is looking great for his age.

Tell us a little bit more about Rev. Sa Sun Whang.

I remember he had a laundry cleaning store on Mason Street. When his son, Paul Whang, graduated from State College, he couldn't find a job. He tried to find a job when he went back home to the city, near

155

Dora Yum Kim
(second from left),
Paul Whang, Ruth
Shin Whang.

Chinatown. The city was full of discrimination and that was the story of our life, growing up with discrimination. Someone said, "Couldn't you have done anything?" I said, "What could you do?" I mean you can get beat up and what's the sense of that? So we all had to keep quiet.

Can you remember any activities, specific activities, in the Korean community?
The Korean Methodist Church was the only religious order, and it was a place for the Koreans to get together socially. Only a few Koreans were in San Francisco. There were more than a hundred total. It was more like a community where everybody knew each other and most of our parents couldn't speak English. The only way was to get together in the church. The children all went to Sunday school there and went to all the activities. Their parents went there.

My father was the president of the Korean National Association and was a member of the Hungsadan. [Ahn Changho established this organization as part of the KNA Independence Movement Program to concentrate on the educational needs of Koreans abroad regarding their homeland.] After my father passed away, I found his books that were printed in Korean. My father was in it, saying that there are eight provinces in Korea. Since he came from Kangwondo, he was one of eight delegates from Kangwondo. Ahn Changho was one of them. They were very active, and so the children were active, too, along with

156

their parents. We never said "No" to our parents, whether we wanted to or not. We took it for granted and went to church with them all the time. When Ahn Changho passed away in 1938 in a Japanese prison, they couldn't hold a funeral for him in Korea because we were still under Japanese rule. So my father, who was the president of the Korean National Association in San Francisco at that time, had a memorial service for Ahn Changho with a big picture of him. I remember I was the piano player for that ceremony. I was the piano player when Rev. Whang Sa Son was a minister there also. So we have many fine memories from the Korean Methodist Church.

You mentioned that there were over a hundred Koreans then. To your knowledge was that the largest number?

That's the largest I remember before 1965. After the immigration laws were relaxed in 1965, the influx of new immigrants began. Now there are over ten thousand Koreans here in San Francisco. It's hard to believe.

Getting back to the old days, I understand the Koreans at that time dwindled down because of what? Why?

No. They didn't dwindle down.

Ahn Changho was here in San Francisco. And then he moved down to LA with a lot of his followers, right? His family moved down to LA.

Yes.

Could you tell us a little bit about the group of Koreans in San Francisco that moved down to LA?

Well, you know, all the Koreans were active together. Some moved down to Los Angeles like Ahn Changho's family did. But I think he went to Korea soon after he went to Los Angeles and he was in prison in Korea. Yes? His family settled down in Los Angeles.

Were there many other families who went down too?

That moved down? Yes, the Lee family was a family of ten children. They had a cleaning store on Canal Street and they all moved down to Los Angeles.

Did quite a number of Koreans move down there?

There were still Koreans here.

Was Syngman Rhee here also?

Oh, yes. Syngman Rhee was here.

What do you remember of Dr. Syngman Rhee?

Just that he was a visitor here. When he was in San Francisco, he stayed at Yang Choo Eun's home. So when Rhee became president of Korea, he invited Yang Choo Eun to come to Korea.

Who is Yang Choo Eun?

He was a man who had a restaurant on Third Street, which is in a not-too-good area. But he was good to the Koreans who would come by because after the 1924 Exclusion Act only scholars, ministers, and students could come over. He had to feed them because they didn't have money. He even fed Syngman Rhee. Of course, Syngman Rhee had done some great work in Hawaii before coming here.

What other leaders were there in San Francisco?

The one main person I can think of is Rev. Lee Dae Wi. He was a minister who married my parents and many others here. He was, I think, the first Korean to graduate from UC Berkeley, in 1916. He actually graduated from Portland Academy because his son gave me his diploma, an ornate diploma. He was a big help to all the Koreans here. He is well remembered. But he died an untimely death because he worked so hard for the Korean community. I remember once I met a man from Chicago who got his PhD from some college and he said he came with a group of students and they were ready to deport him back to Korea. Then Rev. Lee came down and did or said something, and they all got to stay here because of him.

Were the leaders all connected with a church?

Yes. All began at that church. Ahn Changho started his independence movement there. Many things started from that Korean Methodist Church.

Uncle Sam Shop owned by Choo Eun Yang and his wife (on his right).

You mentioned something to the effect of groups giving money to the Independence Movement?

Oh, the bachelors. We had a few bachelors here at that time. And then they were working for wealthy families. They would get one day off a month. They wanted to make much money, to give all the money to the Korean Independence Movement. They were really gung ho.

Who did they give the money to for the Independence Movement?

I think it was the Korean National Association.

Can you remember any of the presidents of the Korean National Association besides your father?

Uhm, they were mostly local people. But I don't remember their names.

Do you remember any other activities that they did as members of Kuk Min Hur?

Well, we had picnics once a year. And all the Koreans would come.

Did you mention something about a language school?

Oh, my father was like Mr. Choo Eun Yang. He felt sorry for the Korean students and scholars coming over. So he said to them, "I'll feed you for free if you teach my children Korean." So we had to go to *kukeo hakgyo* 국어 학교, Korean language school, every vacation time. I guess that's how I learned Korean and I remember the Korean language. I can still read and write, but I don't understand completely.

What kind of hours did the school have?

I think just a few hours a day and during the summer.

Were they quite consistent?

Uh-uh. Well, nobody wanted to learn Korean at that time. Naturally, because we were kids. But we all had to, so we did. However, my younger brother, Henry—while in the U.S. Army and when he was sent oversees on his way to Korea—they pulled him out from the airplane in Japan and sent him to Camp Dewy to learn Korean. He had six months of training and he went to Korea. And he became an interpreter at Panmunjeom. Later he went on to the U.S. Army Intelligence Agency in Washington, D.C. By the way, he was the first Korean-American kid to be drafted by the U.S. Army for the Korean War.

Tell us about the Korean families whom you think were icons in San Francisco.

Well, if you go by outstanding figures in businesses, my father had a restaurant and the Shins had a restaurant across the street. Above them was a barbershop run by Henry Shin. And there was another barbershop on Washington Street run by the Cha family, and there was Kim Dongwoo on Clay Street. And there was a cleaning shop on Kearney Street, Powell Street, and Mason Street and Pacific Avenue. Pacific Avenue was where the Moon family lived. They had a hard time. But the brother became a doctor, Dr. Henry Moon. He was a well-known pathologist and very intelligent. The Chinese doctors said they were all afraid of him at school because he was so intelligent. And he got a grant for cancer research, and yet he died from throat cancer himself. It was sad. His youngest brother's name was Shiny, but later he changed it to William because if he kept Shiny, his full name would be Shiny Moon. Instead, he changed it to William Moon. He's an anesthesiologist in Britain right now. And he's well known there, too, I understand.

So how many families were active in San Francisco that you've mentioned so far?
The two Shinn families, the Chars, and Dongwoo Kim was quite a leader, too. And there was a Chun family who had a bathhouse on Stockwood Street. We didn't have bathtubs in the 1920s. So people would pay to go there and take a bath.

Was it *ofuro* style—Japanese style—many people in one big tub?
No. I know that there were individual tubs in each room.

Tell us a little more about the children.
They all had children. My parents had the least number of children—three. The Shinns had five children; the others had four children, and there was a family of ten, the Lees on Kearney Street, who later moved to Los Angeles.

The Moon family moved. Did they have children here, too?
They passed away here.

No descendents still here?
There is one in Britain, and the girl is on Stockton Street, married to a doctor, Dr. Philip Park, and he passed away. Most of even the second generation were beginning to move away.

How about the Char family?
Oh, they moved to Nevada. I was telling their daughter that all I remember is that she was a cute little girl. And that their mother was

beautiful. They moved to Nevada because the father was jealous of all the attention she was getting from the other Korean men here.

Did you know the Har family from way back? Tell us a little bit what you know about that family.
They had two girls and two boys also. They had a cleaning store on Fillmore Street. My mother and I used to go visit them there. But they were sort of aloof. They were not too friendly with the community, although they participated. There was another Kim family with three boys and two girls. But they didn't come around too much until later in life, when they felt like they needed to be among Koreans.

How about the Shin family? Who did the Shins marry? Philip Shin's family?
They had five children. One was a famous boxer, Richie Shin, and he passed away. I guess he passed away from Alzheimer's, from being punched on the head so much when he was a boxer. Peter, the oldest son, is still alive. Helen, the oldest daughter, is still alive, and there is Pauley. The younger son died. The parents are gone, of course. The others are still alive and they have children.

Paul Whang has a daughter, Gale, who is interested in Korean history. She went down to Mexico and wrote a short paper on what she discovered there—Koreans in Mexico, speaking Korean and Spanish.

Now let's get to the new immigrants. Do you remember the first consul general, Choo Younghan?
Yes, he came from Gangwondo, the same province as my father. So they became pretty close. But he wasn't popular among the new Korean immigrants. He used to invite me to all his affairs. When he had his first celebration, I helped him find the first building the consulate bought. It still exists at 3500 Clay Street. I remember they paid only $40,000 at that time. It was in 1949 after the war. That was the first consulate.

He was not popular? Why? Can you give me your version?
I don't know what he was. He was sort of crude and rude. The students didn't like him because he didn't grant the visas fast enough or

not at all. I didn't know that until after he passed away. With him, we participated in a lot of city community activities. We had the first parade in 1949. It was the first time the Koreans were invited to participate, so we had all the Korean girls assigned to come. We had a float and we had a beautiful Korean girl, Laney Park, as a queen. So it was nice.

At that time, there was an increase in the number of new Korean immigrants in San Francisco. Tell us about how they assimilated.

Nobody knew what a Korean was when we were growing up and they always asked us, "What are you? Are you Chinese?" I said, "No." "You must be Japanese." I said, "No." "Then what are you?" And I would say, "Korean." "Korean? What's that?" I would tell them how Japan came over and murdered the queen and annexed our country in 1910 and tried to eliminate Korea from the map entirely. We were known as the Hermit Nation. Remember, we could never find Korea on the map in our geography books, in our history books. When the Korean influx began, the teachers had a lot of Korean students. They could not speak English, Chinese, or Japanese, and then they realized that they were Koreans. But the teachers didn't know what Koreans were until the Korean War.

At that time, I was working for the State Department of Employment, starting before 1965. Apparently, I was the only Korean-speaking person. So I had to do all the interpretation, translating, and giving the Koreans their first jobs. These were for the immigrants. I don't know how they knew I was working at the State Department of Employment. Someone said that she asked someone for help and they saw my name at the airport on the board for Korean translation. Koreans coming in today don't realize that there were generations of Koreans before them. Some would say, "Oh, we're the first Koreans here." I said, "Oh, no. You're not. I'm the second generation already." They couldn't believe me. The first applicant I had to work with was a Korean pharmacist. I didn't know that pharmacists, professional registered nurses, and engineers could come over without a sponsor. But they had a tough time. They could read and write English. But they just couldn't communicate orally. I spoke to them in Korean. One would

163

say, "Gee, you were born here. How come you have an accent from the northern province 평양도 사투리?" I thought for a moment and I said, "Well, my mother came from Pyongyang." And they'd say, "Oh!" I guess I learned from my mother. It was really funny.

Did you get a feel of where these new Koreans came from, what part of Korea?

All I know is they all came from Seoul.

Tell us little bit more about growing up, when you went to school. Were there other Korean students in your class?

No, I was always the only one. When I entered UC Berkeley, there were only two Koreans: Mabel Park and myself. We had to join that Chinese Club because there was no Korean Club. Now I hear there are thousands of Koreans there in Berkeley.

How did it feel to be Korean among the Chinese? Were they good to you?

We were discriminated against by the Chinese at Berkeley but having grown up in Chinatown, we were accepted by the Chinese there. So we got along with the Chinese in San Francisco Chinatown. For instance, when I called my Chinese friend on the telephone and her mother answered, I could hear her mother say, "Oh, your Korean girlfriend is on the phone." The Chinese in Chinatown used to say, "Oh, all the same . . . Chinese and Koreans . . . all the same." So that was fine in San Francisco Chinatown.

In the early days, did you know anything about Korea and being Korean yourself? I mean, did you know much about what was happening in Korea besides the Japanese invasion?

Well, we heard terrible stories about what the Japanese were doing in Korea. I remember my mother telling me that the Japanese soldiers would come down the hill and the dogs would bark to warn them that they were coming. They had only one knife among three families or something like that. When the Japanese came down they took everything, and they killed their little dog. And she never forgot that.

164

How about Korean history? Do you know any Korean history besides the war?

We learned about history in Korean school 국어학교.

What did you learn?

The Lee Dynasty and Han Dynasty. And we learned the alphabet. They said the Koreans are stubborn like the Irish. You know, stubborn and like to drink—like the Irish.

Tell me a little bit about your contact with your father's family or your mother's family in Korea. Was there any contact before the war began?

No. Up until 1924, I remember my father was sending money to his sister and to her family in Gangwondo. I have a picture of their family, but of course, I never saw them in person. When I went to Korea last time, I met the mayor of Gangwondo. He said, "I'll take you to meet your relatives." Someone said, "No, you'd better not go. They all want to go to America."

And your mother's family?

My grandmother. All I know is that I have a picture of her and her maid and that's all.

Who were your best friends when you were a youngster?

I think a Chinese girl. Because I was the youngest among the Korean girls here, I had to find girls my age. My Chinese and Korean friends all had sisters and I didn't.

Do you remember hearing about an important person who came from Washington, D.C., who was supposed to marry a descendent of the Korean royal family? Do you remember that?

Was that the one in the Min family?

Yes. That's the family. Do you remember the family at all? How did you know about them?

I just knew that there was somebody here of royalty. But they never came around much. The only way I knew of any Korean is if they were here permanently and coming to the church. We would meet them at the church to get to know them. I don't remember them at all except that the wife was royalty or something to that effect.

What else would you like to tell us?

Just about growing up without all the things that are happening with the new immigrants. Now it's surprising to see all the Korean restaurants. We never had this many Korean restaurants before. You have to give them credit. They all are doing well. The new immigrants have better opportunities than we had—except for the English language. All my children were born in San Francisco, grandchildren and great grandchildren. They can't speak Korean. They sort of always ask me, "Why didn't you teach us?" I never knew they had a use for it or even had an interest in it. Now there are Korean schools here. My son, Tom, was the one who wrote the proposal for what is now the Korean Center. It was called the Multi-Service Center for Koreans at that time. Gale Whang was one of them. And Melanie Han; Dr. Steve Shon; and Tom Suh, the attorney; they all got together. They wanted to do something for the new Koreans who were coming over. But something went wrong. We noticed, Gale and I, we couldn't get along with the new Koreans. They were different. And so we all resigned and that's when they moved the office a couple of times and went to Margaret Street. Now they are at Post Street.

What is this about not getting along? Why? What do you think started it?

I have no idea. At first, when we were going to meetings, all they were doing was fighting. We didn't like that.

Was it miscommunication?

That had something to do with it because the third generation here couldn't speak Korean. The new Koreans would make fun of them. Their ideas just didn't match. When we lost that program, we opened the Korean Community Service Center. That's when I started the Korean Senior Meal Program. Later the Korean Center took it over.

12

Interview with Eleanor Chun You

My name is Eleanor Chun You, and I'm a third-generation Korean born in Hawaii in 1918.

My maternal grandparents are Mary Chun Park and Mr. Park. They had three children: two daughters, Young Nani and Sela Won, who was my mother, and a son, Kwon Jin. They brought Young Nani and Kwon Jin to Hawaii. However, they left my mother, Sela, in Korea so that she could go to school there. Sela was left in Korea with a Korean family to finish her education. However, my grandmother found out through the grapevine that she was taken out of school and was being used as a maid. They were upset. They decided that my grandfather should go back to Korea and bring Sela to Hawaii. And so he did. But, on the way coming back, he got typhoid fever on the ship. Unfortunately, my grandfather died and he was quickly buried at the seaside, where the grave site was. Shortly after burial, his coffin got washed away during a thunderstorm. It was awfully sad.

In the meantime, my grandmother was thinking of getting a husband for Sela, her youngest daughter. Before Sela ever had set foot in Hawaii, she already had a fiancé. Why? Because my grandmother thought that Chin Wha Chun, who worked on the sugar plantation on Kauai, would make a good husband for her daughter. He was smart and industrious, although he was about fifteen years older. Anyway, Chin Wha Chun liked what he saw and agreed to marry her. So they became my parents.

Chin Wha Chun with bowler hat and Sela (in front of him on his right) on the Koloa, Kauai, Planation when Sela arrived in Hawaii, 1908.

There were six children in our family: three daughters and three sons. My sisters Hazel and Margaret and myself, and my brothers Soon Ho, Soon Sung, and Soon Tae. Soon Tae died at an early age.

After a few years my father took us out of the plantation on Kauai and bought a furniture store on Fort Street in Honolulu after saving all their money when they came to Honolulu. My two brothers, Soon Ho and Soon Sung, would go to the furniture store and help unpack boxes of furniture parts from the Mainland and assemble the furniture. I also would go there after school to collect money for my father whenever furniture was sold.

My mother took all the laundry there to wash the clothes in the back of the furniture store. She was always there, cooking or washing laundry. She was busy bringing up the family, seeing that we were brought up with the right disciplining. She was a wonderful mother. My father was very protective towards her. They all worked hard. We

Hazel, Sela, Margaret, and Chin Wha Chun, circa 1918.

168

Chin Wha Chun family;
left to right: Eleanor (You),
Margaret, Sela, Soon Tae
(on lap), Hazel, Soon Sung,
Chin Wha, Soon Ho,
circa 1926.

were so busy. My father later moved us to Beretania Street and opened another store near Aala Park. During the war, there was no furniture being shipped to Hawaii, so my father retired from the furniture business. And instead he invested in real estate and rental properties. Although we came from a large family, we had a comfortable existence from his wise investments and hard work.

Chin Wha Chun, circa 1915.

In the meantime, when we were on the island of Kauai, my grandmother remarried. Remember my grandfather died when he went back to Korea to bring my mother to Hawaii. So my grandmother remarried a few years later. She married Kim Dong-gun, who was a good friend of her first husband. They used to know each other at the sugar plantation on Kauai. They later moved to Honolulu also and worked at the Goodale Estate, a remote area of Kapai, on the island of Oahu. They were caretakers of the three acres that the Goodales owned

169

there. Grandmother also raised chickens there. She fed the chickens centipedes. So we used to go and catch centipedes for Grandmother. She gave us all a big, tall glass to catch them to feed the chickens. So I happily went with my brothers to catch them cause we had fun catching them for the chickens. We would have a contest to see who would catch the most centipedes among my sisters and my brothers. So it was a joyous occasion then. The poor chickens. Grandmother also grew their own vegetables; our parents were very resourceful. They grew chili peppers, green onions, string beans, cabbages, and turnips.

Where was this again?
Kapai. That's on Oahu. It's a remote area. Past Waialua. Every Sunday my mother and my father would drop us off over there every summer. They taught us how to catch crabs also. My grandpa would get a big square can and plant it on the sand and he would put fermented seawater in the can. The crabs would climb in. We'd go off and play about two hours. When we came back, the can was full of crabs. My grandmother would pickle them with shoyu and garlic. It was so good.

What did your step-grandfather do? For a living?
For a living? He was a caretaker for the Goodales and that's because the Goodales would come every other Sunday to relax and play there. Then Grandfather would take care of the property while they were gone and would get the place ready for them and clean up after all that. We would help him rake the road leading to the beach house.

Tell us about your father. What is his background?
He was just a smart man. That's why I admired him. He made something of himself. He loved his wife, my mother, so much. We loved them both so very much.

Where was he from? Did he have any relatives here?
He had about five brothers in Korea, I understand. I have never been to Korea to meet them.

Did they write? Did they communicate?
Not that I know of.

Was he active in the Korean Methodist Church?

Not really. He was active in his furniture store.

Did he belong to the Dongji Hoi, the Kuk Min Hur, or the Korean Christian Church?

As far as I can recall, he may have been, but it doesn't click in my mind. He wasn't active; he was more a family man. The family came first with him because he loved my mother so much. My mother would cook some food and we would go over and eat it out in the forest. He was strictly a family man.

You didn't go to church?

Yes, I did. I even taught at the Sunday school at the Korean Methodist Church. That's where I am from. I was taught at Sunday school and I taught there when I grew up. I took my children to the church every Sunday.

When did you start attending the Methodist Church? When did you start?

No, my parents did go to the church also. The Methodist Church. My memory's coming back. They did go to church. They were very gracious and loved to meet people.

At church when I was young, I remember my father would say to me, "Soonyeeya, you always sleep when you are in the church. Don't do that." Yeah, my memory is coming back. And he would say to me "Don't talk, talk in church and don't look all over. You're always looking over to see who is in the back of you. Don't do that. Just sit still in one place."

Was your father a member of the Kuk Min Hur or Dongji Hoi?

I don't remember. I don't remember those things too well because he was busy.

Let's talk about your husband. Who was he and how did you meet him?

Dr. Richard You was my husband. Richard's father had a rooming house across my father's furniture store in Honolulu. He was young. I saw him for the first time across the street going to his father's furniture room to help clean it. I didn't know this at that time, but he told me after we got married that he saw me, too.

How did I meet him? He was in the same class as my sister Margaret from years back. She said he was a wonderful, wonderful boy. She always admired Richard You. He said he was going to become a doctor. Very ambitious. One day I was going home from school and I felt like somebody was looking at me. So I turned around and there was this young man smiling. So I ran home and told Margaret, "You know, there was a tall, good-looking boy staring at me." She said, "That's Richard You. He is a good boy." Then we started dating. One day he said to me, "What kind of flowers do you like?" I said, "Why? What kind of flowers do you like?" He said, "Tulips." I said, "Tulips?" He looked at my lips and kissed me while I said, "Two lips." And that was our first kiss. We got engaged. Then he went away to go to medical school. I waited for him for four years. When he came back, we got married. [Richard You became a medical doctor and was appointed one of the international medical doctors for the Olympics for many years.]

Dr. Richard You.

Dong Men You, father of Dr. Richard You.

Dong Men and Mary You family, circa 1924; left to right: Henry, Melvin, Won Young, Mary, Minnie, Katie, Dong Men, Wonsik, Richard.

What can you tell us about his father, Dong Men You?

My father-in-law. I remember him. Not too much. The only thing I remember of him is when I went to the airport to see my husband go off to medical school, he was there also.

What do you know about him?

Not too much. All I know is what his mother told me about him. They were sort of separated, so to speak.

Let's talk about your childhood. What school did you graduate from?

McKinley High School.

Tell us about your brothers.

It makes me sad when I think about my brothers cause they died so young. My sister Hazel married young to Peter Kim from Waialua. Margaret was married to Young Hee Ko because she wanted the richest man in Hawaii. Although his family sent him to Korea to look for a wife, he came back without a wife because he liked my sister Margaret. They got married.

173

My paternal grandfather, I understood, had three wives back in Korea. He brought his favored wife, Mary, my grandmother, to Hawaii. That's what I understood when I was young.

Whanjin, my youngest uncle, went off to California for the gold rush before his father, my grandfather, died. Then he came back after several years to honor his father. But the grave site was washed away. So he was very upset, and he went back to California. We never heard from him ever again. He was very upset. That's what I heard when I was young, from the family. He never came back again. So my grandmother used to always cry about him. "What happened to Whanjunee?" she used to cry. She used to be so sad, talking about him. She talked about him all the time.

Did you hear about any community activities and leaders such as Syngman Rhee?

Not really. That's a different group. We were Methodist. We were not affiliated with things like that.

13

Interview with Agnes Rho Chun

My name is Agnes Eunsoon Rho Chun. My father, Hee Chang Rho, was also known as Hee Gyeom Rho. He came from Ong Jin, Hwanghaedo, sometime in 1903. My mother was left behind. This is a story I heard from my mom: My mother and dad married in Korea and had three children. My parents were very young when the children all died. One day, my mother was told that my dad had gone to Hawaii with Mr. Lee Hong Gee. I understand that Mr. Lee Hong Gee was the one who was instrumental in getting

Hee Chang Rho, circa 1925.

my father here. My dad had come here with the understanding, I believe, that my mother was going to be taken care of by her sister, who was quite wealthy in the same village, while he was gone.

Upon arrival in Hawaii, my father was sent to the Kauai Plantation with Lee Hong Gee. I don't know when they came out here, but they later went to Honolulu, the capitol of Hawaii. After ten years my father sent for my mother to come here. She came here sometime in 1913 and lived in the Palama District of Honolulu. As far as I know, my mother did not have any experience on the plantation.

Family Photograph;
left to right: Flora
Keum Soon, Violet,
Jung Sun, Hee Chang
Rho, Jung Han.

They had five children born here in Honolulu. My siblings were Jung Han Rho; my second brother, Jung Sun Rho; my sister Flora Keum Soon Rho Park; and my second sister, Violet Rho. Violet's name is actually Violet Oksun Rho Cho. I was the last one in the family living. We had one other brother who was right above me who died very young. The first time that I was aware of the family *chokbo* 족보, which is the genealogy of the family, was in 1950, when my sister-in-law had a cousin who came from Korea and said that this document was a *chokbo*, a genealogy record. This *chokbo* was with my mother at that time. My father had passed away in 1935, when I was nine years old. I was not aware of the *chokbo* until I heard my mother say that she had given this *chokbo* to my brother so that his wife's cousin could do some translation of it, and I never saw it since then.

Later on, I found out from my mother that this *chokbo* was lost. Somehow, they lost track of it. That's what I heard. So my mother went to her grave in 1953, thinking that this *chokbo* was lost and she was very upset about it. However, when my brother passed away in 1997, my sister-in-law gave it to me and said that I should have this document because it is part of our Rho family tree. I was very surprised. I understood now that the *chokbo* is a part of each family in Korea. This *chokbo* actually shows it as *seygye* 세계, meaning "from the beginning." As far as I know, the first grandfather who is noted here is recorded to have lived during the Koryo Dynasty. I understand there are

176

Left to right: Jung Sun, Agnes, mother, Jung Han, Hee Chang Rho, Violet, Flora, circa 1933.

several pieces here which indicate the family tree. There are some pieces that show the names and the dates of death of the family members.

We have one item in the *chokbo* which is very unique. I found out from Dr. Youngho Chae at the University of Hawaii that this is not usually part of the *chokbo*. We couldn't understand what this was, but evidently, I remember according to my mother, one of the family used to be a city clerk. From what I understand this appears to be a mathematical booklet, probably for taxation purposes because it does indicate here the military taxes, other land and grain taxes. So this is a very unique part of our *chokbo* document. This is something that someday I hope someone we will be able to translate to let us know exactly what it is.

From what I understand, my grandfather, the progenitor of the Rho clan, was very instrumental in helping the king of the Koryo Dynasty. This is supposed to be what is called *seygye*. This is the main *chokbo*, listing all of the members of our family and they also have it graded by class. First class, second class, third class. This one here is a taxation book.

Tell us a little bit more about your father, what he was doing here and about his affiliations.

I remember my mother telling me that when my father came here, he worked at the Del Monte Pineapple Cannery. I believe he was also a security guard. I know that he was contracted by the company for the stacking of cans. The modern way of doing it is to have it mechanized by having all of the cans come on palettes. But I understand in those days they had to have pineapples stacked by hand. So I guess my father must have contracted a few people to work with him. The funny part of this story is what my mother told me about my father's honesty. What he would do when he was in charge of a working group is that when he got paid, he had to distribute the money amongst them. Whenever there were a few pennies left, my father would buy these horse matches. When I say horse matches, I mean those little boxes of matches with a horse printed on it. He would then divide the matches amongst them. My mother thought it was crazy. She said, "Why couldn't he just keep those few pennies?" But he was that way, he wanted to make everything equitable.

My father was a very good handyman. One day his friend recognized my father's potential for fixing things. The friend thought of fixing broken things and selling them for a profit. So he propositioned my father to go into a second-hand business with him. They embarked on this idea. The gentleman said that he would be responsible for collecting the items, and my father would be responsible for having them refurbished. My father went into the business, but my mother said after a while they had to dissolve it because there was a lot of friction between those two. What happened was that my father could not see selling an item that the fellow purchased for 15¢ and sell it for like $2.50 or $3.50. The profit margin was so great that my father said it was very dishonest. That's the way he was. So we were sure he would never become a millionaire.

In 1935 my father passed away after a long illness. My brother Jung Han, who was the eldest, was pulled out of high school in his junior year. My sister also was pulled out. They both worked to support the family. My mother then had to start to learn how to sew trousers. We had many other Korean friends who had become tailors, and they were running the shops. They delivered trousers and my mother would sew them. At a very young age, too, I learned how to sew buttonholes and help my mother. She also worked at the pineapple cannery as a trimmer. During those days, we were very poor and were not able to even have my brothers continue school. My second brother became a tailor. My sister, also, did not finish school. My sister Violet and myself, we both finished high school. This was our history about education. Then when the war broke out, we were not able to continue high school.

How about activities at the church? Tell us about the church.

As far as I can remember, I was a member of the Korean Christian Church on Liliha Street since I was born. I remember going to the church and the Korean language school located on School Street in Kalihi. We had another church on School Street. That is where the present Korean Care Home is located. We had buildings there, which were torn down to build the Korean Care Home. That's as far as I can remember. Then when we built the church on Liliha Street, I was there, helping them clean the yard, as far as I can remember. That was probably in 1938 or 1939, when the church was first built. I've been going there since and during the war. It was very difficult for me to be at church steadily because I was employed full time at Pearl Harbor.

What about your father? Do you remember him being active in church?

As far as I can remember, I was only nine years old when he passed away. I remember him, but I don't remember his activities. Looking at the papers that we have, I see that he was active in the Korean Christian Church and the Dongji Hoi 동지회, I am sure.

How about your mother?

My mother was always very active in church as far as I can remember. She was very active in the Ladies' Society, and she was always there for any kind of programs in support of the founder of our Korean Christian Church, Dr. Syngman Rhee. I can say that actually my mother, myself, and my sister Violet, and my brother Junghan—just those are the ones I can remember going to church.

What about contacting relatives in Korea?

As far as I know, our relatives were in the northern part of Korea. They did come down to the southern part of Korea, but I lost track of them.

179

Is that both on your father's and mother's side?
I think it's only my mother's side.

Do you think your parents had a lot of family members in Korea?
I am not sure. All I can remember is my mother saying that there was a very talented young man in that family. While he was very young, he may have been kidnapped or simply disappeared. He was so very talented, my mother said, that he may have been kidnapped by someone who knew of his real talent. Another thing is I still remember my mother saying that my grandfather used to be a *jusa* 주사. I guess it was a clerk, like a city hall clerk.

Recognizing my heritage didn't start until after my mother passed away. I wish things like this had begun earlier so that we would be aware of these documents.

Many people missed the chance.
Exactly. I had thought of interviewing my mother several times but never got around to it. It was really sad. My mother was a typical housewife. It was when she came to Hawaii that she was able to read and write. She learned to do that all by herself.

One example was so funny. One day I came home from work and she said, "Oh, I wrote a letter to your sister." This sister was in California and could read simple Korean characters. I read it, and as I was going along, I asked, "What is this? 이거 뭐야?" She said, "*Sutoa* 수토아." I asked again, "What is *sutoa* 수토아가 뭐야?" And then she told me indignantly, she said, "*Sutoa.*" Then it dawned on me what she really meant was "store." So I told her, "Oh, my goodness 아이구! Why didn't you write *jeombang* 왜 점방 안썼어?" [*Jeombang* is "store" in Korean.] She was kind of hurt, but she laughed. This showed that all of a sudden she was trying to use English words: "store" instead of the Korean word, *jeombang.* I said to myself, "Well, at least she is kind of Westernized in a little way." I was very surprised that through diligence she was learning on her own, how to read the Korean newspaper, *Dongji Hoi Sinmun* specifically. So that is a story that I carry in my heart about my mother.

The last time we talked about your neighborhood friends, you said they were mainly Episcopalians.

Yes. We lived on Pua Lane for many, many years in the Palama area of Honolulu. I realize now that many of the Koreans there, many, many Koreans, were mostly members of the St. Luke's Episcopalian Church on Kanoa Street. They lived all around in the Pua Lane area. I had so many friends in that area who were from the Episcopal Church. They were also store keepers. They had little shops on King Street. We had cleaning shops, shoemakers, furniture stores, and several Korean grocery stores on King Street.

Why do you think there were many Korean Episcopalians in that area?

I really don't know. Could it have been that it was in the vicinity of the Episcopal Church that brought them there? And usually friends who go to the same church get to live there also. Or it could be that because they already lived in that area, they went to the nearest church. I think that's probably what happened there. I really don't know for sure. That seems to have happened at the Korean Christian Church. We, more or less, made friends around the church.

Could you name some friends among the Episcopalians there?

Yes, there was the Charles Choo family, Anita Choo. There was Moon Young-whan, who was one of the grocery store people. There was Adam Lee's family, whose parents were running a cleaning shop. We had Molly Chung and Jonny Chung. They were living across us. We had Patsy Kim and Calvin Kim, Audrey Kim. Those families were there.

Were they all Episcopalians?

They were all Episcopalians—and several others in that vicinity. I remember Mrs. Mary Kang. Her daughter was Rosline Shida. Her mother went to the Episcopalian Church and eventually Rose came to our church.

I think you are old enough to have witnessed the turbulence at the Korean Christian Church in 1940 and 1960.

We had a couple of them, I remember, but like I said, I was playing low-key about politics most of the time. During the first disturbance

I was busy working. In fact, all along I was working, so I never did take an active part in it. I remember many of the incidences that happened there. Going back to the incidences at the church, much of it was, I think, among the older group that were involved in the turbulence. As I said, I was working and hardly went to church regularly at that time. So I really don't know too much. I knew the outcome of the actual disturbances but not much about the reasons for them. I know that we had these disturbances at church which were very unnerving at times. I remember my parents, my mother especially, were more involved in those incidences. The second incidence, as far as I know, had to do with the minister again. I really can't remember the very specific incidences that happened. It was sort of a general feeling amongst the people that this was going on. The elderly persons were key players in the Liliha Church.

Tell us about the arrival of the new immigrants after 1950s. I can recall a rather large number of them went directly to the Korean Christian Church.

Oh, yes. I understand what you're talking about. When the war broke out, I believe most of us were in the busy downtown and Makiki areas.

For a long time, Honolulu city was small. As the circumference of the city widened beyond Kaimuki and Kahala, the new areas beyond Aina Haina came up. Koreans who were in the more wealthy circle moved to those areas. As the years went by, we noticed many of the children of the original immigrant families were moving outward from the immigrant areas. Many of them decided that it was too far to come to their original church and their working hours did not allow it. So many of them joined local churches within their neighborhoods. We, who remained in the old area, noticed that our membership was growing smaller and smaller until the newer immigrants came, I guess, in the late '50s and early '60s. We noticed that many of the new immigrants joined our church. The congregation was getting bigger in the way of the new immigrants versus the locals. I guess in many of the other churches, too, this was going on. We had a good report among new immigrants who joined us. Although many of the immigrants felt that our church was not as warm in some ways.

Back to the past. You were beginning to tell us that the church was started by Dr. Syngman Rhee. Tell us a little bit more. Why did he split?

From what I understand, through the years, Dr. Syngman Rhee was not happy with the Methodist Church hierarchy. We were told that many of the the Methodist decisions were made at the Methodist National Office on the Mainland. Rhee felt that for the Koreans this was not enough for them. So I guess he left the Methodist Church and started his own group. I believe my mom and dad were one of those who went with him and have been with him throughout the years. We stayed with him as part of the Korean Christian Church.

Any other historic events that you can remember? You were born in the 1920s. You were in Honolulu, where most of the activities were taking place, whereas lots of other Korean families were still on the outer islands.

Well, as far as I am concerned, I tried to become a part of the Korean community, also. I was very active with the Korean Community Council and I joined the Korean Chamber. This was back in the 1970s that I joined the Chamber. I've been with the Chamber until a couple of years ago. I don't believe I am still on their roster. I just kind of slowly gave up. The Chamber's membership is now mostly young people and so I just kind of dropped out. The Korean Community Council had many activities in which I was very active. Whenever they had any kind of programs, I was always there for them. That's all I can remember.

How about the leaders of the Korean Christian Church? Who were the leaders way back then—way, way back?

I can remember old names like Dr. You Chan Yang, Nodie Kimhaekim Sohn, Syung Woon Sohn [Nodie's husband], Dr. Y. K. Kim [the Korean ambassador to the Philippines, appointed by Dr. Rhee after WWII]. We had Sung Dae Choi, You Sil Lee, Inez Kong Pai and her mother. They were very active, too. I remember those people. And there was this Mr. Ahn Hyun-Kyung, Salome Han's stepfather. I know they were involved in a lot of activities for the independence of Korea. We were just youngsters going to church at that time.

My husband, Soon Ho Chun, was a member of the Methodist Church when I married him. When we met, it was just getting to know each other, and I don't think there was any distinguishing Methodists from Korean Christians. It was nothing like that. We got married at the Korean Christian Church. He eventually became part of our Korean Christian Church. Women are stronger than men.

Last time you mentioned something to the effect that there may still be some sort of negative feelings between the two groups, among the younger set as well.
I think so, but very subtle. I think they still considered them as Methodist or Korean Christian Church members. I think there is still the subtleness.

Can you tell us little bit more?
You mean the differences? Okay. When you talk about our age group, this is the second generation now, we have older second generation, too, which I think are more knowledgeable about the split, right? But with us, the younger second generation, we still once in a while talked about Rooke Avenue, the headquarters of the Korean National Association [also known as Kuk Min Hur] versus not being a member of that association. The KNA was associated with the Methodist Church.

Could you explain Rooke Avenue?
Rooke Avenue, I believe, is the meeting place for the Methodist group. They bought the Rooke Avenue building.

You mean Kuk Min Hur?
Kuk Min Hur, which is equivalent with the Dongji Hoi for the Korean Christian Church. It's a political association, right? Kuk Min Hur are the Methodists, and the Korean Christian Church are the Dongji Hoi. I think Kuk Min Hur has their headquarters for meetings on Rooke Avenue. I've been there. I was invited to attend one of the gatherings. But the third generation probably would not have made any distinction between the two organizations. Even I, a second generation, didn't know too much. I never knew that there was such a

The Korean Military Brigade was founded in Hawaii in 1914.

thing as a Korean military in Hawaii out here, sponsored by Kuk Min Hur. That was way before my time as far as I can remember. Only after I got involved in the seventy-fifth anniversary of the Korean immigration to Hawaii and the ninetieth anniversary that I realized that there was a military organization of Koreans out here in Hawaii.

Interview with Hazel Pahk Chung on Her Husband, Rev. Euicho Chung

Euicho was born in Korea, I think in Busan, and came to Hawaii with his parents when he was about two or three years old. The Hawaiian Islands were wanting laborers for the cane fields and his parents joined the immigration group. Euicho's family was assigned to the island of Kauai. So he grew up on the island of Kauai. His mother and father opened a tailoring business.

Ho Young Chung family, circa 1912; left to right: Euicho, Ho Young, Margaret, Ellen, mother.

Euicho Chung, circa 1922.

When Euicho came from Korea with his parents, Korea was under Japan. And so he was considered as a Japanese citizen. For all those years that he went to school in Hawaii, he was classified as a Japanese because as I said Korea was under Japan and all children born in Korea during the Occupation and Annexation by Japan were automatically Japanese citizens.

After going to grade school in Hawaii, Euicho's parents wanted a better education for him, so he was sent to Iolani School, which was an Episcopal school. The principal of Iolani felt that this young Oriental boy had much potential. After graduating from Iolani High School, Euicho and his parents agreed that he should still further his education. Euicho went to Oregon University.

Euicho's father was Ho Young Chung 정호영. His younger brother, Choon Young Chung 준영, came from Korea also. I remember the first thing after Euicho introduced me to his father was that his father asked me what church I attended. I told him I attended the Korean Methodist Church. He didn't say anything, but apparently he must have been a part of that church, too. As far as I can remember, I don't think the family ever were members of Kuk Min Hur.

When I got married to Euicho, I automatically lost my American citizenship because of the law about marrying an alien, even though I was born here in Hawaii. And through the years after I married Euicho, I was registered as a Japanese citizen because the male spouse's citizenship determines the wife's citizenship according to the American law. Being a Japanese was sort of a handicap but still, it didn't make much difference to me. In spite of that, I decided to get married. I had to go to Kauai to get married because his parents were living there. His mother and father were very upset that he was getting married to me because he was a college graduate and I was just a high school graduate, so his parents kind of frowned on me. It was felt that he could have done better than marrying a girl not as well educated as he was. He got his master's degree in North Dakota, living with Norwegians up there. We got married on Kauai.

Why was it difficult to be classified as Japanese?

I think the difficulty was just between the Koreans and the Japanese, not the whole islands. We lived in a camp, a Korean camp. There were Okinawan camps, Filipino camps, Japanese camps. And somehow, as I remember, we were classified, when we were going to school, as Japanese. My parents did not like the idea, but we couldn't help it. And it went on and on like that until we finished high school.

About the time I was living in Hilo on the Big Island of Hawaii, my sisters in Honolulu wrote to me and said that my two sisters who were born in Korea were becoming naturalized Americans because of a new immigration law, the McCarran–Walter Act. I didn't know what naturalization was. My sisters explained that I needed to go to the U.S. Courthouse in Hilo to apply for American citizenship, called "naturalization." They said that it would be easier for me to apply where I lived. So I went to the U.S. Court in Hilo to be naturalized, feeling confident that all would be fine.

Something funny happened there in court. Because Hilo was a small town, everybody knew each other. Even "big people" and "little people" would go to the YWCA and play games like badminton and

Rev. Euicho Chung and Hazel Pahk Chung with their children Winchell, Eldene, and in front, Afton, circa 1932.

188

tennis and things like that. I had been playing badminton with Judge Frank McLaughlin. He was the big judge in the town of Hilo. Imagine, me playing with a judge at the badminton court nearly everyday. My sisters from Honolulu wrote to me and told me that I could be naturalized easier in Hilo because my name was already mentioned in their naturalization papers—all I had to do was go to the local courthouse in Hilo to be sworn in and sign the paper. So I went to the courthouse to be sworn in. When I got to the courthouse, I was told that I had to sit up on the witness chair. I went up and sat down. And of all things! The judge walked in the room and it was Judge Frank McLaughlin. So I said to myself, "This is going to be easy for me." But Judge McLaughlin pounded his gravel, "pong pong," and he said, "Stand up, Mrs. Chung. I didn't give you permission to sit down." I felt so embarrassed in the whole big courtroom of the United States of America. So I stood up straight. Then after he asked me questions, he told me I could sit down. I sat down and I said to myself, "Wait till I get him at the badminton court tonight."

So I was naturalized as a American citizen, which I insisted I always was. That was a funny, humiliating incident. I liked Judge McLaughlin very much, but I was ready to scold him that night at the badminton court. After I arrived at the YMCA, I leaned against the wall where I usually waited my turn. I had my arms crossed with my badminton racket in hand. Then Judge McLaughlin came by and he tapped me with his racket. I said, "Don't talk to me." The judge said to everybody out loud, "She had the audacity to sit down. I didn't give her permission to sit down." Everybody there all laughed. We were friends again.

My stay in Hilo was very, very nice. However, my husband was called by the Methodist Mission Administration to go to the Honolulu Methodist Church because they needed a young English-speaking minister. We were losing a lot of young people in the churches everywhere at that time. Our church, the Korean Methodist Church on Fort Street, was the largest in Hawaii.

Do you remember what year you went there?
I can't remember that far back. I know our kids were little. I have pictures of our children there when Rachel was about four years old in front of the church, sometime in 1934.

Tell me about the early relationship between the Methodist Church and Kuk Min Hur and the Korean Christian Church.

That was long before my time. However, I remember Dr. Rhee. He was head of his Korean Christian Church after he left the Korean Methodist Church in 1918, and his followers were there at his church on Liliha Street.

As kids, it seemed to us that the older people were so nationalistic. Mainly, in the beginning, they were against only the Japanese. When Dr. Rhee came here, it seems like he divided the Koreans. At that time he wanted all Koreans to go to his church, but my sisters felt that we should stay where we were, with the Methodist Church. Religion had nothing to do with being Korean or nationalistic things. A church is a church. So we stuck with the Methodist Church. But *Kydokyo* (Korean Christian Church), which is the other church on Liliha Street, I know it divided a lot of Korean families like my father-in-law's. He stayed with the Methodists, but some relatives became Korean Christian Church members. It's one of those political plus national and Christian things.

I remember so clearly when we were living on a plantation (this was after Rhee had become the president of the Korean Provisional Government), everybody began singing, "Dr. Rhee is leading the Koreans, leading the Koreans." And we began singing that, too. He is leading the Koreans because he was against the Japanese or something. We, as kids, didn't know what it was all about.

At Liliha Street, that's Dr. Rhee's church, and the other church, which was the Methodist Church, we had quite a bit of conflict, in the sense that we were told by Rhee's side that we were joining the "white people." I don't know what they had against the white people, but we were told if you wanted to be a Korean, you have to go to Rhee's church. And I still remember that on the plantations where I grew up, the whole group of Korean children would come and sing the same thing, "We're Koreans, we're Koreans," but we didn't know there was a separation of churches. We just stuck with the Methodists through that fight, right along. We weren't nationalistic. We were more Christians. The Korean Christian Church members worshiped Dr. Rhee as God. When we visited that church on Liliha Street, we noticed that they had a Korean flag instead of the Christian flag. We felt that we were Christians, not this Dr. Rhee thing. So that's the way that division stayed. Living on the plantation then you had two divisions: Dr. Rhee's on one side and the Koreans who stayed with the Methodists. According to the other side, the Methodists were the Americans. That's how much I remember about the division of the churches. Our family chose to stick with our church on Fort Street [the Methodist Church].

We had nothing against Dr. Rhee other than the fact that our parents felt that church should not be mixed with politics. Kuk Min Hur is the people against Dr. Rhee, but we were not politically inclined in that aspect either, but then it became that way when the politics came in with the mixture of churches. So that's how I stayed with the church and with my father and mother-in-law on Kauai, to this day.

But still, my mother and father had Dr. Rhee's picture up on the wall, you know. [This was because Rhee was elected President of the Korean Provisional Government (KOPGO) in Shanghai in 1919. His portrait was given to every Korean family in Hawaii. Out of respect for the Korean Independence Movement, Korean Methodists accepted the KOPOGO election.] They considered him an important man, but we didn't consider him as Christ, you know. And that's why we just went to the Methodist Church.

Tell us anything that you remember of other Korean leaders in the community when you were young. Do you know Pak Young Man?

Yes, he was the leader, the opposite leader against Dr. Rhee. He was impressive, but we were more interested in our own life and our own education. However, there is something I remember as a youngster on Ewa Plantation about Pak Young Man. I remember the Korean men who followed him carrying some wooden things on their shoulders like it was a gun. And before that some young men would come to our Korean camp to meet there, and then they would shout "Mansei, mansei 만세, 만세," and being kids, we wouldn't know what was going on. Pretty soon, they would have drills with the wooden guns, going back and forth on the main streets. What was happening? As kids, we didn't know. It seemed like they were going to invade Korea or whatever. We didn't know what it was. We didn't know what was Kuk Min Hur or what was Dongji Hoi.

191

Let's talk about your family members.

When my sister Nora became the first Korean graduate of the prestigious Normal School of Education, where one is trained to be a teacher, they assigned her to the island of Kauai as a teacher in the public school. They didn't have to go to college for a degree. When she was assigned to the island of Kauai, my father said you cannot go alone; you have to take one of the younger sisters to live with you. Later on, Nora was told that because she was born in Korea and therefore an alien, she could not teach in public schools. This was way before the McCarran–Walter Naturalization Act was passed. So Nora went back to the Normal School to become a nurse. She was the first Korean nursing supervisor in Hawaii.

My father and mother were one of the few people who came as husband and wife with children. The plantation didn't know what to do with this wife and two children. They decided that the bachelors, the Korean bachelors in Ewa, had to have someone to cook for them. So my father and my mother became the cooks for the Korean camp at Ewa Plantation. I remember as a little child, we had to stretch our little arms out and get all the piles of wood for the burning stoves. One big wok was for making rice, another was for making soup. We always had soup. The other wok was to make a fast stir-fry of vegetables and things. So we had three big woks on that thing, and under the thing we had charcoal burning, wood burning, and at the end of the day all the laborers, the single laborers, would come and have dinner made by my father and mother.

Korean men who emigrated to Hawaii to work in the sugarcane fields were much older than the men from Okinawa or Japan. Ewa Plantation had segregated camps: Japanese camp, Korean camp, and Okinawa camp. But we didn't have any Filipinos in those very early days. Korean men would send their pictures, their young pictures of themselves, to Korea with somebody who was going back and forth to Korea. The women in Korea chose to marry men who would pay their way over to Hawaii. This is why there were many young, pretty girls who married old men. One of them was my uncle. Many women ran away and went to other camps. So that's how I suppose they began to have interracial marriages. But some women were very conscientious, and they stayed with the men with whom they were supposed to, who

Nora Pahk's graduation.

had paid their way over. They became very good housewives on Ewa Plantation, where a lot of Koreans were.

They built a long house for these Korean men, when the brides arrived in Hawaii, and I remember personally that lots of those pretty ladies were so young. Some would be crying all the time and always crying. They would have to cook on the wooden stoves and men would come after work and chop the wood. So my mother was like the mother superior to the young brides. Some of the young brides stayed, like the one with my uncle. His wife was very, very young, pretty, too. He started right away with a family. Those who stayed all did well, all educated their children, and they all did very well. That's just about what I remember of the picture brides other than the fact that the Methodist Church was packed with young brides.

It was nice because my father was already established. When we were kids, we were always doing what you call *shim burum*—errands, just doing this and doing that. I recall so plainly many things after my mother died. We were still very young: Stella was only four, Agnes was six, I was eight, and my brother was ten. We were all two years apart. Anyway, I remember that when my mother died, lots of these women friends would come to our house and even single, widowed ladies, whom we called "Ah Ju Ma"— "Auntie." They would come and give our father something to eat and say to us, "Give this to your father 아버지 드려라." And for some reason, we felt very suspicious, we wouldn't give it to our father to eat; we would eat it all up. And we

Susannah Wesley Home students, circa 1915.

would wash the plates and take it back to her, and the lady 아주끄니 would say, "Did you give it to your father 아버지 드렸니?" And we would say, "Yes 예" and we'd just run away. My father never knew who ever gave him anything. We ate it all up. This is what our oldest sister told us to do because we didn't want a stepmother. We younger ones didn't know why, but we just did what the older sisters told us. Those were incidents that are very, very vivid in my mind.

What do you know about the Korean Christian Institute, the girls' dormitory.
KCI? I don't know very much about that. I know that KCI was a very good thing for young Korean girls. As for the Methodist families, a lot of the Korean Methodist girls went to the Susannah Wesley Home, on Liliha Street. [It was the first boarding home and school for girls, started long before KCI began.] My sisters went to Susannah Wesley. There was a dividing line, I guess. It seems that at Susannah Wesley Home there wasn't any conflict of any kind at all.

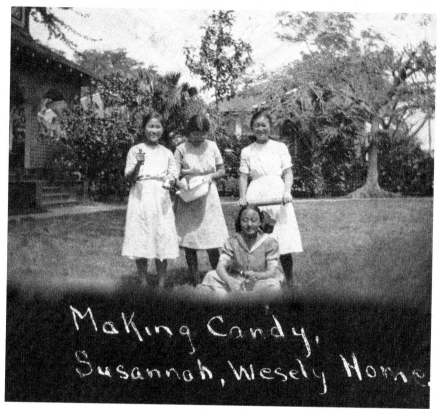

Susannah Wesley Home students, circa 1920.

What was Susannah Wesley all about?

Susannah Wesley was a Methodist place like an orphanage home. They used to accept young girls from all the plantations to live there and learn English, a trade or something, sewing, cooking, something like that. A lot of Koreans went there. John Wesley, the founder, was a Methodist preacher, so many Methodist people were at Susannah Wesley. When our older sisters went to Susannah Wesley from the plantation, they learned to sew, learned to cook, and learned all those domestic things. You could learn more in that atmosphere than you could at your own home. Today, Susannah Wesley is as a recreational center on Liliha Street.

15

Interview with Mary Kim Halm

My name is Mary Kim Halm. I was born in Korea and brought to Hawaii when I was six months old under an unusual circumstance.

Picture bride Choo Chei Lee longed to see her parents and left Hawaii with her firstborn, not knowing she was pregnant. Japanese passport for her and the children's return in 1921.

Upon arrival in Hawaii, I had to register for immigration papers although my parents lived in Hawaii when I was conceived. Upon receiving the citizenship certificate that was granted to me, the U.S. Immigration Bureau requested that we write down what we would like to be known as legally. So I omitted my Korean name and just used "Kim," which was my surname and "Halm," my married name.

My father's name was Si Ho Kim. He was a bachelor who arrived in Honolulu from Pyongyang in 1903, as was the case with most of the other Korean bachelors who immigrated to Hawaii about the same time. They were lonesome, living by themselves, so they wanted brides. From what I understand from my mother, the men

Marriage certificate of Si Ho Kim and Choo Chei Lee, 1917.

sent pictures of themselves to the women in Korea. They appeared quite young in their pictures, younger than what they actually were in age. Their pictures were disseminated in the village where they lived. Her parents granted their permission to accept Si Ho Kim's proposal for their daughter as a picture bride.

My mother's name was Choo Chei Lee. She arrived in Honolulu in 1917. I think she was in her teen years. She met my dad at the pier, and of course, she was a little disappointed because he didn't appear like his picture. He was a little older in years. But they were married anyway, and they went to live in Wahiawa, Oahu. Before she arrived, he was working in the sugar fields and lived on the plantation as far as I know. I can recollect my mother saying that. Later he left the sugar plantation and moved to Wahiawa, which was near the pineapple fields where he worked. While there, she said, he was injured one day by the spikes of a pineapple leaf near his eye. Sugar and pineapple fields make for very different kinds of work.

My mother was very lonesome when she first came. She eventually became pregnant with my sister Martha. Martha was born in 1918. Her Korean name is Guiyeom, which means "loving and adorable." My mother was so busy raising my sister. My mother also worked. I think she helped working on the plantation for a while. She didn't write to her parents in Korea for two years. Her parents were quite worried, wondering what happened to her, whether she was alive or dead. They wrote to her one day and when she received the letter, she was so sad and so shocked. They thought that she was not alive. So, in spite of her financial condition, she somehow scraped together enough money to return to Korea to visit her parents. She didn't know she was pregnant with me before she left. My older sister, who was three years old, went with her.

My father remained here in Hawaii when she went to Korea. When she arrived there, she discovered that she was pregnant. She stayed with my grandparents until she was about six months pregnant, then she tried to return to Hawaii. When she got to Japan, she went through customs, but they wouldn't let her go on the ship fearing that something would happen on the ship with her pregnancy. She was sent back to my grandparents' home in Pusan, Korea. There, she gave birth to me; therefore my name is Oesu, meaning "Whai Kut Jip," meaning the home of the mother's parents. My mother stayed there until I was old enough to travel, which was about six months or so. She brought my sister and me back to Hawaii, and according to what she told me, there were a lot of other

Three sisters; left to right: Pil Duk Lee, Choo Chei Lee, Young Soon Lee.

picture brides on the ship coming back with her. They helped take care of my sister because she was about three years old, running all over the ship. They had to help take care of her.

When she arrived at the port, she heard my father calling and calling me because he had learned of my name. He called all over the port until the ship landed. My parents were reunited. I forgot to mention that my mother said she was so lonesome living in Hawaii that she asked her parents to send her two younger sisters to live with her in Hawaii. So her two sisters were eventually sent here as picture brides also. When they arrived, they lived together near each other in neighboring places. I don't know what city or what town. It could have been Wahiawa.

How old were they when they arrived?
[Howard Halm, Mary's son, answers: "I think that my auntie, Young Soon Lee, was probably about seventeen years old. Her younger sister

was, maybe, fifteen years old or so."] I was born in 1921, so they came a little after that.

Please tell us the names of the two sisters, your aunts.
My middle aunt's name was Young Soon Lee. My younger aunt was Pil Duk Lee. They treasured their surnames. I guess most of the Korean women from Korea like to keep their surnames. My aunts used their surname, Lee, throughout their whole married life, until they died. I've never seen "Kim" used, but officially, they had to use "Mrs. Kim."

I don't recall too many things about the early years when I grew up. The earliest experience I remember was when we moved into the big city, Honolulu. At that time, I guess my dad had fulfilled his contract with the plantation and was able to move us to Honolulu.

Somehow, picture brides and other immigrants gathered in the area near St. Luke's Korean Mission. The church at that time was called "Mission." They all lived in cottages around the church. Therefore, we, the children of the immigrant women, became very good friends, like one big family. We all went to the church very religiously with our parents. My father really didn't go too often, but my mother did with her sisters. I recall going to Sunday morning services and Sunday evening services. Before St. Luke's Church was built, we went to St. Elizabeth's Church. I think I was about four years old when I was enrolled at St. Elizabeth's Preschool. It was a Chinese Congregational Church. But our St. Luke's Church, which was built later, was purely Korean. So we fitted in with each other after it was built. I recall being very frightened when I went to St. Elizabeth's Preschool because I was asked to recite the alphabet by the teacher. On the next day, we had to know how to write and read the alphabet. I was very nervous, so I didn't go to school. I asked another friend of mine to go to the park and pretend that we went to school. At that time, there was the Palama Settlement playground, where all the immigrant children went to play with the equipment. My friend and I were happily riding swings all day. And then my mother came and caught us, fetched us, and took us back home. Of course, I had a good spanking, and so I went straight to school the next day.

Somehow, I survived that year. When I was six years old, I was taken to Kalihi Elementary School, a government public school, which was in our neighborhood. I was given a test to enroll. The principal, I recall, was sitting on a chair at a desk. She asked me to read from a book. I read about four or five pages fluently. So they sent me straight to the third grade instead of the first grade. I was very frightened when I went to the third-grade class because they were sitting at desks, individual desks. I wondered why they were all putting their heads down on the desk. I thought that they were crying. Later I found out that it was rest period. I must have done well because from the third grade onward I was promoted and I graduated from high school at age sixteen.

Then I enrolled in nursing school. I thought that I wanted to become a nurse. It was at that time I met my husband. I was about eighteen-and-a-half years old. He was already finished with his dental school education. We dated for about half a year before he said he wanted to get married. I said, "No, I have to finish my education." He said, "Oh." We couldn't get married then because of the nursing school rules, which did not permit students to marry while they were still students. It's not like now. The nursing school rules have changed since then. After much thought, I decided to quit nursing school and we got married. Then my husband said, "Why don't you go to the University of Hawaii?" It was a good idea, so I did enrolled at the university in teacher education studies. We were married in 1940. Howard, my first child, was born in 1942.

On December 7, 1941, World War II broke out. My husband was instantly called into the activated military reserves because he was already in the Reserved Officers Contingent at the University of Southern California, where he had attended dental school on a scholarship for the military reserves. And from then on, he was in the military services until the end of World War II, in 1945. In the meantime, my daughter was born two years later. Then, when my husband returned from the war, he started a private dental practice. He always wanted to return to California to practice dentistry. He had taken his dental examination there and he passed it. He came back to Honolulu just to look around more or less, to make a final decision where to set up his practice. He thought of Honolulu because this is where he had grown up and lived for many years. While in Honolulu, he took the Hawaii dental examination and passed it. So we decided to stay and work at the dental clinic at Palama Settlement. But he always wanted to return to the Mainland, so he had to persuade me to return to California because I, being an island person, didn't want to leave. So he took us on a vacation trip in 1956 to the Mainland. We enjoyed it very much. The next year, in 1957, we moved to California. Howard, our son, was close to fifteen years old at that time.

Tell us what happened to your sister and your aunts. When and whom did your two aunts marry?

They married "picture husbands," men who had sent their pictures to my aunties, just like my mother and father. When they chose their husbands and moved to Hawaii, we all lived near each other, and they were very close, like real good friends throughout their whole lives. My mom died first, then my youngest aunt, and then Aunt Young Soon Lee.

What were their names? Do you recall?

Pil Goo Low was Aunt Young Soon Lee's husband. I think it's Sang Ho Kim for my other aunt. I don't really recall. I think the tombstone will tell us.

Lee Donohue next to his mother, Pil Duk Lee, and his aunts Choo Chei Lee and Young Soon Lee.

Were these two men also among the first immigrants who came to Hawaii before 1905?

They must have come before 1905 because they were old enough. I think most of the age differences were about twenty years between the men and their brides. The men would be forty years old and the women, twenty years old. Then, as they grew older, the men died first, resulting in a lot of Korean widows.

Do you know where they lived? Did they live near you?

We were always living close to each other—not in one house together—but always different houses in the same area. So we cousins were like one family.

I see. So then those two uncles' and aunts' families were already settled in Honolulu by the time you were growing up?

Yes, my Aunt Young Soon Lee had one daughter, Naomi, and Pil Duk Lee had four children: Bessie, John, Gracie and Kerry. Then her husband passed on and she married Alva Donohue and had one son, Lee Donohue.

Lee Donohue was Chief of Police of Honolulu, 1998–2004.

Tell me about the ages of your parents and what province they came from.

My father came from Pyongyang and my mother came from Pusan. And her sisters came from Pusan also. Where the other men came from, I don't know.

Exactly how old do you think was your father when they married?

He must have been close to forty. Maybe thirty-eight. And she was about like seventeen, eighteen, I think.

Tell me a little bit about growing up. You said you were pretty active at St. Luke's Church when you were young. How long and until what age do you think you were active?

I was active until I left the islands to live on the Mainland. I didn't go to St. Luke's Episcopal Church in Honolulu all the time because when we married, we moved to the other side of the island, Kailua, and went to the Episcopal church there. We've been Episcopalians ever since. And so were my husband and his parents.

Let's talk about Korean school.

My mother enrolled me, in spite of the hardships, at an American-language school in the third grade, at age six. My mother sent us to Korean-language school also, saying we must learn her language. So all the neighborhood Korean children attended the Korean language school. And I was about seven years old. I think I went there until I was in the eighth grade. I learned a lot of Korean history and Korean geography at that school. I must have excelled because I got perfect A's on my report card. My mother was real proud of me. But it was a lot of rote memory type of thinking. The children came not only from the neighborhood, but from other areas also. They walked to school from far places. Then there was a choir at the church that came from the language school. A lot of activities emanated from this language school group. I have pictures of the group taken at the language school.

Tell me about outstanding Korean leaders of that time.

Well, I can't recall. I've heard only Dr. Rhee's name often. My father-in-law was very active. He was always sending money to Korea or whatever organization for the Korean Independence Movement.

So he was a supporter of Dr. Syngman Rhee?

No, I don't think so. He was a supporter of the Korean Independence Movement, not of Dr. Rhee. It was another faction. I can't recall the factions.

There's Kuk Min Hur.

Yes, and what other faction?

Dongji Hoi.

Kuk Min Hur. That must be the one. That's the one that my aunts were very active in it, especially my Aunt Young Soon Lee Rho, who was one of the officers in that club. As far as Korean politics, I was not interested. So I didn't keep track. My father, as I recall, was not interested in Korean politics also. He was a well-educated man in Korea. He loved to read. All I remember is that during his spare time he was reading Korean books. My mother actively participated in Kuk Min Hur with her sisters. But my father-in-law was the one who was more actively involved with financial support and activities of Kuk Min Hur. He didn't talk much about it though.

Let's talk about the country-side Koreans and the town-side Koreans.

What about them?

About how difficult was it to know town Koreans and country Koreans and vice versa?

I don't recall any difference.

So you were not aware of what was going on in the community then? Did you join any Korean organizations?

Not when I was a teenager. After I married, we belonged to the Korean University Club and the Delta Frat Club, two social organizations. When I was a teenager, I was more involved in the Girl Reserves; Miss Ha Soo Whang was the counselor and advisor. She came to our elementary school after school and gathered us up and took us to the park. When we had our meetings, she brought desserts and refreshments. We enjoyed ourselves. I always considered her as a real much older person. Another incident I recall was when Miss Whang recruited me as a six-year-old into the Korean Dance Group. She came and asked my mother if I could join. So I had to practice and practice, I think, once a week. I learned how to dance Korean dances. And when we had performances, I recall my mother really giving me a good bath and cutting my hair and putting on my Korean dress before going there. I don't know who we danced for. That's the big cultural thing that I was involved in because Miss Whang wanted me to be in it.

It was such a long time ago. I would say I was only six years old then or maybe about seven years old.

Did Whang Ha Soo teach you herself?

No. It was another woman. Miss Whang's nieces were in it. Mary Whang [married name Choy] was in my class. I think Mary was a few years older than I was. I think I was one of the younger ones. I recall going through emotions while dancing.

Talk about your mother's theatrical productions.

I recall, vaguely, going to see my mother's productions, and I recall the ladies ... they all said that they came from the same province in Korea, so they were very close knitted. They dressed up in costumes. They gave benefit shows. My youngest aunt, Mrs. Low, was very active in it.

What about Moksa Pyong Yo Cho, the leader of the Korean St. Luke's Church?

Pyong Yo Cho was Jackie Young's grandfather. I don't recall too much, but I know that he sometimes substituted at St. Luke's Church, when Rev. Noah Cho went to Korea on trips to visit his family. Rev. Cho's family lived in Korea, so once in awhile, he went to visit his family. His father died in Korea. Pyong Yo Cho took his place in church when Rev. Cho went to Korea.

Do you recall if there was any intermingling between the youngsters from the different churches?

As I recall, there were the Korean Methodists and there were the Korean Christians. We were the "St. Luke's Episcopal Koreans." The church group youngsters never saw each other socially except at the public schools. Even then, we weren't close. We really didn't know each other. I think the other churches had their own Korean-language schools. So we mingled within our own group of friends in the neighborhood and with the children that went to our church and the same language school.

Were you aware of any kind of clash in the Korean community?

Well, I would hear once in a while that they had clashes in the Korean Christian Church because they were trying to have the minister leave or whatever. But our church focused a lot on religion. We didn't have social problems like the Korean Christian Church congregation, as far as I can understand. The Methodists, some of them were my high school friends. But we really didn't socialize that closely.

What high school did you go to?

I went to McKinley High School. The Korean students were an entity by themselves but were separated from each other because they went to different churches. And more or less, they did not focus on their religion when at school. But the Korean Christian Church students were kind of focused on Dr. Rhee and Dr. Rhee's politics.

Anything else you remember about Dr. Rhee and his wife?

All I can remember is that they stayed at our good friend Wilbert Choi's house. Wilbert Choi took care of Rhee, when he was ill and when he ended his presidency.

How did you become a friend of Wilbert Choi?

We became friends at Delta Frat Club.

Did you belong to the Delta Frat?

Yes. I was an officer of the Korean Delta Frat Club at one point. We just went there to enjoy ourselves. Frat Club was mainly a social club for young adults, second-generation Korean Americans who already graduated from high school. We met once a month at different homes. We had dinner after the social meetings, and we played mahjong and poker and bridge and whatever. It was a social club with a short business meeting. It was unlike the Korean University Club, which gave out yearly scholarships for deserving students to attend the university.

Tell us a little bit more about the Korean University Club (KUC).

The Korean University Club, as far as I can remember, the members had to be university graduates except for associate members, who didn't graduate from the university but were the spouses of members. At this present time, I understand, the membership has changed.

A lot of the members are now newly arrived Korean immigrants from Korea but still highly educated. The purpose of the KUC is the same: to raise funds for higher education scholarships for young Koreans.

In the old days, aside from raising funds for scholarships, what kind of activities did you do with the Korean University Club?
More or less like Delta Frat Club, it was a social group except the KUC members were university graduates with professional occupations. At the KUC meetings we talked about scholarships and the usual procedures about money in the treasury, then minutes of the past meeting, and so forth. We had an elaborate inaugural banquet once a year at one of the hotel ballrooms.

Was your husband a member of the Korean University Club also? Was he active in it?
Yes. Mostly he loved to go and play cards there. With all the men, they stayed and enjoyed themselves, playing cards. So, after the formal meeting broke up, they'd just go in groups to do their own thing. It was a club that focused on scholarships for deserving Korean students.

16

Interview with Dorothy Kim Rudie

My name is Dorothy Kim Rudie. My Korean name is Bomsik Kim. I'm the third child and third daughter of the family. My father's name was Kim Kyung Pok. I believe he came from Kangwha, Korea, and arrived in Hawaii in December of 1901.

It so happened that when the book *In My Footsteps* was being published, there was an article in the *Sunday Star-Bulletin* newspaper about the book. My husband went to the bookstore to purchase that book. It was then that we found out that the Koreans in Hawaii were celebrating the hundredth anniversary of their arrival in Hawaii in 1903. I was stunned to see that they had no information about the few men that came to Hawaii in 1901. I have a document saying that my father had come to Hawaii in 1901.

So we quickly went to the Hawaiian archives to try to check the manifest of the ship that he told us he came on. There was no mention of him or the passenger list. I believe that he came over in 1901 as a worker on board ship because he was a sailor when he lived in Korea. He left his family because he was orphaned at an early age and lived with his aunt. I don't know in what village in Korea, but they had chestnut farms because he told us that they had chestnuts at home. Then he ran away from his aunt and went to sea. He knew a great deal about the sea because Kanghwa is an island. Then, from there, he came to Hawaii, passing through Yokohama, I believe.

At that time, there were no Koreans here in Hawaii, so he gravitated to the Chinese community. I found among his personal possessions red squares with gold lettering on them. I asked him what was that gold lettering? He said

Kyung Pok and Aki Kim family; left to right: Daisy, Kyung Pok, Dorothy (Rudie), Andrew, Aki, Rose, circa 1928. After Kyung Pok Kim, a seaman, jumped ship from the SS *Mongolia* in 1902, he remained in Hawaii. He continued working as a seaman on interisland ships. He married a seventeen-year-old Korean picture bride at the age of thirty-five in 1913.

he belonged to a Chinese *tong,* which is an organization like a *hoi* for Koreans. He joined that group because there were no Koreans here to form a group. He naturally gravitated to the Chinese while he still continued working for steamship lines here in Hawaii, going to other islands along the Hawaiian chain of islands. The last company that he worked for was the Inter-Island Steamship Lines Company as a fireman.

My father retired from sailing and worked in the rice fields with the Chinese people. I remember my father's friends, whom we called "Paki" [Chinese grandfathers] because when my father had a rice plantation in Kaneohe, I was born on that rice plantation among his closest friends, who were all Chinese. He worked with Chinese workmen there, cultivating the rice fields. When he gave up rice field work, he and a lot of Chinese bachelors then went to the Kapahulu area and had truck farms. So we would go on a three-day break to Kapahulu to see our Paki grandfathers. They would kill a chicken and cook it with peanuts, which was strange to us. It was the first time we ate peanuts with meat. Then they would take us to the corner grocery store to buy us animal crackers, so that was a nice outing for us. There were also younger Chinese bachelors whom we considered our uncles.

After some time in Hawaii and after other shiploads of Koreans came, my father wanted to find a Korean bride. By then, there were more Koreans coming to Hawaii who were bachelors like him. He got to know the new arrivals, and they all talked about getting Korean brides. The Methodist Church helped such an arrangement, but there were not enough Korean women in Hawaii. Then the church and friends helped the men arrange picture brides from Korea. My father finally found a young picture bride willing to marry him.

My mother came from the Pusan–Masan area in 1913. In those days, it was a tragedy because many of the girls were only in their late teens. Their husbands sent pictures of themselves when they were young and not as they were then. So when my mother got off the ship, she said she was very afraid. When she found the man that she was supposed to marry, she was very pleased because he was only twice her age, not like the other couples. Twice the age still seems rather strange to us, but my mother said he was so handsome and did not look too old. We giggled and laughed to hear our parents talk that way about when they first met, married, and had children. The first three children were girls, not too happy for Korean families. They were married on the same day that she got off the ship because there was no way that she could stay unless they married immediately.

What year was that?

That was 1913, I believe. I gave you a document pertaining to that. We three girls, the first three children, used to question my mother about the past while our father was away at sea. He would be gone for two weeks at a time. When he was on his free time, he would throw great big hooks over the ship and catch fish. Big fish. So big that it took two men to bring it home. When we were children, we didn't realize what a luxury that was to have such delicious fish. All we'd say when fish was served was, "Uh, fish again." We didn't realize that it was a luxury. Even our neighbors all loved it, when our father went fishing, because everybody shared in the fish. Now that I am older, I have to pay $20 a pound for fish. That was quite a free feast at that time.

As a whole, we knew and saw very little of our father because he was gone to sea most of the time. A few times when he came home from a trip, he wanted to see us right away because he missed us so much, but sometimes school was in session. A couple of times, he would come to the school directly from the ship with a switch in his hand and ask the teachers to let us out of the school. He would tell the teachers that he must see us so that he could discipline us about something. My older sister, who was a very obedient girl, would go with my father regardless of what she saw—that switch, thinking that she's going to get spanked. She would go with him anyway. But I would refuse to go with him because I did not want to get spanked for something that I didn't do. So I wouldn't go with him. Then, after school, when I went home, my sister would tell me, "Oh, you should've gone with me because we went into town, and Papa bought me lunch . . . he bought me this and that. He didn't spank me. He just wanted our company because he missed us children while he was away overseas." He would pull pranks like that on us many times.

Other times whenever he was in town for a long time, he enjoyed time with his closest friend who was a Hawaiian man, his drinking companion. He was used to being a very good friend of Hawaiian men because he was in Hawaii for two years when there were no Koreans around at that time. After 1903, when many Koreans came, he made new friends. After he married, he met more Koreans.

When my father died, I asked my mother how come he had one of the largest funerals I ever saw in Hawaii. It was so large that the service couldn't be held at our normal-size church, at St. Luke's. It had to be held at St. Elizabeth's Church, which was very large. Mother said that he was well liked because every man in that church owed my father money. I couldn't understand how they owed him money when we were so poor. We couldn't possibly lend them money. Later on I realized what she meant. The Korean men owed him because he had helped them get settled in Hawaii since he was here earlier than thousands of Koreans who arrived in the next four years. He would give them things and help them understand their new environment.

My father was able to die happily because there were Korean immigrants around him. He was only twenty-five years old when he first came here. He was on his own for many years during the prime of his life, when he traveled as a sailor on foreign ships before he first came to Hawaii. So he was able to guide these people around in Hawaii. That's why people remembered how he helped them and why he had such a big funeral. That's why, in mother's way of thinking, everybody owed him money. But it was more than that; he was well liked.

211

After he and my mother married, the first three children were girls. My father was very disappointed. When my mother had come to Hawaii as a very young picture bride, the men were much older than the women. I asked my mother how come so many of their contemporaries were divorced. She said you must realize that these were arranged marriages. Then, after two years of living in Hawaii, the woman knew their way around in Hawaii. There was a shortage of women. So some divorced their older husbands and married younger men. She told us life in Korea was very different from life in Hawaii. My father was more Americanized by the time the other men came. From 1901 to 1913 he lived as a bachelor in Hawaii. Things that he expected of my mother were contrary to what she had been brought up with, such as when they sat down to table to eat in Korea, the men would be served first. But my father insisted that she eat at the table with him. She was embarrassed at first. She would take a bowl of rice and then hold it in one hand and get the *panchan* 반찬 to put it in the rice bowl. She would immediately turn her back to him and then eat her dinner that way. He made her change her ways to be modern.

We would tease her about having only girls born to her . . . we'd tell her teasingly that we wanted more sisters. We also wanted to hear more about her life in Korea. We'd giggle and roll on the floor laughing when she would tell us about these strange customs in Korea. We told her that we wouldn't be shy eating with men, especially husbands. We would sit there and eat with them. Then she told us that while it may be strange to us, we must realize that she was brought up in the old way and not the new way and that our father was Americanized before 6,000 Korean immigrant men came to America with the old way of life.

Our father went to sea and left her in Kaneohe with the Chinese farmers for two weeks at a time. She was still shy when she saw him after a long trip coming up the road over the mountains—in those days they didn't have a good road, they only had a kind of trail, going up the mountain. She'd get flushed and excited, seeing him coming home. She got embarrassed looking flushed so she'd run to the neighbor's house. She didn't want to face him because she knew what was going to happen . . . that he would want to sleep with her immediately or something like that. He would go home, and she wouldn't be there.

So he would go to the neighbor's house and out in the yard he would call out in Korean, "Send my wife home." Of course, she would have to go home. She was still young and embarrassed.

Then we asked her about what her life was like when she first came, before we were born, and she said that when she was pregnant with me she had a craving for mangoes. You would find her sitting under a mango tree, eating mangoes like crazy. That discussion about pregnancy led to talk about sex because we asked her how come . . . if he lived in Hawaii for twelve years before you came, how come we don't have any half-Hawaiian brothers or sisters like other Korean men had before their picture brides came. She scolded us; we shouldn't be talking like that. We laughed and kept asking her what happened when she was pregnant and couldn't take care of him. She said that she sent for a maid. "He was a good man, and I couldn't take care of him when I had so many babies. So I sent a maid." We began to realize that their culture was so different from the one in which we were brought up. Mother said that while she was pregnant with me, my father felt sure that I was going to be a boy. In preparation, he left a standing order with a butcher in Kaneohe, where there was a piggery, to send pig's feet to my mother. A boy needs to have pig's feet right away. We didn't know what kind of Korean custom it was.

Even though our parents were not educated people, they went to school in Hawaii and learned things that we'd learn in school. They had their basic common sense because they knew that when my mother was pregnant with me that she had to have good food and a certain kind of food if you expect to have a healthy child. So, when I was born, my father was very disappointed that I was girl—even though I was my mother's biggest and healthiest child. You must realize that he got married so that he could have sons. When my brother came after my birth, of course he was very pleased about that.

Mother told us that her mother said that if she left Korea, she may never see her alive. That came true because my grandmother passed away in the meantime. By the time my mother did go back to Korea to visit, she had been in Hawaii about ten years. The life span in the Orient was much shorter then what it is now. These things which we learned from our mother were contrary to the customs with which we were brought up. However, I will say this: Whatever we were taught

213

in school and came home and told my mother about, whether it was about health, or social science, or geography, she would question us about it to learn the new ways herself because certain subjects were not discussed back in Korea. Also she was trying to make sure that what we were learning was not something that would hurt Korean customs. We told her that we learned these things in school so it was all right. As long as we learned it in school, it was okay to discuss it.

When my father retired as a sailor-merchant marine, he became a landlord. He leased rooming houses. My sister and I would spend quite a bit of time with my father when we very young at the rooming houses, playing or helping him while he did the maintenance. I was about ten years old. We learned how to fill out receipts, how to pay taxes, where to go for the city water department, where to go to find the electric company—all of these things were taught to us by him. We would be his assistants because we could read and write English. We learned business at a very early age, and we learned how and who paid the rent and who didn't pay the rent.

He still kept his Chinese friends even though he had many Korean friends after they began arriving. But his very close bosom buddies were the Hawaiian men that he had known for so long. The name of one of them was Kealoha, his drinking companion, and then there was this Chinese man on Alapai Street, a part of Chinatown where the rooming house was. They had a lot of Chinese restaurants there. He used to eat or get his meals there near his rooming house when we were not with him because sometimes our mother made us stay home. Sometimes my father stayed at the rooming house overnight.

Just before my father retired, he decided that he would take my sister and me to see the ship that he was working on. He knew his plan was to retire soon, so he took us to the harbor. He was working at that time on the Inter-Island Steamship Line. We had to go down to the haul of the ship on a iron stepladder. We kept going down and down to the bottom of the ship and there were huge boilers that he had to use as gauges to feed oil in it. There were catwalks between the boilers. Nowadays, you would have to be a certified engineer to do that kind of the work, but in those days, if you could handle it, that was your job. Life then was different. They had captains who would have the first cup of coffee from the pot they brewed. The lower officers would have the second cup, and then the crew would have the third or fourth cup made from the same grounds. They had salt water showers for the men to cool off. He didn't work all the time because they worked only when they were going from island to island. Then on his day-off he would do some fishing—deep-sea fishing. They used great big hooks.

He told us once that he almost drowned because the men were on the deck gambling. Those that didn't gamble were standing around, watching them gamble. At one time when they were gambling, there was a brawl. My father just happened to be there, and they threw him off the ship. Life on the ship was different from life on shore, but he liked that. He worked at sea so long that we could recognize his footsteps, a sailor man's footsteps. He had that sailor's walk, bowlegged, you know, so we could recognize him anywhere from the noise of his bowlegged footsteps.

Tell me about the church. You said something about being an Episcopalian from way back. Could you tell us little bit more?
Well, I was told that a lot of the men came from Gangwha and they were Episcopalians because that is where the Episcopal missions were. The Episcopalians had a stronghold there in Gangwha. A lot of the other men came from around Seoul and Incheon. But they were Methodists, whereas the women came from the far southern part of Korea. We children went to churches we were told to go to by our parents.

So it was your father who seemed to have influenced the family to go to the Episcopal Church.
Yes. My father's choice was that we go to the Episcopal Church. In the other two churches there was a rivalry between them.

Which churches?
That was the Methodist Church and the other church on Liliha. And that church on Liliha Street was about four times bigger than our church. But, the thing is, the Episcopal church we belong to was part of St. Andrew's. We were a mission group of St. Andrew's Church, the main church for Episcopalians from which we received support. But as far as the Korean community was concerned, St. Luke's Church was our father's choice and where the whole congregation was Korean.

215

However, our mothers, the pictures brides, because most of them were brought up in the Methodist Church, it was their choice that the children be brought up in the Methodist Church. But we were brought up in my father's religion. So that's how come we were Episcopalian. But my father went to church only once a year. I couldn't understand that. We all had to go to church and observe all Sundays, holidays, and everything. But once a year, I remember on the first Sunday after New Year's, my father would wear a beautiful gray suit with his dressy shirt, which was silk. Then he'd go to church and the minister would be so glad to see him. And he'd be out there, visiting with him . . . that's when my father took care of all of the tithes and paid all the tuition that we owed the church for the Korean-language school. We didn't realize what my father's background was before he married. Later we found out that even though he went to the church only once a year, he was very much respected by the ministers for the many things he had done in the past.

Do you remember any leaders among the Episcopalians?

I forget. I was gone away so long from Hawaii. There were no Koreans in Minneapolis, where I lived. There was no contact at all after I married and left Hawaii. I forgot faces, people, and the language, and everything because there was nobody to talk to when I left Hawaii with my husband, who was Caucasian.

But you remember going to school . . .

I remember going to language school because my two sisters—they were older than I—the three of us went to Korean-language school. The two younger boys went sometimes. A year after my father died, my mother married a Filipino man. It was a common-law marriage because we children objected very much to a Filipino man for a father. We would have objected to any man that came to the household because we remembered our father. Nobody could step into his shoes. So we protested it, and so my mother made arrangements for the three of us to go to Korea. I, being the oldest who was supposed to have gone, had to memorize all the birth dates of the family, I had to memorize all the birthmarks that they had, just in case the documents were lost or stolen. That way I could prove that we were who we were.

But one week before we were going to sail off, I put my foot down. I said that I was not going. I absolutely refused to go. I refused because someone told me that if I went to Korea, my mother was going to arrange a marriage for me since I was fourteen years old and old enough to marry. She said that there were lots of Korean men—wealthy people who wanted their sons to come to Hawaii. Since there was a chance that I would be forced into a marriage and come back to Hawaii with a husband, I said that I absolutely would not go. And my mother knew from the time I was born that I was very stubborn. I was the worst child that she had. I was the most stubborn child. So I didn't go.

My two brothers went to Korea instead. They were there for two years during the Japanese Occupation. When they were ready to come home, my aunt in Korea took them to Japan, where they had to go first to return to Hawaii. She put them on a ship there to return to Hawaii. We were surprised to see them in Japanese schoolboy uniforms when they came back. Black caps and black cotton outfits. They completely forgot their English. Instead, the teachers in Korea wanted to be taught English by the boys. They taught their teachers what English they could, which was difficult because the boys were only about ten and eight years old. If I had been there, I would have been able to teach them a little bit more because I was in junior high at that time.

I learned from my brothers that their life in Korea wasn't so bad because they were American citizens. In that small town, my mother sent enough money so that they could buy their own bicycles in Korea. That was a luxury for them. Every now and then, she would send crates with sugar, delicacies for the children. My brother told me that there was a bully in that village. Remember, we were under the Japanese rule, and a police officer's son would try to intimidate my brothers. But they couldn't touch my brothers because my brothers were American citizens. So they got away with a lot. They had maids because I was told that the maids in Korea at that time would work for their meals and one suit of new clothing a year. That's how poor the country was. When they came back to Hawaii, they got into the habit of "Get me a glass of water" or "Do this for me" and "Do that for me." I'd look at them, as an older sister, and I'd say, "Remember, you are in Hawaii. You want those things, you get it yourself. You are not in Korea anymore." My mother laughed.

There was a woman living in our neighborhood. She was a picture bride and she had a son about my brother's age. They would fight like children always fight, they play and fight. Then the mother of the neighborhood boy would come out of the house and scold my brothers in Korean for fighting with her son. Since my brothers were fluent in Korean at that time, they could talk back to her in Korean—word for word. My mother, inside the house behind the door, just laughed because she knew that the woman was stunned that my brothers could match her word for word in Korean. As time went by, however, my brothers lost a bit of the Korean language, after they have been back for a while. They were in Korea for two years. It was only because of the Japanese Occupation in Korea that my mother had them come back to Hawaii. Years later, one of my brothers remembered some of the cousins who were their playmates when he returned to Korea after the Korean War. My brother said that he went back to check on the family tomb to see whether it was properly cared for.

You mentioned before that one of your brothers was just about a year old when your mother took him to Korea. Tell us that story.

That must have been about 1924, 1925 when my brother Yongsik, the second boy, was about six or nine months old. My mother took him to Korea. She stayed there quite a long time I think, anyway between six and nine months. When she returned to Hawaii, the immigration officer thought that she was bringing in another child, one that had been born in Korea and not a child who had been born in Hawaii. So she was detained at the immigration station. To see her, we had to go to the immigration station because they would not let her out. Minister Father Cho of the Episcopal Church busily got proper documents saying that the child had been born in Hawaii. It took about a month before she was released from confinement. My brother—he is now seventy-four—does not know that he was confined in the immigration station for that period of time. That's how strict they were about the immigrants coming to Hawaii under unsure passages.

Tell us more about your mother and her relatives in Korea.

Her name was Kim Ok Hee. She was sometimes called Soon-hee.

My sister took her name, Soon Hee. But on her legal documents and everything else she was always Ok Hee. She came from the Pusan-Masan area. The last time I was in Korea, the road between Pusan and Masan was being built. There was heavy construction going on because the 1988 Olympics was going on. I had relatives from that area visit me in the hotel when we were there in 1985. One girl cousin and one of my boy cousins came to visit us in the hotel. So I still have relatives in that area.

When you were growing up, your mother tried to match-marry you? Tell us more about that.

There were Korean families who wanted to immigrate to Hawaii because the Japanese were closing the doors for Korean immigration. They were wealthy families willing to pay the family in Hawaii money if they let the children marry. If I married a boy in Korea, then I could bring him over to Hawaii because he would be my husband. Even in 1983, when I went to Korea on a tour, one of the tour members in my group, who was a divorced Korean girl, was approached by the tour guide to introduce her to a man who offered $11,000 to marry her so that he could come to Hawaii with her as her husband. She told me about it, and she asked me, "Should I do it?" She said it was very tempting for her to do that. The plan was that after he spent a year with her in Hawaii, they could get a divorce. I told her if she accepted the plan and if the authorities found out it was a false marriage, it would be her, not him, who went to prison because he did not know the American laws. You know the American laws, that this is a fraud. I said that she had to weigh the fact that she may go to jail. So she chose not to do it. There were lots of such cases in Hawaii and in the west coast of the Mainland.

Tell me just a little bit about the Episcopalian Korean-language school. Was there a big group of children your age? What year were you born?

I was born in 1920. There was a language school at St. Luke's. They took the children when they were school age. We would go to public school first. Then at 2:30 or 3:00 o'clock we would be dismissed and go home to get a bite to eat. Then we changed into Korean uniforms. Black skirt and white blouse. Later they modified it and it had a button for us so that we, as children, could button the blouse to make it easy for us to play. They put us according to our age group. We learned reading, writing, and Korean history. That was up to about eighth grade.

What public school did you go to?
We went to a public school in the Palama area, Kaiulani School. It still exists today. It's across the street from Kamakapili Church. St. Luke's was on Banyan and Kanoa Streets. My mother's last home was on Banyan Street. We were in that area. I remember that Father Cho would be upset with us because we had explicit instructions not to go to school through the the parish house yard of Kamakapili Church. He had plum trees in his yard and we were told not to pick the fruits. When we came back to the classroom, we all had to stick out our tongues. If we had purple tongues, we got scolding. Picking and eating the plums was the only way we could have gotten our tongues purple. He had a right to scold us. You know how children are.

Where did all your friends come from? Did you have any friends from the Korean Christian Church and the Methodist Church?
Yes, we had friends from the other churches because we all went to the same public school. The Korean community was very small. Even our parents knew the other parents, although they belonged to different churches. Particularly, the women knew each other well because they were all picture brides mainly from the southern areas of Korea; they had something in common. Others came from the Seoul area. They would get together every now and then. During the New Year's holidays, they would make *juk* and *muk*, with the green beans and stuff. Also they would make different kinds of *yakbab*. Even though they could cook those things by themselves at home, they got together at the church or clubhouse and made those Korean goodies together. I remember as a child eating some of those foods. These women all knew how to prepare them. By that time, we children were all old enough to understand how to make them ourselves. At that time, they had been in Hawaii about eight years or ten, so they still cooked the things that they cooked in Korea. Our diet was more Southern Korea than Northern Korea.

220

Tell us about your marriage.

Oh, my marriage . . . My mother didn't want me to marry a Japanese. We young girls were old fashioned enough that before we got married, our fiancé had to ask our parents' permission, particularly our mother's to get married because my mother was the head of the household even though we had a stepfather. We had to get permission from her because my sisters wanted to get married pretty young. Rose got married at age eighteen and I think Daisy got married at either nineteen or twenty, and I got married at age nineteen. During those days the legal age to get married without parents' consent was twenty-one or over. We had to get our parents' consent because we were under twenty-one. My husband and I had to talk to my mother about it. I told him that before I married him or even went out with him, I had to know what his intentions were. I only started dating my husband after we were engaged because I wasn't going to trust a haole [Caucasian]. So he told me his intentions, and then he went to ask my mother. My poor mother did not know who I was dating. She didn't know if I ever went out with him. He bravely went and asked my mother for my hand. My mother gave her consent. At first I was afraid because everyone said it wouldn't work out, being a mixed marriage. We were more determined that it would work out. We were mature enough to make it.

My husband was a volunteer on December 7, 1941, the day of the Pearl Harbor attack. Every military person answered the emergency call, including him. I did not see him for three days. My daughter was at Children's Hospital because she was exposed to my niece, who suddenly died from an unknown cause a few days earlier. Nowadays, we call it SIDS, Sudden Infant Death Syndrome. We didn't know what my niece had died of. It was a precaution to put my daughter in the hospital to be under observation because they had played together closely.

When December 7 came, our first thought was to get her out of the hospital to be with me. It so happened that it was a Sunday. The previous Saturday I had done my weekly grocery shopping, so I had plenty of food at home. We got our daughter home quickly. Then my husband left to do volunteer work at the military barracks. He knew the Pearl Harbor area well because he had served in the military during the 1930s. He liked Hawaii so much that when he was discharged, he came back to Hawaii as civilian. He became our neighbor; that's how come I met him. He drove an ambulance and evacuated the wounded at Pearl Harbor. What he saw that day, he tried to block out in his memory. He began to have amnesia. It was decided to evacuate us away from Hawaii, so we went to Minneapolis, to the Mayo Clinic, which is in Minnesota. Before we left Hawaii, he was told that he should go to Minneapolis because his mother lived there. That was the best place for him, the doctor told him. But he wouldn't go without me. His mother came to get him and me. We were evacuated in 1942. We came back to Hawaii after a few years. Then we returned to Minnesota permanently in 1965.

I had a very good life in Minneapolis, but there were hardly any Asians there. People there thought I was Chinese, Filipino, Indian, everything else. They didn't know what a Korean was. Nobody knew what a Korean was until the Korean War. They even didn't know a nation like that existed.

My social life in Minneapolis was very good because my husband belonged to the Masons and he belonged to the Shriners. There, we belonged also to St. Lutheran Church, which is the largest Lutheran church in the United States. I sang in the church choir. We had about five different church choirs. As a senior choir member, I was the only dark-haired woman in the whole choir. Anybody can spot me in the big church. Also I stood out when we went to my husband's Shriners parties. We belonged to various organization within the Shriners. People knew us because we were the only odd couple, mixed couple. They were very nice people. They were curious and asked us how we met and all of that. Everybody knew us even though the membership was huge. Even though I could not remember all of them, they remembered me everywhere. I entertained them at my home; we had many private parties at our home.

I worked at the Dayton's Department Store in the sales section, where we did all the billing. Eventually, we computerized the data. I was well respected because I learned it quickly. My co-workers at the office came over to my home often because I had a "rickshaw" [Oriental decorated] home. They came there for skating parties, New Year's parties, and things like that. So I had a very good social life there in Minneapolis. It seems that the more educated people are, the more tolerant they are. The Shriners were very tolerant toward non-Caucasians. There were a few isolated cases, when people were not friendly. Those people were more curious than rude. I did not have a problem with that there.

Once you told me that you liked being different.

Yes, no way can a person like me can hide the fact that I am an Oriental. Most of them thought I was Japanese.

When we went back to Minneapolis, we were on a troopship that was converted into a hospital ship. We were supposed to land at Los Angeles, but Japanese submarines were attacking the coast of California. This was in October 1942. Our ship, then, was diverted down to the Gulf of Mexico. We went hugging the coastline and landed in San Diego. San Diego was not prepared for us because we were supposed to land in Los Angeles. When we came into the harbor, all of us were so happy to be getting off the ship. Then we saw on the skyline, anti-aircraft balloons with cables hanging down. They had submarine nets to entangle the submarines if they came in close. All of us went on the shore side. The ship tilted. Then the captain got on the speaker to tell everybody to go back to the state room. When we landed, the Red Cross helped us leave San Diego. We had to take a train cross-country until we reached Minneapolis.

Whenever we went home to Hawaii, I would have Chinese and Korean dresses made, then take them back to Minneapolis. I would wear them to Shriner parties and other functions. My husband was very proud of me, wearing them because everybody knew he married an Oriental. People knew him and knew my name because we were an odd couple. He didn't mind that at all. I remember he encouraged me to wear my native costumes all the time. We went to parties at other homes or other places and I had no problems at social functions.

The first time I went back to Hawaii to visit, I met my mother's insurance agent, John Kim. Suddenly, I remembered him. I asked my mother, "Did he come from California?" She said, "Yes. When you all were children, you spent summers at his family home in Kaneohe." I remembered now his father told us that he and my father had decided that John and I were going to be married when we grew up. As American teenagers, we didn't even think of letting our parents arrange a marriage for us. But John and I got along very well for a while.

223

Then we started fighting like cats and dogs because we did not want to get involved in an arranged marriage. During that time Korean parents tried to arrange marriages. My mother arranged my older sister's marriage. In our family there were only two children among the seven who married Koreans. The rest of us were allowed to marry whomever we chose. My mother realized after the first arranged marriage that we were right, and that she should not interfere with our choices and we've been all successful. We all have been celebrating our fiftieth wedding anniversaries. Only the one who married a Korean through an arranged marriage did not.

What about your father being a good cook?

He could cook Chinese food. When my mother was sick, my father would take over the kitchen and we thought he was a better cook than my mother because he cooked elaborate Chinese food with lots of different vegetables and mushrooms, delicacies that he learned from the Chinese men. He knew his way around the kitchen very well because he had been a bachelor for a long time, until he was thirty-five years old. So he survived that very well.

By the way, those days when you were sick, you didn't go to the hospital. You went to the hospital only when you are dying. The life time of my mother and father was very different. Another example of being different, because I was brought up in their culture, was that when I got married to my husband, I used call him by his last name. My mother, too, used to call my father "Kim Si." My husband did not like that, my calling him "Rudie." He told me to call him what his mother called his father. So I asked, "What does your mother call you?" He said that his mother called him "Honey." So I called him "Honey." But when our daughter was just a toddler and she'd go around the house calling him, "Honey, honey," we decided that this can't be, so between my husband and me, we got to calling each other "Mommy" and "Daddy" because the child was picking up "Honey" when calling her father.

Another funny thing was that it struck me, when I came back to Hawaii for a visit, that my mother had to ask me what my name was. I was stunned to find out that she didn't even know what my name was. I was her third daughter and she had been calling me by that title, "third child" [in Korean *setjae dal*]. This revelation happened when her

224

friends came over to visit her while I was there in Hawaii for a visit. They had never seen me before. So they asked my mother in Korean, "Who is she?" My mother never mentioned my name, but she would say that I was "셋째딸, third daughter." I kidded her and asked her, "Is that my name after all these years?" I was "third daughter" to her. Even in 1947, when I visited her, she asked me what my real name was. I looked at her and I said, "You mean you still don't know my name?" I was still "third daughter"? I guess that is the way we were brought up, living in both cultures. I don't regret it. I think it was nice. And fun.

Tell me about your mother's second marriage. You said that he was a Filipino.

Well, he was a Filipino man. A widower. He had a wife who died in childbirth in the Philippines. He left his daughter with the grandparents and immigrated to Hawaii without relatives. My mother was only thirty-five years old when she became a widow. When they first met, he came over to help her, to do the laundry and to cook for the family. He began wooing her. This was a real love match. Circumstances were different. We children did not want a stepfather regardless who it was. It was only after we were married ourselves that we were willing to accept another man in our mother's life. My mother was ostracized by other Koreans because of marrying a Filipino. However, later on, their marriage made it easier for us children to marry outside of our race, too, because she did that. Strange, she didn't like the idea that we married outside of our race at first. But she knew what it was like, so she permitted us to do that. When she saw that we would better off with our own choice, she agreed that it was better that way.

Did you see any difference in people marrying a Caucasian or a Japanese? How did you feel about that?

Well, the first boy that I went with was Japanese. He was the youngest in the family. So that meant that I would have to cater to all his older brothers. His older brothers were already telling me what I should do, how I should dress, how I should laugh, and how I should behave. I wasn't even engaged, formally engaged to him. I resented that bitterly. Also my boyfriend and I could not announce our engagement or plans to get married until his older brother married. So I thought, all right, if he doesn't want to get married first and he has to wait until his brother gets married first, I won't wait. His brother was dating his girlfriend for seven years. I was not sticking around for seven years. So I married my husband.

What about your mother? Which do you think she preferred? Haole? Or Japanese?

She preferred a haole rather than a Japanese boy at that time. But my other sister Daisy, the second daughter, married a Japanese boy. Our mother was ostracized for marring a Filipino. So what can she say? It was bad enough that my mother married Filipino. Her first daughter was married to a Korean, which was an arranged marriage, but it did not last. If the third daughter, me, married a Japanese, too, my mother would have been in hot water in the Korean community because she was letting her children marry another Japanese: She would rather have me marry a haole. My mother did tell my haole husband before she died that he was a very good man. She thought that he was very nice compared to my older sister's second husband, who was haole. He had a very different personality than my husband. She did compliment my husband that he was a very good son–in–law.

So you left the Islands in 1942?

Going back and forth, I think I made seven trips.

And your mother made quite a number of visits to Korea?

Yes, she made about three trips. I know definitely three . . . maybe four trips. The last trip that she made was as an American citizen. She said that the last trip was wonderful because she was able to go to the museums and to the different places where the Korean artifacts were and visit palaces, too, which she couldn't visit during her previous trips because she was a Japanese citizen. Remember that the picture brides who came to Hawaii came during the Japanese Occupation of Korea. They all had to have a Japanese citizen passport. This was changed many years after Korea was free again.

My mother learned more about Korean culture during these trips after the war because before she left Korea for the first time, she was a farmer's daughter in a small village. Her father had a silversmith shop, working with metals. He and other families in that area had some education but not much. They were middle-class families in Korea. I could show you pictures of my present cousins. I met my two cousins in Seoul after the war. One was an assistant director of the Korean CIA and the other was a vice president of the Samsung Company.

Yes, I was very pleased to meet my extended family. There was some concern about our background because a lot of haole people married Oriental girls who came from the bars or from some poor background. The women wanted to go to the United States. My cousin said that it wasn't the case with us. When he met my family, he realized that we came from a good background, too, as good or better than his own background. My husband's families . . . his background is very good, too. We got banking officials, we got sheriffs, we got everything in the family. But what surprised me the most was to find that a lot of our lost relatives in Korea, the men, they were in the civil services. My family in Hawaii, the majority . . . nearly all of us are in some form of civil service job also. So how is it that two families—thousands of miles apart, who have not been in contact for many years because of the wars—have the same likes and dislikes and that we are all in civil service? We're both sides in business and in civil service work.

Do you remember anything about involvement in the Independence Movement?

No. All I know is that my mother did send donation money, now and then. I would say that the church on Liliha Street, they were more active. Ours was more on the religious side. We didn't get involved in politics very much, but I know about some of the politics because, being such a small Korean community, we knew each other. The children all knew each other even though we belonged to different churches and different language schools.

Aki Kim, Dorothy Rudie's mother, visiting her parents' gravesite in Korea, circa 1960s.

227

Interview with Rosie Kim Chang

My name is Rosie Kim Chang. I am a second-generation Korean. My grandmother arrived here with my mother, who was five years old. They arrived on one of the ships in 1904 from Korea.

Because my mother came with my grandmother, my grandmother was not employed in the sugar fields. My grandmother did not come with her husband. What she did was, she went to do laundry for the Korean single men, while my mother was taken to the Susannah Wesley Home. It was a school for the youngsters of the immigrants. So my mother was brought up in the Susannah Wesley Home. And she went to high school at McKinley High School and graduated there. Later my mother met my father, Chip Chong Kim.

My father, who came the same year as my grandmother and mother, arrived as a young man. Because he was too young to be sent to the fields, he was sent to Mills College, which is the predecessor of the Mid-Pacific Institute. How they met, I am not familiar with. So they got married after high school, and from what I understand, one of my father's early jobs was as a radio operator for CPC, the California Packing Company. While working there he contracted tuberculosis and was sent to Leahi Hospital, where he died. He died when I was about five years old.

There were three siblings in our family. My mother was not able to support herself. So my grandmother did a match marriage for her. My grandmother was very thoughtful in getting a husband for her, a man who had the

Susannah
Wesley Home
and Training
School, circa
1906.

same surname, Kim. So my stepfather came in to the picture about 1924. He was at that time an officer in the Salvation Army. And from that marriage three additional children were born: Betty, Ruth, and Earl. A unique thing happened: My stepfather wanted a better-paying job, so he was sent to California to learn a profession as a barber. When he came back, he was better able to support the family.

Among my siblings from my first father were Clara Kim Emerson, who was the first Korean to become a public school principal, and a brother, Bill Kim, who became a well-known sports editor for the local newspaper. Bill continued his activities with sports throughout his life and was featured in the newspapers often. He graduated from St. Louis High School. He became the editor of the Catholic newspaper. Years later, he studied law at Hastings University to become an attorney. He was about to become a judge when he suddenly died in his early 40s.

Because my grandmother and mother were recruited from the Korean Methodist Church in Korea to go to Hawaii, they affiliated themselves with the Fort Street Korean Methodist Church. So, growing up, I remember that Sundays were spent in church ... in the morning, in the afternoon, and in the evening. As a teenager, we added another day of the week for choir practice. Our whole social activity was immersed in the church. Thus, the church was our social foundation. The church also was where we went to the Korean

Mary Ae Gee Kim and family, circa 1930: left to right, sitting: Rosie, Betty, Ruth, Bill; standing: Clara, Kwan Yer (Mary Ae Gee's second husband), Mary Ae Gee Kim.

school for two reasons: to give support to the church and secondly, to be able to keep up with the Korean language.

However, when World War II came into the picture, all foreign-language schools were eliminated. We joined other social activities that were outside of the church and the children were able to to be affiliated with other young people when we grew older. The church was not as important to the second or third generation as it was with the new immigrants. There were many new immigrants after World War II and the Korean War. They came to the Islands in the late 1960s and the church became their social foundation.

Now, about my own personal background . . . if you recall, Koreans were a small minority in the Hawaiian Islands, not as abundant as the Japanese or the Chinese. The Koreans were termed as "Others" in the census because we were less than one percent of the entire population in Hawaii. We were the first ethnic group that was dispersed in the Islands, in urban Honolulu. And so, because the major Korean Methodist Church was on Fort Street, we lived on the upper part of Fort Street, and later we moved to the Punchbowl area. It was very close to the Korean Methodist Church on Fort Street. Before 1918, there was only one Korean church in Honolulu.

Our home was amongst the Portuguese also. And there, too, was the Catholic church, which the Portuguese attended. We became so close to the Portuguese people that we were able to learn how to eat sweet bread. My brother Bill was sent to St. Louis College, a Catholic school, and since he was immersed in Catholicism, he became a Catholic and was baptized into that church. It was at St. Louis College where he first sold local newspapers and then became the editor of the *Catholic Herald*. He was well known when he grew up.

My sister Clara and I were the only ones in the family that went to a public school. There was a prestigious public high school that would admit non-Caucasian children who could speak English well. It was called Roosevelt High School, the English Standard School. When we were old enough, Clara and I took the exam for Roosevelt and were admitted, so we were both graduates of the English Standard School. Before that school, we were students at Royal School, which is in the Punchbowl area. After high school, I went to the university for two years then was admitted to the Queen's Hospital School of Nursing.

During my first position in the School of Nursing, I won the Director of Nursing Award for Best Bedside Nurse. My first appointed position was as head nurse. Then, in the late 40s, I went to the University of Pittsburgh, where I got my master's degree in nursing education. In fact, I followed my husband, Dr. John Chang, who was in medical school at the University of Pittsburgh. While I was getting my master's degree in Pittsburgh, the director of Queen's Hospital in Honolulu wrote to me and said that they would like to appoint me as assistant director of nursing, which was unthought of at that time; all top positions up to that time were given to Caucasians recruited from the Mainland. No Honolulu local person was given such a high position earlier. So that was my job. Then, after that position, I was appointed Head of the School of Nursing—not as an assistant but the high position because my master's was in administration from the School of Nursing.

Then later I was Director of the School of Nursing there. I was promoted to head the Hawaii State Hospital since I did some testing for the Personnel Services to reorganize nursing there. When the Regional Medical Program came up, a higher position, I was asked to join it. I remained there until 1987. Then I went back to study to receive my doctorate. After that, I was employed at the university, not in nursing but in international health. I did some educational programs there as well as research programs. From there, I retired and continued my volunteer work at the Center of Asia-Pacific Exchange. In this program, I coordinated the teaching programs for people from the Asia-Pacific region and started to do seminars in Seoul and Pusan in South Korea. I enjoyed that very much. The Center of Asia-Pacific Exchange was like a small East-West Center, which was the first large Asian study center in the U.S. I enjoyed it very much and spent a lot of time with Koreans.

Did your mother speak to you sometimes in Korean?

No, my mother spoke English all the time. She spoke in front of the children in Korean only when she and my father did not wish us to understand what they are saying. And I think I adopted the spirit of nationalism about Korea from her because it was through immersion—not because she forced us to be nationalist and so forth. We learned it through our desire . . . she didn't push it on us. We knew about the situation in Korea before they came over to Hawaii: the hardships that they had, the famine, the treatment under the Japanese, and it was, I think, just embedded in us. She didn't have to say, you have to hate the other ethnic groups. And, I think as a whole, Koreans were more liberal than the Japanese or the Chinese. The Japanese and the Chinese, at least among my friends, if they married outside of their race, they were kicked out of the household. But I think the Korean families here were more tolerant, at least that was my understanding.

Do you know anything about the split in the community?

Oh, yes. The thing is that, having gone through the Korean Methodist Church, I heard and saw a lot. Now they didn't really, at that time, say bad things about the other church. But we knew the fallout in the Korean Methodist Church when Dr. Rhee took some of this fallout and set up the Korean Christina Church on Liliha Street. So we knew that, but other than that, we didn't really feel it. Because after all, Bill, my brother, was named by Dr. Syngman Rhee. He named my brother Bill. But I think it was before the fallout. We just had feelings about the fallout. We were too young to be involved. And we knew about Dongji Hoi and Kuk Min Hur, two separate organizations.

How did it come about that Syngman Rhee named Bill?

That I don't know. Because I didn't ask my mother when she said, "Well you know, it was Dr. Syngman Rhee who named him." It was before the fallout, I'm sure. You see, my parents stayed with the Korean Methodist Church.

What year was this?

Bill was born in 1920. A long time ago, so I don't know when the fallout was.

232

It began in 1916, but the final split was in 1918.

Yes. But my mother wasn't that active or had such intense feelings as some of the other people had. Of course, she was partial because of her affiliation with the Korean Methodist Church.

Do you remember some of her friends?

No, I really don't, except that I know that Mary Hong Park . . . her family was very active with the Korean Methodist Church, and my mother was active in the same church work there. As I said, our whole life was immersed in church activities.

What about Ha Soo Whang? Do you remember her?

Oh, absolutely. Ha Soo Whang was a leader, especially for Korean girls. I was very active with the activities that she started; for example, at that time, I remember so clearly, that she set up so many activities at the Academy of Arts. I don't know who taught us Korean dances and so forth. But I remember performing there at that time, and there were other activities that she did, especially for the Korean girls. I remember that when I was in high school, we went back to the Honolulu Academy of Arts and when I was a youngster, I thought the stage was so huge. But now, when I see the stage, it's so small. I had remembered it as being so large. And I also remember Mr. Tai Sung Lee, Pearl Lee Kim's father. He was a very active leader among the Korean young people. He initiated some youth programs, too. He and Ha Soo Whang were both on the YWCA staff as well as active in the YMCA. They were very close to the Korean youngsters in Hawaii. I feel they never should be forgotten because they helped us through the teenage high school years.

18

Interview with Esther Soon Yee Hong Kang

My name is Esther Soon Yee Hong Kang. I was born on June 10, 1917. My father was Hong Young Soo, who was my mother's second husband. He was from Hwanghaedo, Korea. His family spent most of the time in Jejudo. He came to Hawaii to work on the sugar plantation in Kona, which is on the Big Island.

My father was very good with his hands in sewing. So eventually he worked on people's uniforms and clothes. Then he started a tailor shop in Kona on the Big Island.

My mother was Anna Lee. She never had a Korean name that I know of. She came from Seoul, Korea, as a picture bride at age fourteen for her first husband, who was not my father. When she saw her first husband, who was nineteen years old, she refused to marry him because she said he was too old. So she stayed one month in the woman's compound. The women told her, "If you don't marry him, you will have to go back to Korea." So she married him and they had six children. These children were my stepsisters and stepbrothers, that is, my mother's children from her first husband.

Esther Kang at the Korean Cultural & Food Festival, 1983, *Korea Times*.

The first child was Paul Kae Hong. He was an unusually bright fellow. He didn't go to school. But he had an electrical engineering license from the government at that time. My second brother, John, he was a carpenter. He did roofing, and he did all kinds of things to improve houses. My third brother was a contractor. He took jobs taking care of homes. He fixed them up and sold them for a profit.

When my older sister Dora married a Chinese boy, my father didn't approve of her marrying a Chinese boy, so she took my father to court. She told the court, "I want to know why my father won't allow me to marry Charlie Choo. My father told the judge, "I don't want no Pake [Chinese] for a son-in-law." The judge scolded her father and allowed her to marry Charlie Choo, so she was married to Charlie Choo again, this time in front of the judge in court and in front of my father. When they left, it was all amicable. They had three children. They lived very, very happily.

Go on with your story about your mother meeting your father, your mother's second husband. Oh, tell us first what happened to the first husband.

Oh, her first husband decided to go back to Korea. So he told my mother he was going back to Korea and asked her if she wanted to go with him. She said, "No." She wanted to stay in Hawaii. So he took their youngest son with him, leaving five children with her. He returned to Korea and was never heard from again.

When my father, her second husband, saw my mother with her five children, he felt sorry for her, so he helped support them. When they got married, they had six children of their own. I was the oldest.

Name them.

The children are Soon Yee, Soon Ah, Soon Yea, Clara, and Walter. I am the oldest of her second husband.

When did the family move to Honolulu?

I think a few years after he found out that he could sew. My mother could sew, too. So they started their own tailor shop when they came to Honolulu. They went to Fort Shafter. From there, they went to live near Schofield Barracks. And they did very well there, too.

Did they both go to the Korean Christian Church? I know you go to the Christian Church. Did your father go, too?

Yes. Both went to the Korean Christian Church. My father was a great supporter of Dr. Rhee. So my mother went along. And she worked hard for him, too. They went through a lot of heartaches. They went to the Korean Christian Church because they supported Dr. Rhee. Some of the other Koreans in the Korean Christian Church didn't support Dr. Rhee. So they would have arguments right at church [within the Korean Christian Church]. But in the end, it was ok.

What year do you think your family moved to Honolulu? And where were you born?

According to my birth certificate, I was born in Honolulu in 1917. So they must have married earlier than that.

Tell us about their activities in the church. Who was the stronger one in the family regarding church affiliation, your father or your mother?

My father was the stronger one.

Was he the one who chose to follow Syngman Rhee?

Yes, right.

What happened? How did he get to be a Syngman Rhee follower?

My father said he knew Syngman Rhee from Korea. So when they came out here, they already were friends. The Methodist Church Congregation had frictions. So Syngman Rhee said the Korean Methodist Church didn't have their own soul. They were led by the Methodist Church in the United States. They had to go according to that. So Syngman Rhee got mad. And he said, "Why should we have to follow somebody on the Mainland?" So he left. My father was one of the great followers of Rhee.

So then your father was a Methodist at one time.

Yes, they were all Methodists at one time. In fact, all Koreans were Methodists at that time until Dr. Syngman Rhee walked off.

Do you know anything more than that? What did your father do for Syngman Rhee?
Well, I know Syngman Rhee lived at our house for a while, and then they started the KCI.

When was this? What year was it that he lived at your house?
I can't remember.

How old were you?
I think four or five years old.

Tell me more about what you remember, growing up in the Korean Christian Church.
When I went there, they accepted me. I just enjoyed myself there. My father was great; he was a great disciplinarian.

What do you remember of KCI?
I remember it being a rambling building with a lot of students in there. They were very, very royal to Dr. Syngman Rhee. They studied real hard.

Did you ever attend that school?
No, I didn't. Too young. But my older sisters and brothers went to that school.

What do you remember them telling you about that school?
Well, they said that it was a good school. They learned a lot and they were given much opportunity to say what they wanted. They were disciplined.

What significant persons do you remember during that time as the leaders of the Korean community, such as Won Soon Lee? Do you remember Won Soon Lee?
Yes, I remember him. He was a domineering member. I don't remember too much more about him since I was so young. But I do know that he used to come around and tell us what to do, and he'd tell all the people what to do. He was financially well-off, too. So he was able to do much for the Korean community.

Tell me about your husband. Where did you meet him?

He was my brother's very good friend. My brother used to bring him around the house, and we used to go fishing together. Go riding, all this and that. I don't know how we became attached to each other.

What is his full name?

David Taewui Kang. He was born in Kihei, Maui. His father died when he was ten years old. So his mother was left with all his brothers and sisters. He had to quit school and work for the plantation companies, but he was very, very smart, and eventually he became foreman of the sugar plantation. Because he was a foreman, there were certain privileges that other people didn't have. So he said he could have a good life.

Where were his parents from?

They were from Hwanghaedo. His mother? No, I don't know about his mother.

Do you know if his mother was a picture bride?

Yes, his mother was a picture bride.

Do you know when they came to Honolulu?

He was in school when they came to Honolulu. So he must have been about six or seven years old.

Have you ever met David's father?

No, I met his stepfather.

His mother remarried?

Yes. His mother remarried, to Mr. Kim. I lived with them many, many years. He was very good man. Very punctual.

What was his full name?

I can't remember. Kim.

Did they have children?

Yes, they had one son.

Is he still alive?
Oh, yes. Samuel Kim.

Where does he live?
He lives in California.

Where did you live when you were growing up?
I grew up in the Liliha Street area. I remember the Filipino church there, very distinctly.

What schools did you attend?
I went to Liliuokalani School and McKinley High School and to the University of Hawaii. I lived on 19th Avenue at that time. Then my father sold that place.

How about the children of the first husband?
The six above me were all grown up. They all had their own business, working, and one of my sisters was in college so . . .

Tell us more about your youth, anything.
Oh, when I was young, life was very, very hard because I had five younger brothers and sisters. My father would say I couldn't go out on a date with any other nationality but Korean. But my first love was a Japanese boy. I remember this distinctly. One night, we came home, and we sat in the car. We just talked. When I came to the house, my father was sitting at the front door chair. As I came near, he just walked off and I knew he was mad. I told this to my Japanese boyfriend. We just quit dating. But I still think about him. He was a nice guy. He became a dentist. I don't know if he passed away or not. He was really a nice guy.

Tell us a little bit more about activities at the Korean Christian Church.
Oh, the Korean Christian Church was very, very active. We would get together and go down to the Korean Old Folks Care Home to sing for them and take food to them, like cookies and *dok* [Korean rice cakes]. We would make tea and serve them. We would go in and clean up the

239

place. I had my name down there for entrance in the future. If there was a vacancy, I would go there. It was a nice little place. Now the Korean Care Home takes in retirees of any nationality because they are under the state regulations about discrimination.

What kind of activities did you do with Koreans? For instance, with the Wahiawa Korean Christian Church?

Well, I didn't do much with the Wahiawa Korean Christian Church. But we did go on home calls. If somebody was sick, the minister would call one of us to go with him. We would go visit them.

There was a big ruckus at the Korean Christian Church in the 1940s. Do you know anything about that?

Yes. I think that was terrible. I remember I was in church on a Sunday. I think it was a Rev. Park who came. Some ladies got angry and said "You get out of this church, you don't belong to this church." He responded that he belonged to this church because he was a member of the Korean Christian Church and it was under God. They had a big, big argument at church. I remember that distinctly.

So what happened?

I don't know what happened after that.

Can you name some outstanding personalities during the 1940s and even the 1930s? Have you ever heard of Tai Sung Lee? Tell me what you know about him.

Well, he was a soft-spoken man. He was a nice guy. He was very, very disciplined. What he said sometimes was admirable. I have great admiration for that man. I think he was a mid-built man. I thought he was a good-looking guy. Although he had a soft-spoken voice, whenever he was mad, you could hear the rafters ringing.

You don't know what happened to your husband's father? Did you ever find out where David's mother came from?

She came from Seoul, Korea. She came from a well-to-do family, where she had a private tutor and things of that sort. She wasn't used to all this hard work when she came to Hawaii.

240

Did she tell you why she came?

She said she came to Hawaii as a picture bride. Anything to get away from Korea because Korea was very hard on women.

What about your father? Did he still work hard at tailoring or did he change jobs?

He worked at his tailoring job. He was very, very good at his business of tailoring at Fort Ruger. He bought a lot of properties. He made money from rentals. He said that he made money from renting out rooms to the Koreans. He did all right.

Where was that?

In Wahiawa. The building is still there. I still can see the building there.

Did you ever meet Syngman Rhee?

Oh, yes. Like I said, one time he stayed with us.

Oh, that's right. Tell us about that a little bit more.

Well, we were all afraid of him because you know he was the Number One Man. But he was very, very gentle. He talked to us when we had troubles with our parents. Syngman Rhee said you have to respect your parents. He was the man who taught me to have respect for my elders and respect for my teachers. And he was a really wonderful person. He didn't talk much. He didn't socialize much. He only read, read, and read. Even if his food wasn't good, he never complained about his food. He just ate his food. He was an exceptional man, Syngman Rhee.

What about Mrs. Rhee.

She was nice, too . . . although she was haole. Because she was haole, we didn't consider her as one of us, but she was really nice. She tried to make us understand that even though she was haole and Dr. Syngman Rhee was a Korean, it didn't matter. They really proved something to us.

Have you ever heard of Nodie Kimhaekim?

Yes. Nodie Kim. We thought Dr. Rhee would marry Nodie. But he had this haole girlfriend. We knew it was out of the question. Nodie understood and she was very tolerant. She accepted Mrs. Rhee. Nodie was very good. She started a Korean women's group. And we went around singing at the Koreans centers and at all the old peoples' homes not only Koreans. I sang there and we served out Korean *dodeok* 떡. We made tea and had a nice time.

Do you remember Inez Kong Pai?
Inez Kong Pai was definitely for the Korean Christian Church. She claimed that her mother and her father helped start the Korean Christian Church. Her parents donated quite a bit of money to the church. Anytime when there was a social gathering, she was always there. She was a great orator, too. She was a wonderful person.

Who else do you remember in the second generation who was pretty active at Christian Church?
Wilbert Choi's family was very active. He always volunteered and donated time and money to the church. And whenever there was a big occasion you would see Wilbert, right there.

Do you think that the break between the Methodist Church and Korean Christian Church affected the second generation?
You mean our age? No, I didn't think it affected us at all because we were loyal to Syngman Rhee. We knew that he left the church not because of religion but because of the Mainland people telling us what to do in Hawaii and they don't know anything about Hawaii.

Did second-generation intermarry? Did they marry each other, Methodists and Korean Christian Church members?
Oh, yes. They did. Sometimes, it was so difficult. I remember I was a Korean Christian Church member and my husband was a Methodist. When we got married, I wanted to get married at the Korean Christian Church. And his mother wanted her son to get married in the Methodist Church. It was really, really difficult. So what we did was we got married in the Korean Christian Church but had the *moksa* 목사 [pastor] from the Methodist Church perform the ceremony with the help of the Korean Christian Church minister. I remember. It was really, really nice.

When did you marry?

I was married in 1940 to David, who was a good friend of my brothers. How we ever got involved I don't know, but eventually we got married. We had three children and we lived very happily together. He was a very, very considerate person. After we got married we lived with his mother. His mother was very, very good to me. But my father-in-law was even nicer because whenever my mother-in-law would show favoritism he would tell her, "You are not thinking of her, too." I remember those two arguing over that. My father-in-law wasn't a man of much words . . . he didn't say much. But he was a very, very thoughtful man. I loved that man. He did a lot for his children, too.

After I graduated from McKinley High School in 1935, I wanted to go to the University of Hawaii. The school recommended that I go to further my education. But because of our family's financial situation, I just couldn't go to the University of Hawaii. I went to one of the smaller community colleges. David saw me studying at 3, 4 o'clock in the morning and then rushing to school. So he told me one day, "Why do you need that college degree except for your own ego?" I said that's why I need it. He said he couldn't see me studying at 3, 4 o'clock in the morning, rushing to school, coming home, doing my other work, and then studying to go back to school. So I just quit. Later I was sorry that I quit because I could have continued if I had persisted.

What kind of work did you do after that?

Oh, I went into the real estate business.

Where was your husband working?

Oh, my husband was a furniture manufacturer. And I helped him in his business sewing, getting him started. But once he was on his own, I thought maybe it would be better if I wasn't connected with it. So when he hired two more girls who could do the sewing, I left the shop. And he did very fine, too.

19

Interview with Howard Halm on His Paternal Grandparents, Sam Yo Halm and Mary Hong Halm

My name is Howard Halm. I was born in Honolulu, Hawaii, in 1942, the son of Dr. Gilbert Chi Num Halm and Mary Kim Halm.

My parents were born in Honolulu. You have already interviewed my mother about her lineage. I would like to say a few things about my paternal grandparents. My father's parents came to Honolulu in 1904 from the Port of Incheon. They came as a family with one son to work in the Hawaii sugarcane fields. My paternal grandmother's name was Mary Hong Halm. She was from Seoul. My grandfather's name was Sam Yo Halm. He was from Pyongyang.

When they came over from Korea, my grandfather was forty-seven years old and my grandmother was thirty-five years old. So they were one of the few Korean families that came over as a family group. After living in Honolulu, they had four children: Richard, Jane, Henry, and my father, Gilbert.

My father was born in 1912 and his brothers and sister were born about two years apart. My grandfather came to Hawaii with several documents, which are still in my possession. One is a family genealogy, which I think is called a *kongbok*. Recently, I was in Korea for the first time, and I met a lawyer there by the name of Halm. I sent him a copy of the *kongbok*. He's going to look to see if we are related somehow. My grandfather also had a map of Korea which showed the burial sites of his ancestors. The *kongbok* goes back to the year 1503, which is, obviously, within the Chosun Dynasty.

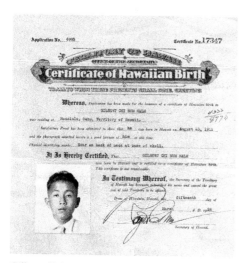

Gilbert Chi Num Halm was born in 1912; birth certificate in 1928.

He also had his passport or his immigration document, which indicated that he left Incheon on September 7, 1904. From what I understand, my grandfather, being a sort of senior citizen even at that time, was very involved in the Korean Independence Movement, supporting and sending back a lot of money to some coalition. I was told by my friends that if, instead of sending back money, he had invested in real estate here in Honolulu, especially at that time, we'd be very well off today. But he instead supported the Korean Independence Movement. He never did go back to Korea; he died in Honolulu in 1925. My grandmother, who died in Los Angeles in 1956, is buried next to him at the Oahu Cemetery in Honolulu.

I recall when I was twelve years that I sat down with my grandmother and asked about her life story. We could only communicate with stick figures because I didn't speak Korean, but we communicated in simple pidgin English. That way she told me the story I told you of her coming to Honolulu with with her husband. She said when she came from Seoul to Honolulu, her first work was to wash the clothes for the sugarcane workers and she made money that way. She also was very good at making the *mook*. She was obviously a much older woman, having been born in 1869. So she was older than many of the men who came over as sugarcane field workers. Most of the men were born in the 1870s and the early 1880s. Her husband was born in 1857 so they were sort of the oldest couple in the community.

Did she have a Korean name?

I'm sure she did. I'm not clear why she used only the name Mary.

I recall just a few months ago, when I was at Oahu Cemetery, I looked up the index card of everybody who was buried at the cemetery. This goes back to the 1850s. They have a Korean section up there. The Korean section is not categorized by denomination in the sense of religion or church affiliation. They do not have Korean Christians,

Korean Methodists, Korean Episcopalians. They all are buried together there. So I looked through the index cards. I was interested in the index cards of the Halm family. I saw, for example, 1925. The cards fold out by the name of my grandfather and my grandmother when he died and her name was listed simply as "Mary Hong." So, at least as of 1925, she preferred to be called "Mary Hong."

And no Korean name with it?
I don't know any Korean name. There's no Korean name on her gravestone either, which is interesting.

Is there any hint that they were Christians before they came?
There is no hint. I am not clear exactly what they did, except that I understand my grandfather was a school teacher who traveled. That's what brought him from Pyongyang down to Seoul. He was a traveling school teacher.

A number of Incheon people were Methodist who were recruited for the plantations in Hawaii—especially if they were married couples.
Well, you know, I am not that clear as to whether or not my grandparents were even Episcopalians. Do you know, Mother, whether or not they were? [Mary Halm replies: "Yes, they went to our church."]

OK. I never really knew my grandmother was a really religious person. My mother remembers that they attended St. Luke's Church in the early days at least.

You mentioned something about a child who was born in Korea and came later to Hawaii.
Yes. Uncle William was born in Korea. He was born probably in 1902 or 1901. But he came over around 1904, so he was probably born in 1903.

Did you mention that he was your grandmother's child?
My grandmother's child from another husband. What my grandmother told me was that she had three children. William was her youngest. She met my grandfather. They fell in love and decided to leave Seoul and come to Hawaii.

246

Leaving the other two children?
I believe so.

Anything else about your paternal grandmother's family?
No, but I could probably learn a lot more if I could get somebody to translate the *kongbok*. The *kongbok* is written in old Korean so it's hard unless you're a scholar of the language back in the 1500s and 1600s. I'm working on this genealogy as I said through this attorney that I know, and once I am able to unravel that, then I can actually go back several centuries.

Tell us about your life in Hawaii.
I was born in Honolulu. We lived near the corner of McCully and Wilder. And then we moved when I was about five or six years old to Nehoa Street, near Roosevelt High School. And then we moved from there to Kailua in 1949. Kailua then was a small town with about maybe 5,000 people. My father was the second dentist to move to that area. We lived on the outskirts of town, where the cow pastures and swamps were in our neighborhood. I attended Kailua Elementary School, which was where my mother began working as a teacher, when I was in the fifth grade.

My father had his dental practice office in our large house, so when I came from school, my father would be there. My mother was at that time pursuing her college degree in education. In 1952 I started attending Punahou School until 1957, which was when we moved to Los Angeles.

What happened to your maternal grandfather? Was he living with the family?
My maternal grandfather died in 1942, before I was born. He died because of an industrial accident. My paternal grandmother was very much like a lot of the Koreans that we see today. Very energetic, very much like an entrepreneur for many years. She must have bought and sold real property almost every year or maybe, on the average, every other year. She was able to do that without any appreciable education, without being able to speak English, without having a car, without having a lawyer, so to speak. She was able to buy and sell property,

get the equity from one property to invest in the other property. She owned ten units by subletting in the Punchbowl area without problems. To me, that's a great story of perseverance. She died in 1971. I saw a lot of that kind of energy in the Korean people when I was in Korea recently.

Who did she live with?
She lived by herself. She was a very self-sufficient woman and she did not want to be dependent on any of her children, even after she had a stroke in 1964. She preferred to live alone. Her son lived close by and took care of her.

Which son?
Noel. He is actually the only son.

What do you remember about the Korean community?
Well, I don't remember anything about the Korean community, at least not in Honolulu back then. I know a lot now about what the Korean community must have been like back in the past because I do a lot of reading and I talked to a lot of people. I know that at some point in the time and history of Koreans that among Koreans in Hawaii there was a split between the organizations that they followed. What's his name? Youngman Park?

Youngman Park.
And Dr. Syngman Rhee. And Ahn Chang Ho. I know that the divisiveness still persists today.

We had this conference in 1999 and one of the topics was about the history of Koreans in Hawaii. We had a professor from Philadelphia who talked about twenty minutes about history, history of Koreans in the United States or at least in Hawaii. He did not once mention Syngman Rhee. That was my first realization that I had of how that conflict has persisted. I mean even until today people can have their debates about that. I don't know if you met Charles Kim yet, but Charles is the executive director of Korean American Coalition (KAC). Charles Kim is the president of the KAC right now, and he is here to talk at the conference at the University of Hawaii.

Tell us what's happening in Los Angeles and in KAC.

I'm the chairman of the Board of Directors this year. And this is my last year. Bill Min is going to take over as the chairman of the Korean American Coalition. Our president is Joseph Ahn, who would be in Hawaii, and our executive director is Charles Kim. What we are going to be doing in Hawaii is having a conference.

This is an annual conference. We call it a winter conference that we have each year. It is our hope that this conference will become a national conference, a meeting just like the JACL national meeting or the OCA national meeting. We've been having this conference that has been primarily a local Los Angeles conference. But this is going to be the first year when we have more from around the country. At the present time, the Korean American Coalition has about seven or eight chapters. We have affiliates in Washington D.C., and Seattle. We have a chapter in Anchorage, Alaska; Sacramento; Soritos; Orange County; and Torrence. We have a new member on the board, her name is Helen B. Kim, who came from New York. We are hoping to try to work out

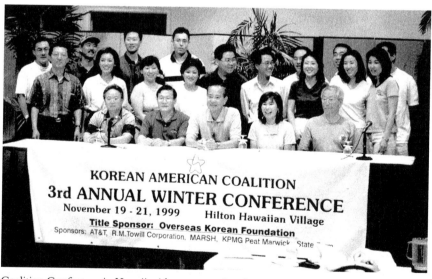

Coalition Conference in Hawaii with representatives from several states, 1999; left to right, first row: Alvin Kang, Keith Kim, Howard Halm, Janis Koh, William Min; second row: Vice Consul Gerald Oh, Young Kim, Helen Kim, Nita Song, Joon Song, Byung Kwon Kim, Hyepin Im, Julie Lee, Cathy Choi; third row: Mark Keam, Russell Park, unidentified, unidentified, Jimmy Lee, unidentified, unidentified.

something with the people from New York. But our goal is to have a national organization that will do several things. First of all, it's to continue the programs for full-time citizenship assistance for those who wish to become citizens. Next, once you become a citizen, we encourage them to become registered voters. We have a voter registration drive at different times of the year.

Then we have community education once a month. We have a general meeting where we have whatever the key issue is, whether it's some immigration reform or whether it's the mayoral election or some aspect of Los Angeles life that we have. The primary protagonist at the meeting is in support of Korean medias to get the word out to the community and to educate the community about what's going on. We also believe that it is very important to develop leaders for the future. We have a very strong group—as you know there are over a million Koreans in other countries. About 75 to 80 percent of them are first generation, the others are second and third generation. But the first generation, most of them have come over only recently, primarily since the 1970s, even 1980s, as we speak. So these are the people that we are focusing on. We will try to to develop leaders. And we have about thirty to forty young college students that we bring in during the beginning of the summer. We send them to attend a leadership training camp. And then about ten of them go out into different jobs and work as interns. We have a budget of about $600,000 a year and we have twenty-two full-time and part-time staff people.

When did KAC begin?

In 1983. We have an office in Washington, D.C. We want to expand our office because Korean American Alliance became an affiliate of KAC. They are the Korean American group in Washington, D.C. We are hoping that they will become a KAC chapter next year to help us build that office so that we can have a national voice.

One of the things I am sure you're familiar with about Korean history is that at the turn of the century, when Koreans and Korean Americans went to Washington, D.C., we couldn't get it because we had no voice and no power, we had nothing. So I think a lot about how the first-generation and second-generation Koreans must have felt powerless, especially following the riots of 1992. A typical example of the lack of power was when the riots were beginning. We called the governor's office, asking them to immediately calm down nationally. Hundreds of businesses were destroyed . . . millions of dollars were lost. So we want to avoid that situation in the future. That's why it's very important for the Korean-American community nationally to organize and to become voters and to join other coalitions and become a more powerful voice, so that Koreans will be represented until the point of time where there is no first generation any more. It will be primarily an American—Korean American—community.

Today, KAC is represented by chapters in Alaska, San Francisco, Sacramento, Los Angeles, San Diego, Colorado, Dallas-Fort Worth, Arizona, Chicago, Atlanta, and Washington, D.C. Since 2006, Bill Min, Duncan Lee, and Chong Choe have lead KAC nationally.

Profile of Howard Halm

The youngest of our interviewees, Howard Halm told us about his passionate commitment to Korean communities throughout the U.S.

In 2000, Howard served as president of the National Asian Pacific American Bar Association, which represented the interests of 40,000 Asian American lawyers throughout the country. As an active participant in local bar associations for over twenty-five years, he served as the inaugural president of the Asian Pacific American Bar Association, president of the Korean American Bar Association, and president of the Japanese American Bar Association. Governor Arnold Schwarzenegger appointed Howard to the Los Angeles Superior Court on January 23, 2009.

Before taking the bench, Howard represented national and international clients, practicing complex civil litigation. At the same time, he began starting his practice as a deputy attorney general with the State of California Department of Justice for five years. Howard is a graduate of UCLA and the University of San

Judge Howard Halm, Superior Court of California, 2009 to present; grandson of Choo Chei Kim.

Diego School of Law, where he served as an editor of the *Law Review.*

Howard is the recipient of the NAPABA Trailblazer Award, APABA President's Award, and a commendation from Mayor Tom Bradley for his leadership in the Japanese American Bar Association. He was selected as the Outstanding Judge of the Year 2000, presented by the Korean Community Lawyers' Association.

Appendix ———————————
Early Korean Churches and Organizations in Hawaii

1 The Korean Methodist Church, formally established 1905

Korean Methodist Church, Honolulu, 1905; visiting Korean Vice Minister of Foreign Affairs, Chi Ho Yun (front row, wearing light suit), at the Korean Day School.

Korean Methodist Episcopal Church, Honolulu, 1915; Rev. Hong Kan Sik and Dr. William Fry (both front row, with folded arms).

Korean Methodist Church, Honolulu, 1933; Rev. Lim Doo Wha (middle, in dark suit).

Korean Methodist Church, Wahiawa, 1936: the "Down Church."

2 The Korean Episcopal Church, established 1905

CHUN HEUNG HYOP HOI — 1905
St. Luke Episcopal Church

St. Luke's Korean Church and School, Kanoe Street, Honolulu, circa 1920.

St. Luke's Episcopal Church, circa 1930s; Rev. Noha Cho.

St. Luke's Episcopal Church, circa 1954.

3 The Korean National Association, established 1909

Korean National Association's first officers in 1909 in front of the Ahana Building near Miller Street; first president, Won Myung Chung (middle, sitting).

Korean National Association headquarters, 1915.

Korean National Association Membership Certificate. The association had 2,000 members at its peak in 1910.

Korean National Association, April 14, 1913.

Korean National Association, Kuk Min Hur headquarters, Miller Street, Honolulu, circa 1915.

Korean National Association, Rooke Avenue, Honolulu, circa 1995.

4 The Korean Military Brigade, established 1914

Korean Military Brigade, Honolulu, circa 1915.

Korean Military Brigade training base at Ahuimanu, Oahu, in 1915. Korea Independence Hall Collection.

Commander Youngman Pak (second from right) training recruits in Nebraska, circa 1911.

Youngman Pak, commander of the Korean
Military Brigade in Hawaii, 1912–1918.

5 Dr. Syngman Rhee's Major Organizations

**DONGJI HOI,
1918**

Dr. Rhee (at desk) and Dongji Hoi members (including Nodie Kimhaekim, the only woman) at the Korean Christian Church, circa 1920.

**THE KOREAN
CHRISTIAN
CHURCH, 1918**

Korean Christian Church, Liliha Street, circa 1923.

Korean Christian Church, Wahiawa, circa 1935: the "Up Church."

WAHIAWA KOREAN CHRISTIAN CHURCH
DECEMBER 21, 1986

Korean Christian Church, Liliha Street, Honolulu, circa 1993.

THE KOREAN CHRISTIAN INSTITUTE, 1918

THE KYOMINDAN, 1921

Kyomindan officers, circa 1921.

6 The Korean American Club, established 1925

Korean American Club members, 1926.

Korean American Club members, 1935.

Cloud Owen, president
and founder of the Korean
American Club, circa 1930.

7 The Korean University Club, established 1926

Korean University Club members, circa 1934.

8 The Taeguk Club, established 1933

Taeguk Club officers, circa 1950: Mickey Shon, Harold Kim, Charles Lee, Smith Choi, Duke Duk Man Moon. Mary Moon Han Album.

9 The Delta Fraternity and Sorority, established 1934

Delta Fraternity and Sorority picnic, circa 1930; left to right: Tai Hee Hong, Mary Hong (Park), Sarah Sur, Ernest Park, unidentified, unidentified, Fannie Nahm. Mary Hong Park Album.

Although hostilities among these organizations deeply disturbed the Korean community abroad and had serious implications for the current unrest in Korea, we have not found any meaningful research regarding their impact on the liberation of Korea. Undoubtedly, they were all a part of or were affected by the turbulent years of the Korean Independence Movement, a precursor to the devastating division of Korea. The present division in Korea is still fraught with dissension. Further discussion and research are needed to understand fully the place of these past organizations in the Korean dilemma. The interviews recorded in this book shed some light on what it was like when the Korean world in Hawaii was young.

INDEX

ABOUT THE AUTHORS

Roberta W. S. Chang, the principal researcher for this book, is a second-generation Korean American born in Hawaii. Chang is a graduate of the University of Hawaii, with master's degrees in social work and public health administration. As a Catholic missionary, Chang worked in Korea from 1960-1969 and witnessed the beginning of the second wave of Korean emigration to the USA. She has applied her research to a variety of projects, including documentaries profiling Koreans in Hawaii. Her short pictorial story on a new immigrant family coming to Hawaii in 1974, *We Want to Be Americans,* was published in 1985. The National History Compilation Committee of the Korean Ministry of Education published her research on Korean politics in Hawaii, *The Korean National Association and Syngman Rhee, 1915–1936*, vol. 45. Her documentary, *The Legacy of the Korean National Association*, was presented at the Hawai'i International Film Festival in 1999. Over 900 photographs of Koreans in America were collected and nearly 100 Koreans above the age of sixty were interviewed for her book *The Koreans in Hawaii: A Pictorial History, 1903–2003.*

Dr. Seonju Lee, the major coordinator for the publication of this book, is a HK research professor at Ewha Institute for the Humanities, Ewha Womans University. She received her PhD in English literature at Ewha Womans University in 1997 and was a professor of tourism English at Songho University. Lee authored *Dickens and Social Position and Capital,* which was selected as an Excellent Academic Work by the Ministry of Culture and Tourism. Her translation of I. A. Richards' *Principles of Literary Criticism* into Korean was also selected as an Excellent Academic Work by the National Academy of Sciences. Among her articles are "Korean-American's Diasporic Imagination," "Suki Kim and Chang-rae Lee as Performative Subjects in a Hybrid Culture," "Charles Dickens and Modernity," and "Invisibility and Empowerment of Migrant Women's Labor."

CPSIA information can be obtained
at www.ICGtesting.com
Printed in the USA
FSOW04n2303130515
7123FS